Congo Business Law Handbook

Just The facts101

Textbook Key Facts

by cram101

Textbook NOT Included

Table of Contents

Title Page

Copyright

Foundations of Business

Management

Business law

Finance

Human resource management

Information systems

Marketing

Manufacturing

Commerce

Business ethics

Accounting

Index: Answers

Just The Facts101

Exam Prep for

Congo Business Law Handbook

Just The Facts101 Exam Prep is your link from
the textbook and lecture to your exams.

**Just The Facts101 Exam Preps are unauthorized and comprehensive reviews
of your textbooks.**

All material provided by CTI Publications (c) 2019

Textbook publishers and textbook authors do not participate in or contribute to these reviews.

Just The Facts101 Exam Prep

Copyright © 2019 by CTI Publications. All rights reserved.

eAIN 444421

Foundations of Business

A business, also known as an enterprise, agency or a firm, is an entity involved in the provision of goods and/or services to consumers. Businesses are prevalent in capitalist economies, where most of them are privately owned and provide goods and services to customers in exchange for other goods, services, or money.

:: Contract law ::

A _____ is a legally-binding agreement which recognises and governs the rights and duties of the parties to the agreement. A _____ is legally enforceable because it meets the requirements and approval of the law. An agreement typically involves the exchange of goods, services, money, or promises of any of those. In the event of breach of _____, the law awards the injured party access to legal remedies such as damages and cancellation.

Exam Probability: **Medium**

1. *Answer choices:*

(see index for correct answer)

- a. Liquidated damages
- b. Contract
- c. Perfect tender
- d. Condition precedent

Guidance: level 1

:: Health promotion ::

_____, as defined by the World _____ Organization, is "a state of complete physical, mental and social well-being and not merely the absence of disease or infirmity." This definition has been subject to controversy, as it may have limited value for implementation. _____ may be defined as the ability to adapt and manage physical, mental and social challenges throughout life.

Exam Probability: **High**

2. *Answer choices:*

(see index for correct answer)

- a. Health impact assessment
- b. Vianova
- c. Patient navigators
- d. HealthEquity

Guidance: level 1

:: Identity management ::

_____ is the ability of an individual or group to seclude themselves, or information about themselves, and thereby express themselves selectively. The boundaries and content of what is considered private differ among cultures and individuals, but share common themes. When something is private to a person, it usually means that something is inherently special or sensitive to them. The domain of _____ partially overlaps with security, which can include the concepts of appropriate use, as well as protection of information. _____ may also take the form of bodily integrity.

Exam Probability: **Low**

3. *Answer choices:*

(see index for correct answer)

- a. Privacy-enhancing technologies
- b. Certification on demand
- c. Password manager
- d. Mobile Signature Roaming

Guidance: level 1

:: Energy and fuel journals ::

In physics, energy is the quantitative property that must be transferred to an object in order to perform work on, or to heat, the object. Energy is a conserved quantity; the law of conservation of energy states that energy can be converted in form, but not created or destroyed. The SI unit of energy is the joule, which is the energy transferred to an object by the work of moving it a distance of 1 metre against a force of 1 newton.

Exam Probability: **High**

4. *Answer choices:*

(see index for correct answer)

- a. Energy Procedia
- b. International Journal of Hydrogen Energy
- c. The Energy Journal
- d. Fuel Cells

Guidance: level 1

:: Product management ::

A _____, trade mark, or trade-mark is a recognizable sign, design, or expression which identifies products or services of a particular source from those of others, although _____ s used to identify services are usually called service marks. The _____ owner can be an individual, business organization, or any legal entity. A _____ may be located on a package, a label, a voucher, or on the product itself. For the sake of corporate identity, _____ s are often displayed on company buildings. It is legally recognized as a type of intellectual property.

Exam Probability: **Low**

5. *Answer choices:*

(see index for correct answer)

- a. Promise Index
- b. Mature technology
- c. Trademark
- d. Obsolescence

Guidance: level 1

:: ::

_____ or accountancy is the measurement, processing, and communication of financial information about economic entities such as businesses and corporations. The modern field was established by the Italian mathematician Luca Pacioli in 1494. _____ , which has been called the "language of business", measures the results of an organization's economic activities and conveys this information to a variety of users, including investors, creditors, management, and regulators. Practitioners of _____ are known as accountants. The terms "_____" and "financial reporting" are often used as synonyms.

Exam Probability: **Medium**

6. *Answer choices:*

(see index for correct answer)

- a. similarity-attraction theory
- b. cultural
- c. interpersonal communication
- d. empathy

Guidance: level 1

:: Business law ::

A _____ is an arrangement where parties, known as partners, agree to cooperate to advance their mutual interests. The partners in a _____ may be individuals, businesses, interest-based organizations, schools, governments or combinations. Organizations may partner to increase the likelihood of each achieving their mission and to amplify their reach. A _____ may result in issuing and holding equity or may be only governed by a contract.

Exam Probability: **Medium**

7. *Answer choices:*

(see index for correct answer)

- a. United Kingdom commercial law
- b. Limited liability limited partnership
- c. Partnership
- d. Companies law

Guidance: level 1

:: Accounting software ::

_____ is any item or verifiable record that is generally accepted as payment for goods and services and repayment of debts, such as taxes, in a particular country or socio-economic context. The main functions of _____ are distinguished as: a medium of exchange, a unit of account, a store of value and sometimes, a standard of deferred payment. Any item or verifiable record that fulfils these functions can be considered as _____ .

Exam Probability: **High**

8. *Answer choices:*

(see index for correct answer)

- a. Microsoft Money
- b. Money
- c. NewViews
- d. Moneydance

Guidance: level 1

:: ::

An _____ is a contingent motivator. Traditional _____ s are extrinsic motivators which reward actions to yield a desired outcome. The effectiveness of traditional _____ s has changed as the needs of Western society have evolved. While the traditional _____ model is effective when there is a defined procedure and goal for a task, Western society started to require a higher volume of critical thinkers, so the traditional model became less effective. Institutions are now following a trend in implementing strategies that rely on intrinsic motivations rather than the extrinsic motivations that the traditional _____ s foster.

Exam Probability: **Medium**

9. *Answer choices:*

(see index for correct answer)

- a. deep-level diversity
- b. personal values
- c. Incentive
- d. process perspective

Guidance: level 1

:: Management ::

_____ is the process of thinking about the activities required to achieve a desired goal. It is the first and foremost activity to achieve desired results. It involves the creation and maintenance of a plan, such as psychological aspects that require conceptual skills. There are even a couple of tests to measure someone's capability of _____ well. As such, _____ is a fundamental property of intelligent behavior. An important further meaning, often just called " _____ " is the legal context of permitted building developments.

Exam Probability: **Low**

10. *Answer choices:*

(see index for correct answer)

- a. Planning
- b. Business workflow analysis
- c. Corticon
- d. Business process interoperability

Guidance: level 1

:: Marketing ::

_____ or stock is the goods and materials that a business holds for the ultimate goal of resale.

Exam Probability: **High**

11. *Answer choices:*

(see index for correct answer)

- a. Inventory
- b. Price
- c. Carrying cost
- d. Corporate anniversary

Guidance: level 1

:: Generally Accepted Accounting Principles ::

An _____ or profit and loss account is one of the financial statements of a company and shows the company's revenues and expenses during a particular period.

Exam Probability: **Medium**

12. *Answer choices:*

(see index for correct answer)

- a. Engagement letter
- b. Income statement
- c. Financial position of the United States
- d. Consolidation

Guidance: level 1

:: Classification systems ::

_____ is the practice of comparing business processes and performance metrics to industry bests and best practices from other companies. Dimensions typically measured are quality, time and cost.

Exam Probability: **Medium**

13. *Answer choices:*

(see index for correct answer)

- a. Carnegie Classification of Institutions of Higher Education
- b. Benchmarking
- c. Systematized Nomenclature of Medicine
- d. TUN

Guidance: level 1

:: Consumer theory ::

_____ is the quantity of a good that consumers are willing and able to purchase at various prices during a given period of time.

Exam Probability: **Medium**

14. *Answer choices:*

(see index for correct answer)

- a. End-of-life
- b. Compensated demand
- c. Demand
- d. Demand vacuum

Guidance: level 1

:: Loans ::

In finance, a _____ is the lending of money by one or more individuals, organizations, or other entities to other individuals, organizations etc. The recipient incurs a debt, and is usually liable to pay interest on that debt until it is repaid, and also to repay the principal amount borrowed.

Exam Probability: **Medium**

15. *Answer choices:*

(see index for correct answer)

- a. VA loan
- b. Loan
- c. Secured loan
- d. Collateralized loan obligation

Guidance: level 1

:: Evaluation ::

_____ solving consists of using generic or ad hoc methods in an orderly manner to find solutions to _____ s. Some of the _____ -solving techniques developed and used in philosophy, artificial intelligence, computer science, engineering, mathematics, or medicine are related to mental _____ -solving techniques studied in psychology.

Exam Probability: **Medium**

16. *Answer choices:*

(see index for correct answer)

- a. Advocacy evaluation
- b. Educational evaluation

- c. Continuous assessment
- d. Quality assurance

Guidance: level 1

:: Commerce ::

> _____ relates to "the exchange of goods and services, especially on a large scale". It includes legal, economic, political, social, cultural and technological systems that operate in a country or in international trade.

Exam Probability: **High**

17. *Answer choices:*

(see index for correct answer)

- a. Bill of sale
- b. Oxygen bar
- c. Straw purchase
- d. Commerce

Guidance: level 1

:: Employment ::

The _____ is an individual's metaphorical "journey" through learning, work and other aspects of life. There are a number of ways to define _____ and the term is used in a variety of ways.

Exam Probability: **High**

18. *Answer choices:*

(see index for correct answer)

- a. Career
- b. Job security
- c. Working parent
- d. BA-X

Guidance: level 1

:: Association of Southeast Asian Nations ::

The Association of Southeast Asian Nations is a regional intergovernmental organization comprising ten countries in Southeast Asia, which promotes intergovernmental cooperation and facilitates economic, political, security, military, educational, and sociocultural integration among its members and other countries in Asia. It also regularly engages other countries in the Asia-Pacific region and beyond. A major partner of Shanghai Cooperation Organisation, _____ maintains a global network of alliances and dialogue partners and is considered by many as a global powerhouse, the central union for cooperation in Asia-Pacific, and a prominent and influential organization. It is involved in numerous international affairs, and hosts diplomatic missions throughout the world.

Exam Probability: **High**

19. *Answer choices:*

(see index for correct answer)

- a. ASEAN
- b. Emblem of the Association of Southeast Asian Nations
- c. Enlargement of the Association of Southeast Asian Nations
- d. ASEAN Intergovernmental Commission on Human Rights

Guidance: level 1

:: Generally Accepted Accounting Principles ::

Expenditure is an outflow of money to another person or group to pay for an item or service, or for a category of costs. For a tenant, rent is an _____ . For students or parents, tuition is an _____ . Buying food, clothing, furniture or an automobile is often referred to as an _____ . An _____ is a cost that is "paid" or "remitted", usually in exchange for something of value. Something that seems to cost a great deal is "expensive". Something that seems to cost little is "inexpensive". " _____ s of the table" are _____ s of dining, refreshments, a feast, etc.

Exam Probability: **Low**

20. *Answer choices:*

(see index for correct answer)

- a. Net income
- b. Depreciation
- c. Expense
- d. Long-term liabilities

Guidance: level 1

:: Management accounting ::

_____ s are costs that change as the quantity of the good or service that a business produces changes. _____ s are the sum of marginal costs over all units produced. They can also be considered normal costs. Fixed costs and _____ s make up the two components of total cost. Direct costs are costs that can easily be associated with a particular cost object. However, not all _____ s are direct costs. For example, variable manufacturing overhead costs are _____ s that are indirect costs, not direct costs. _____ s are sometimes called unit-level costs as they vary with the number of units produced.

Exam Probability: **High**

21. *Answer choices:*

(see index for correct answer)

- a. Hedge accounting
- b. Total benefits of ownership
- c. Variable cost
- d. Fixed assets management

Guidance: level 1

:: Analysis ::

_____ is the process of breaking a complex topic or substance into smaller parts in order to gain a better understanding of it. The technique has been applied in the study of mathematics and logic since before Aristotle, though _____ as a formal concept is a relatively recent development.

Exam Probability: **Medium**

22. *Answer choices:*

(see index for correct answer)

- a. Water pinch analysis
- b. Situational analysis
- c. Analysis
- d. SWOQe

Guidance: level 1

:: Marketing ::

A _____ is the quantity of payment or compensation given by one party to another in return for one unit of goods or services.. A _____ is influenced by both production costs and demand for the product. A _____ may be determined by a monopolist or may be imposed on the firm by market conditions.

Exam Probability: **Low**

23. *Answer choices:*

(see index for correct answer)

- a. Competitor indexing
- b. Cannibalization
- c. Double-loop marketing
- d. Democratized transactional giving

Guidance: level 1

:: Materials ::

A _____ , also known as a feedstock, unprocessed material, or primary commodity, is a basic material that is used to produce goods, finished products, energy, or intermediate materials which are feedstock for future finished products. As feedstock, the term connotes these materials are bottleneck assets and are highly important with regard to producing other products. An example of this is crude oil, which is a _____ and a feedstock used in the production of industrial chemicals, fuels, plastics, and pharmaceutical goods; lumber is a _____ used to produce a variety of products including all types of furniture. The term " _____ " denotes materials in minimally processed or unprocessed in states; e.g., raw latex, crude oil, cotton, coal, raw biomass, iron ore, air, logs, or water i.e. "...any product of agriculture, forestry, fishing and any other mineral that is in its natural form or which has undergone the transformation required to prepare it for internationally marketing in substantial volumes."

Exam Probability: **Low**

24. *Answer choices:*

(see index for correct answer)

- a. Aramid
- b. Orthotropic material
- c. Raw material
- d. Slag

Guidance: level 1

:: Project management ::

Some scenarios associate "this kind of planning" with learning "life skills". _____s are necessary, or at least useful, in situations where individuals need to know what time they must be at a specific location to receive a specific service, and where people need to accomplish a set of goals within a set time period.

Exam Probability: **High**

25. *Answer choices:*

(see index for correct answer)

- a. Requirements traceability
- b. Hammock activity
- c. Assumption-based planning
- d. Schedule

Guidance: level 1

:: ::

_____ is the collection of mechanisms, processes and relations by which corporations are controlled and operated. Governance structures and principles identify the distribution of rights and responsibilities among different participants in the corporation and include the rules and procedures for making decisions in corporate affairs. _____ is necessary because of the possibility of conflicts of interests between stakeholders, primarily between shareholders and upper management or among shareholders.

Exam Probability: **Low**

26. *Answer choices:*

(see index for correct answer)

- a. Sarbanes-Oxley act of 2002
- b. personal values
- c. imperative
- d. functional perspective

Guidance: level 1

:: Alchemical processes ::

In chemistry, a _____ is a special type of homogeneous mixture composed of two or more substances. In such a mixture, a solute is a substance dissolved in another substance, known as a solvent. The mixing process of a _____ happens at a scale where the effects of chemical polarity are involved, resulting in interactions that are specific to solvation. The _____ assumes the phase of the solvent when the solvent is the larger fraction of the mixture, as is commonly the case. The concentration of a solute in a _____ is the mass of that solute expressed as a percentage of the mass of the whole _____. The term aqueous _____ is when one of the solvents is water.

Exam Probability: **Medium**

27. *Answer choices:*

(see index for correct answer)

- a. Ceration
- b. Sublimation apparatus
- c. Solution
- d. Fermentation in food processing

Guidance: level 1

:: ::

_____ is the administration of an organization, whether it is a business, a not-for-profit organization, or government body. _____ includes the activities of setting the strategy of an organization and coordinating the efforts of its employees to accomplish its objectives through the application of available resources, such as financial, natural, technological, and human resources. The term " _____ " may also refer to those people who manage an organization.

Exam Probability: **Medium**

28. *Answer choices:*

(see index for correct answer)

- a. Sarbanes-Oxley act of 2002
- b. levels of analysis
- c. personal values
- d. co-culture

Guidance: level 1

:: Business planning ::

_____ is an organization's process of defining its strategy, or direction, and making decisions on allocating its resources to pursue this strategy. It may also extend to control mechanisms for guiding the implementation of the strategy. _____ became prominent in corporations during the 1960s and remains an important aspect of strategic management. It is executed by strategic planners or strategists, who involve many parties and research sources in their analysis of the organization and its relationship to the environment in which it competes.

Exam Probability: **Low**

29. *Answer choices:*

(see index for correct answer)

- a. Joint decision trap
- b. Exit planning
- c. Strategic planning
- d. Gap analysis

Guidance: level 1

:: Decision theory ::

A _____ is a deliberate system of principles to guide decisions and achieve rational outcomes. A _____ is a statement of intent, and is implemented as a procedure or protocol. Policies are generally adopted by a governance body within an organization. Policies can assist in both subjective and objective decision making. Policies to assist in subjective decision making usually assist senior management with decisions that must be based on the relative merits of a number of factors, and as a result are often hard to test objectively, e.g. work-life balance _____ . In contrast policies to assist in objective decision making are usually operational in nature and can be objectively tested, e.g. password _____ .

Exam Probability: **High**

30. *Answer choices:*

(see index for correct answer)

- a. Optimal decision
- b. Decision matrix
- c. Kepner-Tregoe
- d. Cognitive bias

Guidance: level 1

:: Financial risk ::

_____ is a type of risk faced by investors, corporations, and governments that political decisions, events, or conditions will significantly affect the profitability of a business actor or the expected value of a given economic action. _____ can be understood and managed with reasoned foresight and investment.

Exam Probability: **High**

31. *Answer choices:*

(see index for correct answer)

- a. Political risk
- b. Foreign exchange risk
- c. Distortion risk measure
- d. Modern portfolio theory

Guidance: level 1

:: Decision theory ::

Within economics the concept of _____ is used to model worth or value, but its usage has evolved significantly over time. The term was introduced initially as a measure of pleasure or satisfaction within the theory of utilitarianism by moral philosophers such as Jeremy Bentham and John Stuart Mill. But the term has been adapted and reapplied within neoclassical economics, which dominates modern economic theory, as a _____ function that represents a consumer's preference ordering over a choice set. As such, it is devoid of its original interpretation as a measurement of the pleasure or satisfaction obtained by the consumer from that choice.

Exam Probability: **Low**

32. *Answer choices:*

(see index for correct answer)

- a. Action axiom
- b. Taleb distribution
- c. Group decision-making
- d. Applied information economics

Guidance: level 1

:: Costs ::

In microeconomic theory, the _____, or alternative cost, of making a particular choice is the value of the most valuable choice out of those that were not taken. In other words, opportunity that will require sacrifices.

Exam Probability: **Medium**

33. *Answer choices:*

(see index for correct answer)

- a. Sliding scale
- b. Total cost of acquisition
- c. Average variable cost
- d. Opportunity cost

Guidance: level 1

:: Management accounting ::

In economics, _____ s, indirect costs or overheads are business expenses that are not dependent on the level of goods or services produced by the business. They tend to be time-related, such as interest or rents being paid per month, and are often referred to as overhead costs. This is in contrast to variable costs, which are volume-related and unknown at the beginning of the accounting year. For a simple example, such as a bakery, the monthly rent for the baking facilities, and the monthly payments for the security system and basic phone line are _____ s, as they do not change according to how much bread the bakery produces and sells. On the other hand, the wage costs of the bakery are variable, as the bakery will have to hire more workers if the production of bread increases. Economists reckon _____ as a entry barrier for new entrepreneurs.

Exam Probability: **High**

34. *Answer choices:*

(see index for correct answer)

- a. Institute of Management Accountants
- b. Standard cost
- c. Fixed cost
- d. Extended cost

Guidance: level 1

:: Strategic alliances ::

A _____ is an agreement between two or more parties to pursue a set of agreed upon objectives needed while remaining independent organizations. A _____ will usually fall short of a legal partnership entity, agency, or corporate affiliate relationship. Typically, two companies form a _____ when each possesses one or more business assets or have expertise that will help the other by enhancing their businesses. _____ s can develop in outsourcing relationships where the parties desire to achieve long-term win-win benefits and innovation based on mutually desired outcomes.

Exam Probability: **Low**

35. *Answer choices:*

(see index for correct answer)

- a. Strategic alliance
- b. Bridge Alliance
- c. Defensive termination
- d. Cross-licensing

Guidance: level 1

:: Statistical terminology ::

_____ is the magnitude or dimensions of a thing. _____ can be measured as length, width, height, diameter, perimeter, area, volume, or mass.

Exam Probability: **Low**

36. *Answer choices:*

(see index for correct answer)

- a. Empirical probability
- b. Statistical error
- c. Gompertz function
- d. P-value

Guidance: level 1

:: Fraud ::

In law, _____ is intentional deception to secure unfair or unlawful gain, or to deprive a victim of a legal right. _____ can violate civil law, a criminal law, or it may cause no loss of money, property or legal right but still be an element of another civil or criminal wrong. The purpose of _____ may be monetary gain or other benefits, for example by obtaining a passport, travel document, or driver's license, or mortgage _____, where the perpetrator may attempt to qualify for a mortgage by way of false statements.

Exam Probability: **Medium**

37. *Answer choices:*

(see index for correct answer)

- a. Voice phishing
- b. misleading advertising
- c. Transcript fraud
- d. Fraud

Guidance: level 1

:: Management ::

_____ is a process by which entities review the quality of all factors involved in production. ISO 9000 defines _____ as "A part of quality management focused on fulfilling quality requirements".

Exam Probability: **Medium**

38. *Answer choices:*

(see index for correct answer)

- a. Nonconformity
- b. Process management
- c. Concept of operations
- d. Economic production quantity

Guidance: level 1

:: Currency ::

A _____, in the most specific sense is money in any form when in use or circulation as a medium of exchange, especially circulating banknotes and coins. A more general definition is that a _____ is a system of money in common use, especially for people in a nation. Under this definition, US dollars, pounds sterling, Australian dollars, European euros, Russian rubles and Indian Rupees are examples of currencies. These various currencies are recognized as stores of value and are traded between nations in foreign exchange markets, which determine the relative values of the different currencies. Currencies in this sense are defined by governments, and each type has limited boundaries of acceptance.

Exam Probability: **Low**

39. *Answer choices:*

(see index for correct answer)

- a. Circulation
- b. Currency
- c. Demurrage
- d. Swan diagram

Guidance: level 1

:: ::

_____ is the study and management of exchange relationships. _____ is the business process of creating relationships with and satisfying customers. With its focus on the customer, _____ is one of the premier components of business management.

Exam Probability: **Low**

40. *Answer choices:*

(see index for correct answer)

- a. Character
- b. levels of analysis
- c. Sarbanes-Oxley act of 2002
- d. functional perspective

Guidance: level 1

:: Telecommunication theory ::

In reliability theory and reliability engineering, the term _____ has the following meanings.

Exam Probability: **High**

41. *Answer choices:*

(see index for correct answer)

- a. Articulation score
- b. Availability
- c. Net gain
- d. Noise power

Guidance: level 1

:: Generally Accepted Accounting Principles ::

In business and accounting, _____ is an entity's income minus cost of goods sold, expenses and taxes for an accounting period. It is computed as the residual of all revenues and gains over all expenses and losses for the period, and has also been defined as the net increase in shareholders' equity that results from a company's operations. In the context of the presentation of financial statements, the IFRS Foundation defines _____ as synonymous with profit and loss. The difference between revenue and the cost of making a product or providing a service, before deducting overheads, payroll, taxation, and interest payments. This is different from operating income .

Exam Probability: **Low**

42. *Answer choices:*

(see index for correct answer)

- a. Reserve
- b. Matching principle
- c. Provision
- d. Net income

Guidance: level 1

:: Payments ::

A _____ is the trade of value from one party to another for goods, or services, or to fulfill a legal obligation.

Exam Probability: **Medium**

43. *Answer choices:*

(see index for correct answer)

- a. Subsidy
- b. VersaPay
- c. KlickEx
- d. Thirty pieces of silver

Guidance: level 1

:: Money ::

In economics, _____ is money in the physical form of currency, such as banknotes and coins. In bookkeeping and finance, _____ is current assets comprising currency or currency equivalents that can be accessed immediately or near-immediately. _____ is seen either as a reserve for payments, in case of a structural or incidental negative _____ flow or as a way to avoid a downturn on financial markets.

Exam Probability: **Medium**

44. *Answer choices:*

(see index for correct answer)

- a. Lump sum
- b. Standard of deferred payment
- c. Cash
- d. Crorepati

Guidance: level 1

:: Management ::

A _____ is a method or technique that has been generally accepted as superior to any alternatives because it produces results that are superior to those achieved by other means or because it has become a standard way of doing things, e.g., a standard way of complying with legal or ethical requirements.

Exam Probability: **Medium**

45. *Answer choices:*

(see index for correct answer)

- a. Managerialism
- b. Line manager
- c. U-procedure and Theory U
- d. Best practice

Guidance: level 1

:: Business ::

A _____ is a mathematical object used to count, measure, and label. The original examples are the natural _____ s 1, 2, 3, 4, and so forth. A written symbol like "5" that represents a _____ is called a numeral. A numeral system is an organized way to write and manipulate this type of symbol, for example the Hindu–Arabic numeral system allows combinations of numerical digits like "5" and "0" to represent larger _____ s like 50. A numeral in linguistics can refer to a symbol like 5, the words or phrase that names a _____ , like "five hundred", or other words that mean a specific _____ , like "dozen". In addition to their use in counting and measuring, numerals are often used for labels , for ordering , and for codes . In common usage, _____ may refer to a symbol, a word or phrase, or the mathematical object.

Exam Probability: **High**

46. *Answer choices:*

(see index for correct answer)

- a. Number
- b. Policy capturing
- c. Resource slack
- d. Ian McLeod

Guidance: level 1

:: Marketing ::

A _____ is a group of customers within a business's serviceable available market at which a business aims its marketing efforts and resources. A _____ is a subset of the total market for a product or service. The _____ typically consists of consumers who exhibit similar characteristics and are considered most likely to buy a business's market offerings or are likely to be the most profitable segments for the business to service.

Exam Probability: **Medium**

47. *Answer choices:*

(see index for correct answer)

- a. Commercial planning
- b. Kronos Effect
- c. Demand signal repository
- d. Target market

Guidance: level 1

:: Business models ::

_____es are privately owned corporations, partnerships, or sole proprietorships that have fewer employees and/or less annual revenue than a regular-sized business or corporation. Businesses are defined as "small" in terms of being able to apply for government support and qualify for preferential tax policy varies depending on the country and industry. _____es range from fifteen employees under the Australian Fair Work Act 2009, fifty employees according to the definition used by the European Union, and fewer than five hundred employees to qualify for many U.S. _____ Administration programs. While _____es can also be classified according to other methods, such as annual revenues, shipments, sales, assets, or by annual gross or net revenue or net profits, the number of employees is one of the most widely used measures.

Exam Probability: **High**

48. *Answer choices:*

(see index for correct answer)

- a. Legacy carrier
- b. Sustainable business
- c. Freemium
- d. Small business

Guidance: level 1

:: Quality management ::

_____ ensures that an organization, product or service is consistent. It has four main components: quality planning, quality assurance, quality control and quality improvement. _____ is focused not only on product and service quality, but also on the means to achieve it. _____ , therefore, uses quality assurance and control of processes as well as products to achieve more consistent quality. What a customer wants and is willing to pay for it determines quality. It is written or unwritten commitment to a known or unknown consumer in the market. Thus, quality can be defined as fitness for intended use or, in other words, how well the product performs its intended function

Exam Probability: **High**

49. *Answer choices:*

(see index for correct answer)

- a. Institute of Standards and Industrial Research of Iran
- b. Quality management
- c. Flemish Quality Management Center
- d. TL 9000

Guidance: level 1

:: Competition regulators ::

The _____ is an independent agency of the United States government, established in 1914 by the _____ Act. Its principal mission is the promotion of consumer protection and the elimination and prevention of anticompetitive business practices, such as coercive monopoly. It is headquartered in the _____ Building in Washington, D.C.

Exam Probability: **Medium**

50. *Answer choices:*

(see index for correct answer)

- a. Queensland Competition Authority
- b. Federal Trade Commission
- c. Industrial Commission
- d. Australian Competition and Consumer Commission

Guidance: level 1

:: Monopoly (economics) ::

A _____ is a form of intellectual property that gives its owner the legal right to exclude others from making, using, selling, and importing an invention for a limited period of years, in exchange for publishing an enabling public disclosure of the invention. In most countries _____ rights fall under civil law and the _____ holder needs to sue someone infringing the _____ in order to enforce his or her rights. In some industries _____ s are an essential form of competitive advantage; in others they are irrelevant.

Exam Probability: **High**

51. *Answer choices:*

(see index for correct answer)

- a. Patent
- b. Quasi-rent
- c. Barriers to exit
- d. Cost per procedure

Guidance: level 1

:: Customs duties ::

A _____ is a tax on imports or exports between sovereign states. It is a form of regulation of foreign trade and a policy that taxes foreign products to encourage or safeguard domestic industry. _____ s are the simplest and oldest instrument of trade policy. Traditionally, states have used them as a source of income. Now, they are among the most widely used instruments of protection, along with import and export quotas.

Exam Probability: **High**

52. *Answer choices:*

(see index for correct answer)

- a. Immigration tariff
- b. Duty-free shop
- c. Malaysian motor vehicle import duties
- d. Court of Exchequer

Guidance: level 1

:: Land value taxation ::

_____, sometimes referred to as dry _____, is the solid surface of Earth that is not permanently covered by water. The vast majority of human activity throughout history has occurred in _____ areas that support agriculture, habitat, and various natural resources. Some life forms have developed from predecessor species that lived in bodies of water.

Exam Probability: **Medium**

53. *Answer choices:*

(see index for correct answer)

- a. Prosper Australia
- b. Land
- c. Georgism
- d. Physiocracy

Guidance: level 1

:: Management ::

The _____ is a strategy performance management tool – a semi-standard structured report, that can be used by managers to keep track of the execution of activities by the staff within their control and to monitor the consequences arising from these actions.

Exam Probability: **Medium**

54. *Answer choices:*

(see index for correct answer)

- a. Coworking
- b. Enterprise planning system
- c. Submission management
- d. Balanced scorecard

Guidance: level 1

:: Real estate valuation ::

_____ or OMV is the price at which an asset would trade in a competitive auction setting. _____ is often used interchangeably with open _____, fair value or fair _____, although these terms have distinct definitions in different standards, and may or may not differ in some circumstances.

Exam Probability: **High**

55. *Answer choices:*

(see index for correct answer)

- a. Rate base
- b. Market value

- c. Lamudi
- d. Highest and best use

Guidance: level 1

:: Data collection ::

A _____ is an utterance which typically functions as a request for information. _____ s can thus be understood as a kind of illocutionary act in the field of pragmatics or as special kinds of propositions in frameworks of formal semantics such as alternative semantics or inquisitive semantics. The information requested is expected to be provided in the form of an answer. _____ s are often conflated with interrogatives, which are the grammatical forms typically used to achieve them. Rhetorical _____ s, for example, are interrogative in form but may not be considered true _____ s as they are not expected to be answered. Conversely, non-interrogative grammatical structures may be considered _____ s as in the case of the imperative sentence "tell me your name".

Exam Probability: **Medium**

56. *Answer choices:*

(see index for correct answer)

- a. Data scraping
- b. European Social Survey
- c. Question
- d. Crude Oil Data Exchange

Guidance: level 1

:: Human resource management ::

_____ is the corporate management term for the act of reorganizing the legal, ownership, operational, or other structures of a company for the purpose of making it more profitable, or better organized for its present needs. Other reasons for _____ include a change of ownership or ownership structure, demerger, or a response to a crisis or major change in the business such as bankruptcy, repositioning, or buyout. _____ may also be described as corporate _____ , debt _____ and financial _____ .

Exam Probability: **High**

57. *Answer choices:*
(see index for correct answer)

- a. Organizational orientations
- b. Expense management
- c. Skill mix
- d. Restructuring

Guidance: level 1

:: ::

_____ is the collection of techniques, skills, methods, and processes used in the production of goods or services or in the accomplishment of objectives, such as scientific investigation. _____ can be the knowledge of techniques, processes, and the like, or it can be embedded in machines to allow for operation without detailed knowledge of their workings. Systems applying _____ by taking an input, changing it according to the system's use, and then producing an outcome are referred to as _____ systems or technological systems.

Exam Probability: **Medium**

58. *Answer choices:*

(see index for correct answer)

- a. empathy
- b. Technology
- c. imperative
- d. information systems assessment

Guidance: level 1

:: Organizational behavior ::

_____ is the state or fact of exclusive rights and control over property, which may be an object, land/real estate or intellectual property. _____ involves multiple rights, collectively referred to as title, which may be separated and held by different parties.

Exam Probability: **Low**

59. *Answer choices:*

(see index for correct answer)

- a. Collaborative partnerships
- b. Ownership
- c. Organizational behavior management
- d. Organizational storytelling

Guidance: level 1

Management

Management is the administration of an organization, whether it is a business, a not-for-profit organization, or government body. Management includes the activities of setting the strategy of an organization and coordinating the efforts of its employees (or of volunteers) to accomplish its objectives through the application of available resources, such as financial, natural, technological, and human resources.

:: Management occupations ::

_____ is the process of designing, launching and running a new business, which is often initially a small business. The people who create these businesses are called entrepreneurs.

Exam Probability: **Low**

1. *Answer choices:*

(see index for correct answer)

- a. Chief design officer
- b. Deputy mayor
- c. Entrepreneurship
- d. Corporate trainer

Guidance: level 1

:: Human resource management ::

Frederick Herzberg, an American psychologist, originally developed the concept of `_____` in 1968, in an article that he published on pioneering studies at A T&T. The concept stemmed from Herzberg's motivator-hygiene theory, which is based on the premise that job attitude is a construct of two independent factors, namely job satisfaction and job dissatisfaction. Job satisfaction encompasses intrinsic factors that arise from the work itself, including achievement and advancement; whilst job dissatisfaction stems from factors external to the actual work, including company policy and the quality of supervision.

Exam Probability: **Medium**

2. *Answer choices:*

(see index for correct answer)

- a. Job enrichment
- b. Individual development plan

- c. Broadbanding
- d. Continuing professional development

Guidance: level 1

:: Marketing ::

> _____ comes from the Latin neg and otsia referring to businessmen who, unlike the patricians, had no leisure time in their industriousness; it held the meaning of business until the 17th century when it took on the diplomatic connotation as a dialogue between two or more people or parties intended to reach a beneficial outcome over one or more issues where a conflict exists with respect to at least one of these issues. Thus, _____ is a process of combining divergent positions into a joint agreement under a decision rule of unanimity.

Exam Probability: **Low**

3. *Answer choices:*

(see index for correct answer)

- a. Immersion marketing
- b. Mystery shopping
- c. Content partnership
- d. Negotiation

Guidance: level 1

:: Autonomy ::

In developmental psychology and moral, political, and bioethical philosophy, _____ is the capacity to make an informed, uncoerced decision. Autonomous organizations or institutions are independent or self-governing. _____ can also be defined from a human resources perspective, where it denotes a level of discretion granted to an employee in his or her work. In such cases, _____ is known to generally increase job satisfaction. _____ is a term that is also widely used in the field of medicine — personal _____ is greatly recognized and valued in health care.

Exam Probability: **Low**

4. *Answer choices:*

(see index for correct answer)

- a. Respect for persons
- b. Hong Kong Autonomy Movement
- c. Quebec autonomism
- d. Rhex

Guidance: level 1

:: Business law ::

A _____ is a group of people who jointly supervise the activities of an organization, which can be either a for-profit business, nonprofit organization, or a government agency. Such a board's powers, duties, and responsibilities are determined by government regulations and the organization's own constitution and bylaws. These authorities may specify the number of members of the board, how they are to be chosen, and how often they are to meet.

Exam Probability: **Low**

5. *Answer choices:*

(see index for correct answer)

- a. Official Assignee
- b. TRIPS Agreement
- c. Novation
- d. Board of directors

Guidance: level 1

:: Project management ::

In political science, an _____ is a means by which a petition signed by a certain minimum number of registered voters can force a government to choose to either enact a law or hold a public vote in parliament in what is called indirect _____ , or under direct _____ , the proposition is immediately put to a plebiscite or referendum, in what is called a Popular initiated Referendum or citizen-initiated referendum).

Exam Probability: **Low**

6. *Answer choices:*

(see index for correct answer)

- a. project triangle
- b. Feature-driven development
- c. Project Management Professional
- d. Initiative

Guidance: level 1

:: Training ::

_____ is action or inaction that is regulated to be in accordance with a particular system of governance. _____ is commonly applied to regulating human and animal behavior, and furthermore, it is applied to each activity-branch in all branches of organized activity, knowledge, and other fields of study and observation. _____ can be a set of expectations that are required by any governing entity including the self, groups, classes, fields, industries, or societies.

Exam Probability: **High**

7. *Answer choices:*

(see index for correct answer)

- a. Arts-based training

- b. Boardcast
- c. Fartlek
- d. Practicum

Guidance: level 1

:: Planning ::

_____ is a high level plan to achieve one or more goals under conditions of uncertainty. In the sense of the "art of the general," which included several subsets of skills including tactics, siegecraft, logistics etc., the term came into use in the 6th century C.E. in East Roman terminology, and was translated into Western vernacular languages only in the 18th century. From then until the 20th century, the word "_____" came to denote "a comprehensive way to try to pursue political ends, including the threat or actual use of force, in a dialectic of wills" in a military conflict, in which both adversaries interact.

Exam Probability: **Medium**

8. *Answer choices:*
(see index for correct answer)

- a. Commercial area
- b. Reproductive life plan
- c. Enterprise architecture planning
- d. Group information management

Guidance: level 1

:: Employment ::

_____ is a relationship between two parties, usually based on a contract where work is paid for, where one party, which may be a corporation, for profit, not-for-profit organization, co-operative or other entity is the employer and the other is the employee. Employees work in return for payment, which may be in the form of an hourly wage, by piecework or an annual salary, depending on the type of work an employee does or which sector she or he is working in. Employees in some fields or sectors may receive gratuities, bonus payment or stock options. In some types of _____ , employees may receive benefits in addition to payment. Benefits can include health insurance, housing, disability insurance or use of a gym. _____ is typically governed by _____ laws, regulations or legal contracts.

Exam Probability: **High**

9. *Answer choices:*

(see index for correct answer)

- a. BA-X
- b. Payroll tax
- c. Illicit work
- d. Employment

Guidance: level 1

:: ::

___ refers to the confirmation of certain characteristics of an object, person, or organization. This confirmation is often, but not always, provided by some form of external review, education, assessment, or audit. Accreditation is a specific organization's process of ___ . According to the National Council on Measurement in Education, a ___ test is a credentialing test used to determine whether individuals are knowledgeable enough in a given occupational area to be labeled "competent to practice" in that area.

Exam Probability: **Medium**

10. *Answer choices:*

(see index for correct answer)

- a. information systems assessment
- b. imperative
- c. Certification
- d. Character

Guidance: level 1

:: ::

In sales, commerce and economics, a ___ is the recipient of a good, service, product or an idea - obtained from a seller, vendor, or supplier via a financial transaction or exchange for money or some other valuable consideration.

Exam Probability: **Low**

11. *Answer choices:*

(see index for correct answer)

- a. Sarbanes-Oxley act of 2002
- b. hierarchical
- c. Customer
- d. Character

Guidance: level 1

:: Organizational theory ::

_____ refers to both a body of non-elective government officials and an administrative policy-making group. Historically, a _____ was a government administration managed by departments staffed with non-elected officials. Today, _____ is the administrative system governing any large institution, whether publicly owned or privately owned. The public administration in many countries is an example of a _____ , but so is the centralized hierarchical structure of a business firm.

Exam Probability: **Low**

12. *Answer choices:*

(see index for correct answer)

- a. Bureaucracy

- b. Institutional complementarity
- c. Mary Parker Follett
- d. Contingency theory

Guidance: level 1

:: Management ::

_____ is a method of quality control which employs statistical methods to monitor and control a process. This helps to ensure that the process operates efficiently, producing more specification-conforming products with less waste . SPC can be applied to any process where the "conforming product" output can be measured. Key tools used in SPC include run charts, control charts, a focus on continuous improvement, and the design of experiments. An example of a process where SPC is applied is manufacturing lines.

Exam Probability: **High**

13. *Answer choices:*

(see index for correct answer)

- a. Modes of leadership
- b. Statistical process control
- c. SimulTrain
- d. Overtime rate

Guidance: level 1

:: Systems theory ::

A _____ is a set of policies, processes and procedures used by an organization to ensure that it can fulfill the tasks required to achieve its objectives. These objectives cover many aspects of the organization's operations. For instance, an environmental _____ enables organizations to improve their environmental performance and an occupational health and safety _____ enables an organization to control its occupational health and safety risks, etc.

Exam Probability: **Low**

14. *Answer choices:*

(see index for correct answer)

- a. Management system
- b. Black box
- c. co-design
- d. transient state

Guidance: level 1

:: ::

_____ Corporation was an American energy, commodities, and services company based in Houston, Texas. It was founded in 1985 as a merger between Houston Natural Gas and InterNorth, both relatively small regional companies. Before its bankruptcy on December 3, 2001, _____ employed approximately 29,000 staff and was a major electricity, natural gas, communications and pulp and paper company, with claimed revenues of nearly $101 billion during 2000. Fortune named _____ "America's Most Innovative Company" for six consecutive years.

Exam Probability: **Medium**

15. *Answer choices:*

(see index for correct answer)

- a. similarity-attraction theory
- b. deep-level diversity
- c. Enron
- d. functional perspective

Guidance: level 1

:: Commercial item transport and distribution ::

In commerce, supply-chain management, the management of the flow of goods and services, involves the movement and storage of raw materials, of work-in-process inventory, and of finished goods from point of origin to point of consumption. Interconnected or interlinked networks, channels and node businesses combine in the provision of products and services required by end customers in a supply chain. Supply-chain management has been defined as the "design, planning, execution, control, and monitoring of supply-chain activities with the objective of creating net value, building a competitive infrastructure, leveraging worldwide logistics, synchronizing supply with demand and measuring performance globally."SCM practice draws heavily from the areas of industrial engineering, systems engineering, operations management, logistics, procurement, information technology, and marketing and strives for an integrated approach. Marketing channels play an important role in supply-chain management. Current research in supply-chain management is concerned with topics related to sustainability and risk management, among others. Some suggest that the "people dimension" of SCM, ethical issues, internal integration, transparency/visibility, and human capital/talent management are topics that have, so far, been underrepresented on the research agenda.

Exam Probability: **Low**

16. *Answer choices:*

(see index for correct answer)

- a. Roll-on/roll-off
- b. Supply chain management
- c. Affreightment
- d. Slip sheet

Guidance: level 1

:: Management ::

In business, a _____ is the attribute that allows an organization to outperform its competitors. A _____ may include access to natural resources, such as high-grade ores or a low-cost power source, highly skilled labor, geographic location, high entry barriers, and access to new technology.

Exam Probability: **Medium**

17. *Answer choices:*
(see index for correct answer)

- a. Competitive advantage
- b. Continuous-flow manufacturing
- c. Control
- d. Swarm Development Group

Guidance: level 1

:: Electronic feedback ::

_____ occurs when outputs of a system are routed back as inputs as part of a chain of cause-and-effect that forms a circuit or loop. The system can then be said to feed back into itself. The notion of cause-and-effect has to be handled carefully when applied to _____ systems.

Exam Probability: **Low**

18. *Answer choices:*

(see index for correct answer)

- a. feedback loop
- b. Positive feedback

Guidance: level 1

:: Management ::

A _____ is a formal written document containing business goals, the methods on how these goals can be attained, and the time frame within which these goals need to be achieved. It also describes the nature of the business, background information on the organization, the organization's financial projections, and the strategies it intends to implement to achieve the stated targets. In its entirety, this document serves as a road map that provides direction to the business.

Exam Probability: **Medium**

19. *Answer choices:*

(see index for correct answer)

- a. Business plan
- b. Vendor relationship management
- c. Product differentiation
- d. Force-field analysis

Guidance: level 1

:: Security compliance ::

A _____ is a communicated intent to inflict harm or loss on another person. A _____ is considered an act of coercion. _____ s are widely observed in animal behavior, particularly in a ritualized form, chiefly in order to avoid the unnecessary physical violence that can lead to physical damage or the death of both conflicting parties.

Exam Probability: **High**

20. *Answer choices:*

(see index for correct answer)

- a. Attack
- b. Vulnerability management
- c. Month of bugs
- d. Threat

Guidance: level 1

:: Life skills ::

_____ , emotional leadership , emotional quotient and _____ quotient , is the capability of individuals to recognize their own emotions and those of others, discern between different feelings and label them appropriately, use emotional information to guide thinking and behavior, and manage and/or adjust emotions to adapt to environments or achieve one's goal.

Exam Probability: **Low**

21. *Answer choices:*

(see index for correct answer)

- a. Social intelligence
- b. coping mechanism
- c. Emotional intelligence
- d. multiple intelligence

Guidance: level 1

:: Supply chain management terms ::

In business and finance, _____ is a system of organizations, people, activities, information, and resources involved in moving a product or service from supplier to customer. _____ activities involve the transformation of natural resources, raw materials, and components into a finished product that is delivered to the end customer. In sophisticated _____ systems, used products may re-enter the _____ at any point where residual value is recyclable. _____ s link value chains.

Exam Probability: **Medium**

22. *Answer choices:*

(see index for correct answer)

- a. Supply chain
- b. Supply-chain management
- c. Capital spare
- d. inventory management

Guidance: level 1

:: Telecommuting ::

_____ , also called telework, teleworking, working from home, mobile work, remote work, and flexible workplace, is a work arrangement in which employees do not commute or travel to a central place of work, such as an office building, warehouse, or store. Teleworkers in the 21st century often use mobile telecommunications technology such as Wi-Fi-equipped laptop or tablet computers and smartphones to work from coffee shops; others may use a desktop computer and a landline phone at their home. According to a Reuters poll, approximately "one in five workers around the globe, particularly employees in the Middle East, Latin America and Asia, telecommute frequently and nearly 10 percent work from home every day." In the 2000s, annual leave or vacation in some organizations was seen as absence from the workplace rather than ceasing work, and some office employees used telework to continue to check work e-mails while on vacation.

Exam Probability: **High**

23. *Answer choices:*

(see index for correct answer)

- a. The Conference Group
- b. Telecommuting
- c. Home Work Convention, 1996
- d. IvanAnywhere

Guidance: level 1

:: Outsourcing ::

_____ is the relocation of a business process from one country to another—typically an operational process, such as manufacturing, or supporting processes, such as accounting. Typically this refers to a company business, although state governments may also employ _____ . More recently, technical and administrative services have been offshored.

Exam Probability: **High**

24. *Answer choices:*

(see index for correct answer)

- a. Chinggis Technologies
- b. Service-level agreement
- c. Divestment
- d. Offshoring

Guidance: level 1

:: ::

A _____ is monetary compensation paid by an employer to an employee in exchange for work done. Payment may be calculated as a fixed amount for each task completed, or at an hourly or daily rate, or based on an easily measured quantity of work done.

Exam Probability: **Medium**

25. *Answer choices:*

(see index for correct answer)

- a. similarity-attraction theory
- b. imperative
- c. Wage
- d. corporate values

Guidance: level 1

:: Psychometrics ::

_____ is a dynamic, structured, interactive process where a neutral third party assists disputing parties in resolving conflict through the use of specialized communication and negotiation techniques. All participants in _____ are encouraged to actively participate in the process. _____ is a "party-centered" process in that it is focused primarily upon the needs, rights, and interests of the parties. The mediator uses a wide variety of techniques to guide the process in a constructive direction and to help the parties find their optimal solution. A mediator is facilitative in that she/he manages the interaction between parties and facilitates open communication. _____ is also evaluative in that the mediator analyzes issues and relevant norms, while refraining from providing prescriptive advice to the parties.

Exam Probability: **Medium**

26. *Answer choices:*

(see index for correct answer)

- a. Psychometric function
- b. Person-fit analysis
- c. Adaptive comparative judgement
- d. Opinion poll

Guidance: level 1

:: Evaluation methods ::

In social psychology, _____ is the process of looking at oneself in order to assess aspects that are important to one's identity. It is one of the motives that drive self-evaluation, along with self-verification and self-enhancement. Sedikides suggests that the _____ motive will prompt people to seek information to confirm their uncertain self-concept rather than their certain self-concept and at the same time people use _____ to enhance their certainty of their own self-knowledge. However, the _____ motive could be seen as quite different from the other two self-evaluation motives. Unlike the other two motives through _____ people are interested in the accuracy of their current self view, rather than improving their self-view. This makes _____ the only self-evaluative motive that may cause a person's self-esteem to be damaged.

Exam Probability: **High**

27. *Answer choices:*

(see index for correct answer)

- a. Self-assessment
- b. Quantitative research
- c. Reference class forecasting
- d. quasi-experimental

Guidance: level 1

:: ::

A _____ is an individual or institution that legally owns one or more shares of stock in a public or private corporation. _____ s may be referred to as members of a corporation. Legally, a person is not a _____ in a corporation until their name and other details are entered in the corporation's register of _____ s or members.

Exam Probability: **Medium**

28. *Answer choices:*

(see index for correct answer)

- a. imperative
- b. empathy
- c. Shareholder
- d. deep-level diversity

Guidance: level 1

:: Monopoly (economics) ::

A _____ is a form of intellectual property that gives its owner the legal right to exclude others from making, using, selling, and importing an invention for a limited period of years, in exchange for publishing an enabling public disclosure of the invention. In most countries _____ rights fall under civil law and the _____ holder needs to sue someone infringing the _____ in order to enforce his or her rights. In some industries _____ s are an essential form of competitive advantage; in others they are irrelevant.

Exam Probability: **Low**

29. *Answer choices:*

(see index for correct answer)

- a. Contestable market
- b. Patent
- c. Government-granted monopoly
- d. Competition Commission

Guidance: level 1

:: Game theory ::

To _____ is to make a deal between different parties where each party gives up part of their demand. In arguments, _____ is a concept of finding agreement through communication, through a mutual acceptance of terms—often involving variations from an original goal or desires.

Exam Probability: **Low**

30. *Answer choices:*

(see index for correct answer)

- a. Compromise
- b. Smart market
- c. Chess opening

- d. Open-loop model

Guidance: level 1

:: Evaluation ::

> _____ is a way of preventing mistakes and defects in manufactured products and avoiding problems when delivering products or services to customers; which ISO 9000 defines as "part of quality management focused on providing confidence that quality requirements will be fulfilled". This defect prevention in _____ differs subtly from defect detection and rejection in quality control and has been referred to as a shift left since it focuses on quality earlier in the process.

Exam Probability: **High**

31. *Answer choices:*

(see index for correct answer)

- a. Defence Evaluation and Research Agency
- b. Program evaluation
- c. Knowledge survey
- d. International Association for the Evaluation of Educational Achievement

Guidance: level 1

:: Leadership ::

_____ is a theory of leadership where a leader works with teams to identify needed change, creating a vision to guide the change through inspiration, and executing the change in tandem with committed members of a group; it is an integral part of the Full Range Leadership Model. _____ serves to enhance the motivation, morale, and job performance of followers through a variety of mechanisms; these include connecting the follower's sense of identity and self to a project and to the collective identity of the organization; being a role model for followers in order to inspire them and to raise their interest in the project; challenging followers to take greater ownership for their work, and understanding the strengths and weaknesses of followers, allowing the leader to align followers with tasks that enhance their performance.

Exam Probability: **High**

32. *Answer choices:*

(see index for correct answer)

- a. Transformational leadership
- b. Meta-leadership
- c. Three levels of leadership model
- d. Authentic leadership

Guidance: level 1

:: Product management ::

_____ s, also known as Shewhart charts or process-behavior charts, are a statistical process control tool used to determine if a manufacturing or business process is in a state of control.

Exam Probability: **Medium**

33. *Answer choices:*
(see index for correct answer)

- a. Diffusion of innovations
- b. Consumer adoption of technological innovations
- c. Control chart
- d. Product cost management

Guidance: level 1

:: Meetings ::

A _____ is a body of one or more persons that is subordinate to a deliberative assembly. Usually, the assembly sends matters into a _____ as a way to explore them more fully than would be possible if the assembly itself were considering them. _____ s may have different functions and their type of work differ depending on the type of the organization and its needs.

Exam Probability: **High**

34. Answer choices:

(see index for correct answer)

- a. Tertulia
- b. Fishbowl
- c. Moment of silence
- d. Minutes

Guidance: level 1

:: ::

> _____ refers to a business or organization attempting to acquire goods or services to accomplish its goals. Although there are several organizations that attempt to set standards in the _____ process, processes can vary greatly between organizations. Typically the word " _____ " is not used interchangeably with the word "procurement", since procurement typically includes expediting, supplier quality, and transportation and logistics in addition to _____ .

Exam Probability: **High**

35. Answer choices:

(see index for correct answer)

- a. functional perspective
- b. Purchasing
- c. information systems assessment

- d. cultural

Guidance: level 1

:: Organizational theory ::

_____ is the process of groups of organisms working or acting together for common, mutual, or some underlying benefit, as opposed to working in competition for selfish benefit. Many animal and plant species cooperate both with other members of their own species and with members of other species .

Exam Probability: **High**

36. *Answer choices:*

(see index for correct answer)

- a. The three circles model
- b. Swift trust theory
- c. Cooperation
- d. Sociogram

Guidance: level 1

:: Business terms ::

A _____ is a short statement of why an organization exists, what its overall goal is, identifying the goal of its operations: what kind of product or service it provides, its primary customers or market, and its geographical region of operation. It may include a short statement of such fundamental matters as the organization's values or philosophies, a business's main competitive advantages, or a desired future state—the "vision".

Exam Probability: **Low**

37. *Answer choices:*

(see index for correct answer)

- a. organic growth
- b. back office
- c. Mission statement
- d. granular

Guidance: level 1

:: Unemployment ::

In economics, a _____ is a business cycle contraction when there is a general decline in economic activity. Macroeconomic indicators such as GDP, investment spending, capacity utilization, household income, business profits, and inflation fall, while bankruptcies and the unemployment rate rise. In the United Kingdom, it is defined as a negative economic growth for two consecutive quarters.

Exam Probability: **Low**

38. *Answer choices:*

(see index for correct answer)

- a. Involuntary unemployment
- b. Employment-to-population ratio
- c. Recession
- d. Unemployment Provision Convention, 1934

Guidance: level 1

:: Human resource management ::

_____ is a family of procedures to identify the content of a job in terms of activities involved and attributes or job requirements needed to perform the activities. _____ provides information of organizations which helps to determine which employees are best fit for specific jobs. Through _____ , the analyst needs to understand what the important tasks of the job are, how they are carried out, and the necessary human qualities needed to complete the job successfully.

Exam Probability: **High**

39. *Answer choices:*

(see index for correct answer)

- a. Job analysis

- b. Personal development planning
- c. Health human resources
- d. On-ramping

Guidance: level 1

:: Industry ::

_____ describes various measures of the efficiency of production. Often , a _____ measure is expressed as the ratio of an aggregate output to a single input or an aggregate input used in a production process, i.e. output per unit of input. Most common example is the labour _____ measure, e.g., such as GDP per worker. There are many different definitions of _____ and the choice among them depends on the purpose of the _____ measurement and/or data availability. The key source of difference between various _____ measures is also usually related to how the outputs and the inputs are aggregated into scalars to obtain such a ratio-type measure of _____ .

Exam Probability: **Medium**

40. *Answer choices:*
(see index for correct answer)

- a. Productivity
- b. Tube and clamp scaffold
- c. Eco-industrial development
- d. Recommended exposure limit

Guidance: level 1

:: Stochastic processes ::

_____ is a system of rules that are created and enforced through social or governmental institutions to regulate behavior. It has been defined both as "the Science of Justice" and "the Art of Justice". _____ is a system that regulates and ensures that individuals or a community adhere to the will of the state. State-enforced _____ s can be made by a collective legislature or by a single legislator, resulting in statutes, by the executive through decrees and regulations, or established by judges through precedent, normally in common _____ jurisdictions. Private individuals can create legally binding contracts, including arbitration agreements that may elect to accept alternative arbitration to the normal court process. The formation of _____ s themselves may be influenced by a constitution, written or tacit, and the rights encoded therein. The _____ shapes politics, economics, history and society in various ways and serves as a mediator of relations between people.

Exam Probability: **High**

41. *Answer choices:*

(see index for correct answer)

- a. Law
- b. Stochastic thinking
- c. Affine term structure model
- d. Self-similar process

Guidance: level 1

:: Quality management ::

_____ ensures that an organization, product or service is consistent. It has four main components: quality planning, quality assurance, quality control and quality improvement. _____ is focused not only on product and service quality, but also on the means to achieve it. _____ , therefore, uses quality assurance and control of processes as well as products to achieve more consistent quality. What a customer wants and is willing to pay for it determines quality. It is written or unwritten commitment to a known or unknown consumer in the market . Thus, quality can be defined as fitness for intended use or, in other words, how well the product performs its intended function

Exam Probability: **Low**

42. *Answer choices:*

(see index for correct answer)

- a. Test bay
- b. Quality policy
- c. Quality Management Maturity Grid
- d. Quality management

Guidance: level 1

:: ::

_____ is the administration of an organization, whether it is a business, a not-for-profit organization, or government body. _____ includes the activities of setting the strategy of an organization and coordinating the efforts of its employees to accomplish its objectives through the application of available resources, such as financial, natural, technological, and human resources. The term "_____" may also refer to those people who manage an organization.

Exam Probability: **High**

43. *Answer choices:*

(see index for correct answer)

- a. cultural
- b. process perspective
- c. Management
- d. open system

Guidance: level 1

:: Workplace ::

A _____, also referred to as a performance review, performance evaluation, development discussion, or employee appraisal is a method by which the job performance of an employee is documented and evaluated. _____s are a part of career development and consist of regular reviews of employee performance within organizations.

Exam Probability: **High**

44. *Answer choices:*

(see index for correct answer)

- a. Workplace wellness
- b. Performance appraisal
- c. Workplace aggression
- d. Toxic workplace

Guidance: level 1

:: Marketing ::

_____ , in marketing, manufacturing, call centres and management, is the use of flexible computer-aided manufacturing systems to produce custom output. Such systems combine the low unit costs of mass production processes with the flexibility of individual customization.

Exam Probability: **High**

45. *Answer choices:*

(see index for correct answer)

- a. LGBT marketing
- b. Concept testing
- c. Inbound marketing automation

- d. Movie gimmick

Guidance: level 1

:: Human resource management ::

_____ is a core function of human resource management and it is related to the specification of contents, methods and relationship of jobs in order to satisfy technological and organizational requirements as well as the social and personal requirements of the job holder or the employee. Its principles are geared towards how the nature of a person's job affects their attitudes and behavior at work, particularly relating to characteristics such as skill variety and autonomy. The aim of a _____ is to improve job satisfaction, to improve through-put, to improve quality and to reduce employee problems.

Exam Probability: **Low**

46. *Answer choices:*

(see index for correct answer)

- a. Job enlargement
- b. Job description management
- c. Domestic inquiry
- d. Job design

Guidance: level 1

:: Marketing techniques ::

In industry, product lifecycle management is the process of managing the entire lifecycle of a product from inception, through engineering design and manufacture, to service and disposal of manufactured products. PLM integrates people, data, processes and business systems and provides a product information backbone for companies and their extended enterprise.

Exam Probability: **Medium**

47. *Answer choices:*

(see index for correct answer)

- a. Locals casino
- b. Angel dusting
- c. Co-promotion
- d. Real-time marketing

Guidance: level 1

:: ::

In organizational behavior and industrial/organizational psychology, proactivity or _____ behavior by individuals refers to anticipatory, change-oriented and self-initiated behavior in situations. _____ behavior involves acting in advance of a future situation, rather than just reacting. It means taking control and making things happen rather than just adjusting to a situation or waiting for something to happen. _____ employees generally do not need to be asked to act, nor do they require detailed instructions.

Exam Probability: **High**

48. *Answer choices:*

(see index for correct answer)

- a. open system
- b. similarity-attraction theory
- c. deep-level diversity
- d. Proactive

Guidance: level 1

:: Human resource management ::

_____ are the people who make up the workforce of an organization, business sector, or economy. "Human capital" is sometimes used synonymously with "_____", although human capital typically refers to a narrower effect. Likewise, other terms sometimes used include manpower, talent, labor, personnel, or simply people.

Exam Probability: **High**

49. *Answer choices:*

(see index for correct answer)

- a. Action alert
- b. Human resources
- c. Talent management
- d. Human resource management

Guidance: level 1

:: ::

_____ is the process of two or more people or organizations working together to complete a task or achieve a goal. _____ is similar to cooperation. Most _____ requires leadership, although the form of leadership can be social within a decentralized and egalitarian group. Teams that work collaboratively often access greater resources, recognition and rewards when facing competition for finite resources.

Exam Probability: **Medium**

50. *Answer choices:*

(see index for correct answer)

- a. Collaboration
- b. Character

- c. similarity-attraction theory
- d. functional perspective

Guidance: level 1

:: Employment ::

The _____ is an individual's metaphorical "journey" through learning, work and other aspects of life. There are a number of ways to define _____ and the term is used in a variety of ways.

Exam Probability: **High**

51. *Answer choices:*
(see index for correct answer)

- a. The Kingdom of Could Be You
- b. Career
- c. Performance improvement
- d. Job shadow

Guidance: level 1

:: ::

_____ or haggling is a type of negotiation in which the buyer and seller of a good or service debate the price and exact nature of a transaction. If the _____ produces agreement on terms, the transaction takes place. _____ is an alternative pricing strategy to fixed prices. Optimally, if it costs the retailer nothing to engage and allow _____ , s/he can divine the buyer's willingness to spend. It allows for capturing more consumer surplus as it allows price discrimination, a process whereby a seller can charge a higher price to one buyer who is more eager . Haggling has largely disappeared in parts of the world where the cost to haggle exceeds the gain to retailers for most common retail items. However, for expensive goods sold to uninformed buyers such as automobiles, _____ can remain commonplace.

Exam Probability: **Low**

52. *Answer choices:*

(see index for correct answer)

- a. levels of analysis
- b. cultural
- c. Bargaining
- d. functional perspective

Guidance: level 1

:: Internet privacy ::

An _____ is a private network accessible only to an organization's staff. Often, a wide range of information and services are available on an organization's internal _____ that are unavailable to the public, unlike the Internet. A company-wide _____ can constitute an important focal point of internal communication and collaboration, and provide a single starting point to access internal and external resources. In its simplest form, an _____ is established with the technologies for local area networks and wide area networks . Many modern _____ s have search engines, user profiles, blogs, mobile apps with notifications, and events planning within their infrastructure.

Exam Probability: **Low**

53. *Answer choices:*

(see index for correct answer)

- a. Ipredator
- b. Intranet
- c. Anonymity application
- d. Real-name system

Guidance: level 1

:: Organizational structure ::

An _____ defines how activities such as task allocation, coordination, and supervision are directed toward the achievement of organizational aims.

Exam Probability: **High**

54. *Answer choices:*

(see index for correct answer)

- a. Automated Bureaucracy
- b. Organizational structure
- c. Organization of the New York City Police Department
- d. Blessed Unrest

Guidance: level 1

:: Human resource management ::

_____ , also known as management by results, was first popularized by Peter Drucker in his 1954 book The Practice of Management. _____ is the process of defining specific objectives within an organization that management can convey to organization members, then deciding on how to achieve each objective in sequence. This process allows managers to take work that needs to be done one step at a time to allow for a calm, yet productive work environment. This process also helps organization members to see their accomplishments as they achieve each objective, which reinforces a positive work environment and a sense of achievement. An important part of MBO is the measurement and comparison of an employee's actual performance with the standards set. Ideally, when employees themselves have been involved with the goal-setting and choosing the course of action to be followed by them, they are more likely to fulfill their responsibilities. According to George S. Odiorne, the system of _____ can be described as a process whereby the superior and subordinate jointly identify common goals, define each individual's major areas of responsibility in terms of the results expected of him or her, and use these measures as guides for operating the unit and assessing the contribution of each of its members.

Exam Probability: **Medium**

55. *Answer choices:*

(see index for correct answer)

- a. Appreciative inquiry
- b. Job design
- c. Enterprise architecture
- d. Job sharing

Guidance: level 1

:: Economic globalization ::

_____ is an agreement in which one company hires another company to be responsible for a planned or existing activity that is or could be done internally, and sometimes involves transferring employees and assets from one firm to another.

Exam Probability: **Low**

56. *Answer choices:*

(see index for correct answer)

- a. Outsourcing
- b. global financial

Guidance: level 1

:: ::

_____ is a form of development in which a person called a coach supports a learner or client in achieving a specific personal or professional goal by providing training and guidance. The learner is sometimes called a coachee. Occasionally, _____ may mean an informal relationship between two people, of whom one has more experience and expertise than the other and offers advice and guidance as the latter learns; but _____ differs from mentoring in focusing on specific tasks or objectives, as opposed to more general goals or overall development.

Exam Probability: **Medium**

57. *Answer choices:*

(see index for correct answer)

- a. open system
- b. interpersonal communication
- c. process perspective
- d. Coaching

Guidance: level 1

:: Management ::

_____ is the process of thinking about the activities required to achieve a desired goal. It is the first and foremost activity to achieve desired results. It involves the creation and maintenance of a plan, such as psychological aspects that require conceptual skills. There are even a couple of tests to measure someone's capability of _____ well. As such, _____ is a fundamental property of intelligent behavior. An important further meaning, often just called " _____ " is the legal context of permitted building developments.

Exam Probability: **Low**

58. *Answer choices:*

(see index for correct answer)

- a. Business workflow analysis
- b. Planning
- c. Management styles
- d. Visual learning

Guidance: level 1

:: ::

An _____ in international trade is a good or service produced in one country that is bought by someone in another country. The seller of such goods and services is an _____ er; the foreign buyer is an importer.

Exam Probability: **Medium**

59. *Answer choices:*

(see index for correct answer)

- a. surface-level diversity
- b. information systems assessment
- c. imperative
- d. hierarchical perspective

Guidance: level 1

Business law

Corporate law (also known as business law) is the body of law governing the rights, relations, and conduct of persons, companies, organizations and businesses. It refers to the legal practice relating to, or the theory of corporations. Corporate law often describes the law relating to matters which derive directly from the life-cycle of a corporation. It thus encompasses the formation, funding, governance, and death of a corporation.

:: Patent law ::

A _____ is generally any statement intended to specify or delimit the scope of rights and obligations that may be exercised and enforced by parties in a legally recognized relationship. In contrast to other terms for legally operative language, the term _____ usually implies situations that involve some level of uncertainty, waiver, or risk.

Exam Probability: **High**

1. *Answer choices:*

(see index for correct answer)

- a. INID
- b. Research tool patents
- c. Disclaimer
- d. Inventions and Their Management

Guidance: level 1

:: ::

An _____ is an area of the production, distribution, or trade, and consumption of goods and services by different agents. Understood in its broadest sense, 'The _____ is defined as a social domain that emphasize the practices, discourses, and material expressions associated with the production, use, and management of resources'. Economic agents can be individuals, businesses, organizations, or governments. Economic transactions occur when two parties agree to the value or price of the transacted good or service, commonly expressed in a certain currency. However, monetary transactions only account for a small part of the economic domain.

Exam Probability: **Medium**

2. *Answer choices:*

(see index for correct answer)

- a. deep-level diversity
- b. imperative
- c. Economy

- d. process perspective

Guidance: level 1

:: ::

According to the philosopher Piyush Mathur, "Tangibility is the property that a phenomenon exhibits if it has and/or transports mass and/or energy and/or momentum".

Exam Probability: **High**

3. *Answer choices:*
(see index for correct answer)

- a. surface-level diversity
- b. imperative
- c. personal values
- d. process perspective

Guidance: level 1

:: Debt ::

A _____ is a party that has a claim on the services of a second party. It is a person or institution to whom money is owed. The first party, in general, has provided some property or service to the second party under the assumption that the second party will return an equivalent property and service. The second party is frequently called a debtor or borrower. The first party is called the _____ , which is the lender of property, service, or money.

Exam Probability: **Low**

4. *Answer choices:*

(see index for correct answer)

- a. Interest
- b. External financing
- c. Debt relief
- d. Creditor

Guidance: level 1

:: Insolvency ::

_____ is the state of being unable to pay the money owed, by a person or company, on time; those in a state of _____ are said to be insolvent. There are two forms: cash-flow _____ and balance-sheet _____ .

Exam Probability: **High**

5. *Answer choices:*

(see index for correct answer)

- a. Insolvency
- b. Liquidation
- c. Official Committee of Equity Security Holders
- d. Financial distress

Guidance: level 1

:: Progressive Era in the United States ::

The Clayton Antitrust Act of 1914, was a part of United States antitrust law with the goal of adding further substance to the U.S. antitrust law regime; the _____ sought to prevent anticompetitive practices in their incipiency. That regime started with the Sherman Antitrust Act of 1890, the first Federal law outlawing practices considered harmful to consumers. The _____ specified particular prohibited conduct, the three-level enforcement scheme, the exemptions, and the remedial measures.

Exam Probability: **High**

6. *Answer choices:*

(see index for correct answer)

- a. Clayton Antitrust Act
- b. Mann Act
- c. Clayton Act

Guidance: level 1

:: Project management ::

A _____ is a source or supply from which a benefit is produced and it has some utility. _____ s can broadly be classified upon their availability—they are classified into renewable and non-renewable _____ s. Examples of non renewable _____ s are coal, crude oil natural gas nuclear energy etc. Examples of renewable _____ s are air, water, wind, solar energy etc. They can also be classified as actual and potential on the basis of level of development and use, on the basis of origin they can be classified as biotic and abiotic, and on the basis of their distribution, as ubiquitous and localized. An item becomes a _____ with time and developing technology. Typically, _____ s are materials, energy, services, staff, knowledge, or other assets that are transformed to produce benefit and in the process may be consumed or made unavailable. Benefits of _____ utilization may include increased wealth, proper functioning of a system, or enhanced well-being. From a human perspective a natural _____ is anything obtained from the environment to satisfy human needs and wants. From a broader biological or ecological perspective a _____ satisfies the needs of a living organism.

Exam Probability: **High**

7. *Answer choices:*
(see index for correct answer)

- a. System anatomy
- b. Scope creep
- c. Assumption-based planning
- d. Resource

Guidance: level 1

:: ::

_____ is the body of law that governs the activities of administrative agencies of government. Government agency action can include rule making, adjudication, or the enforcement of a specific regulatory agenda. _____ is considered a branch of public law. As a body of law, _____ deals with the decision-making of the administrative units of government that are part of a national regulatory scheme in such areas as police law, international trade, manufacturing, the environment, taxation, broadcasting, immigration and transport. _____ expanded greatly during the twentieth century, as legislative bodies worldwide created more government agencies to regulate the social, economic and political spheres of human interaction.

Exam Probability: **High**

8. *Answer choices:*

(see index for correct answer)

- a. corporate values
- b. process perspective
- c. Administrative law
- d. personal values

Guidance: level 1

:: ::

A _____ is an individual or institution that legally owns one or more shares of stock in a public or private corporation. _____ s may be referred to as members of a corporation. Legally, a person is not a _____ in a corporation until their name and other details are entered in the corporation's register of _____ s or members.

Exam Probability: **Low**

9. *Answer choices:*

(see index for correct answer)

- a. Shareholder
- b. interpersonal communication
- c. empathy
- d. functional perspective

Guidance: level 1

:: Contract law ::

_____ are damages whose amount the parties designate during the formation of a contract for the injured party to collect as compensation upon a specific breach.

Exam Probability: **High**

10. *Answer choices:*

(see index for correct answer)

- a. Non-repudiation
- b. Liquidated damages
- c. Handshake deal
- d. Acceleration clause

Guidance: level 1

:: ::

In English law, a _____ or _____ absolute is an estate in land, a form of freehold ownership. It is a way that real estate and land may be owned in common law countries, and is the highest possible ownership interest that can be held in real property. Allodial title is reserved to governments under a civil law structure. The rights of the _____ owner are limited by government powers of taxation, compulsory purchase, police power, and escheat, and it could also be limited further by certain encumbrances or conditions in the deed, such as, for example, a condition that required the land to be used as a public park, with a reversion interest in the grantor if the condition fails; this is a _____ conditional.

Exam Probability: **High**

11. *Answer choices:*
(see index for correct answer)

- a. cultural
- b. hierarchical

- c. Fee simple
- d. Sarbanes-Oxley act of 2002

Guidance: level 1

:: ::

_____, often abbreviated cert. in the United States, is a process for seeking judicial review and a writ issued by a court that agrees to review. A _____ is issued by a superior court, directing an inferior court, tribunal, or other public authority to send the record of a proceeding for review.

Exam Probability: **High**

12. *Answer choices:*

(see index for correct answer)

- a. surface-level diversity
- b. deep-level diversity
- c. interpersonal communication
- d. hierarchical perspective

Guidance: level 1

:: Money market instruments ::

_____, in the global financial market, is an unsecured promissory note with a fixed maturity of not more than 270 days.

Exam Probability: **High**

13. *Answer choices:*

(see index for correct answer)

- a. Banker's acceptance
- b. Commercial Paper

Guidance: level 1

:: ::

An _____, for United States federal income tax, is a closely held corporation that makes a valid election to be taxed under Subchapter S of Chapter 1 of the Internal Revenue Code. In general, _____ s do not pay any income taxes. Instead, the corporation's income or losses are divided among and passed through to its shareholders. The shareholders must then report the income or loss on their own individual income tax returns.

Exam Probability: **High**

14. *Answer choices:*

(see index for correct answer)

- a. hierarchical perspective
- b. S corporation
- c. surface-level diversity
- d. imperative

Guidance: level 1

:: Legal doctrines and principles ::

In law, a _____ is an event sufficiently related to an injury that the courts deem the event to be the cause of that injury. There are two types of causation in the law: cause-in-fact, and proximate cause. Cause-in-fact is determined by the "but for" test: But for the action, the result would not have happened. The action is a necessary condition, but may not be a sufficient condition, for the resulting injury. A few circumstances exist where the but for test is ineffective. Since but-for causation is very easy to show, a second test is used to determine if an action is close enough to a harm in a "chain of events" to be legally valid. This test is called _____ . _____ is a key principle of Insurance and is concerned with how the loss or damage actually occurred. There are several competing theories of _____ . For an act to be deemed to cause a harm, both tests must be met; _____ is a legal limitation on cause-in-fact.

Exam Probability: **Low**

15. *Answer choices:*

(see index for correct answer)

- a. Attractive nuisance
- b. Contributory negligence

- c. Proximate cause
- d. Unilateral mistake

Guidance: level 1

:: Contract law ::

In jurisprudence, _____ is an equitable doctrine that involves one person taking advantage of a position of power over another person. This inequity in power between the parties can vitiate one party's consent as they are unable to freely exercise their independent will.

Exam Probability: **High**

16. *Answer choices:*

(see index for correct answer)

- a. Essentialia negotii
- b. Multimarket contact
- c. Warranty tolling
- d. Pactum de quota litis

Guidance: level 1

:: ::

_____ is the act or practice of forbidding something by law; more particularly the term refers to the banning of the manufacture, storage, transportation, sale, possession, and consumption of alcoholic beverages. The word is also used to refer to a period of time during which such bans are enforced.

Exam Probability: **High**

17. *Answer choices:*

(see index for correct answer)

- a. interpersonal communication
- b. levels of analysis
- c. Prohibition
- d. Character

Guidance: level 1

:: Legal procedure ::

_____ , adjective law, or rules of court comprises the rules by which a court hears and determines what happens in civil, lawsuit, criminal or administrative proceedings. The rules are designed to ensure a fair and consistent application of due process or fundamental justice to all cases that come before a court.

Exam Probability: **Medium**

18. *Answer choices:*

(see index for correct answer)

- a. civil procedure
- b. Procedural law
- c. Opening statement
- d. appellate

Guidance: level 1

:: Marketing ::

_____ or stock is the goods and materials that a business holds for the ultimate goal of resale.

Exam Probability: **High**

19. *Answer choices:*

(see index for correct answer)

- a. Gladvertising
- b. Matomy Media
- c. Paddock girl
- d. Commercial planning

Guidance: level 1

:: Business law ::

In the United States, the United Kingdom, Australia, Canada and South Africa, _____ relates to the doctrines of the law of agency. It is relevant particularly in corporate law and constitutional law. _____ refers to a situation where a reasonable third party would understand that an agent had authority to act. This means a principal is bound by the agent's actions, even if the agent had no actual authority, whether express or implied. It raises an estoppel because the third party is given an assurance, which he relies on and would be inequitable for the principal to deny the authority given. _____ can legally be found, even if actual authority has not been given.

Exam Probability: **Low**

20. *Answer choices:*

(see index for correct answer)

- a. Administration
- b. Trusted Computing
- c. Lex mercatoria
- d. Oppression remedy

Guidance: level 1

:: Stock market ::

_____ is freedom from, or resilience against, potential harm caused by others. Beneficiaries of _____ may be of persons and social groups, objects and institutions, ecosystems or any other entity or phenomenon vulnerable to unwanted change by its environment.

Exam Probability: **High**

21. *Answer choices:*

(see index for correct answer)

- a. Stub
- b. Intellidex
- c. Order book
- d. Security

Guidance: level 1

:: Consumer theory ::

A _____ is a technical term in psychology, economics and philosophy usually used in relation to choosing between alternatives. For example, someone prefers A over B if they would rather choose A than B.

Exam Probability: **Low**

22. *Answer choices:*

(see index for correct answer)

- a. Income elasticity of demand
- b. Consumer choice
- c. Elasticity of intertemporal substitution
- d. Preference

Guidance: level 1

:: ::

_____, in United States trademark law, is a statutory cause of action that permits a party to petition the Trademark Trial and Appeal Board of the Patent and Trademark Office to cancel a trademark registration that "may disparage or falsely suggest a connection with persons, living or dead, institutions, beliefs, or national symbols, or bring them into contempt or disrepute." Unlike claims regarding the validity of the mark, a _____ claim can be brought "at any time," subject to equitable defenses such as laches.

Exam Probability: **Medium**

23. *Answer choices:*

(see index for correct answer)

- a. co-culture
- b. Disparagement
- c. functional perspective
- d. open system

Guidance: level 1

:: ::

A _____ is the party who initiates a lawsuit before a court. By doing so, the _____ seeks a legal remedy; if this search is successful, the court will issue judgment in favor of the _____ and make the appropriate court order. "_____" is the term used in civil cases in most English-speaking jurisdictions, the notable exception being England and Wales, where a _____ has, since the introduction of the Civil Procedure Rules in 1999, been known as a "claimant", but that term also has other meanings. In criminal cases, the prosecutor brings the case against the defendant, but the key complaining party is often called the "complainant".

Exam Probability: **Medium**

24. *Answer choices:*

(see index for correct answer)

- a. interpersonal communication
- b. cultural
- c. Sarbanes-Oxley act of 2002
- d. Plaintiff

Guidance: level 1

:: Business law ::

The term is used to designate a range of diverse, if often kindred, concepts. These have historically been addressed in a number of discrete disciplines, notably mathematics, physics, chemistry, ethics, aesthetics, ontology, and theology.

Exam Probability: **Medium**

25. *Answer choices:*

(see index for correct answer)

- a. Perfection
- b. Consumer privacy
- c. Subordination
- d. United Kingdom commercial law

Guidance: level 1

:: International trade ::

A _____ is a document issued by a carrier to acknowledge receipt of cargo for shipment. Although the term historically related only to carriage by sea, a _____ may today be used for any type of carriage of goods.

Exam Probability: **Medium**

26. *Answer choices:*

(see index for correct answer)

- a. Flying geese paradigm
- b. Proexport
- c. Foreign trade multiplier
- d. Asian Clearing Union

Guidance: level 1

:: Legal doctrines and principles ::

_____ is a doctrine that a party is responsible for acts of their agents. For example, in the United States, there are circumstances when an employer is liable for acts of employees performed within the course of their employment. This rule is also called the master-servant rule, recognized in both common law and civil law jurisdictions.

Exam Probability: **High**

27. *Answer choices:*

(see index for correct answer)

- a. Respondeat superior
- b. Res ipsa
- c. unconscionable contract
- d. Res ipsa loquitur

Guidance: level 1

:: Contract law ::

A _____ is an event or state of affairs that is required before something else will occur. In contract law, a _____ is an event which must occur, unless its non-occurrence is excused, before performance under a contract becomes due, i.e., before any contractual duty exists.

Exam Probability: **Medium**

28. *Answer choices:*

(see index for correct answer)

- a. Condition precedent
- b. Domicilium citandi et executandi
- c. Fair Food Program
- d. Synallagmatic contract

Guidance: level 1

:: Real property law ::

A _____ is any legal instrument in writing which passes, affirms or confirms an interest, right, or property and that is signed, attested, delivered, and in some jurisdictions, sealed. It is commonly associated with transferring title to property. The _____ has a greater presumption of validity and is less rebuttable than an instrument signed by the party to the _____ . A _____ can be unilateral or bilateral. _____ s include conveyances, commissions, licenses, patents, diplomas, and conditionally powers of attorney if executed as _____ s. The _____ is the modern descendant of the medieval charter, and delivery is thought to symbolically replace the ancient ceremony of livery of seisin.

Exam Probability: **High**

29. *Answer choices:*

(see index for correct answer)

- a. Deed
- b. Palestinian land laws
- c. Probate
- d. Conveyancing

Guidance: level 1

:: ::

A _____ is monetary compensation paid by an employer to an employee in exchange for work done. Payment may be calculated as a fixed amount for each task completed, or at an hourly or daily rate, or based on an easily measured quantity of work done.

Exam Probability: **Low**

30. *Answer choices:*

(see index for correct answer)

- a. similarity-attraction theory
- b. interpersonal communication
- c. Character
- d. empathy

Guidance: level 1

:: Marketing ::

A _____ is an overall experience of a customer that distinguishes an organization or product from its rivals in the eyes of the customer. _____ s are used in business, marketing, and advertising. Name _____ s are sometimes distinguished from generic or store _____ s.

Exam Probability: **High**

31. *Answer choices:*

(see index for correct answer)

- a. Brand
- b. Field marketing
- c. Global Center for Health Innovation

- d. elaboration likelihood

Guidance: level 1

:: Employment discrimination ::

_____ is a form of discrimination based on race, gender, religion, national origin, physical or mental disability, age, sexual orientation, and gender identity by employers. Earnings differentials or occupational differentiation—where differences in pay come from differences in qualifications or responsibilities—should not be confused with _____. Discrimination can be intended and involve disparate treatment of a group or be unintended, yet create disparate impact for a group.

Exam Probability: **High**

32. *Answer choices:*

(see index for correct answer)

- a. Employment Non-Discrimination Act
- b. Marriage bars
- c. Employment discrimination
- d. MacBride Principles

Guidance: level 1

:: Jurisdiction ::

In United States law, _____ jurisdiction is the subject-matter jurisdiction of United States federal courts to hear a civil case because the plaintiff has alleged a violation of the United States Constitution, federal law, or a treaty to which the United States is a party.

Exam Probability: **Medium**

33. *Answer choices:*

(see index for correct answer)

- a. Removal jurisdiction
- b. Federal question
- c. Appellate jurisdiction
- d. Subject-matter jurisdiction

Guidance: level 1

:: ::

The U.S. _____ is an independent agency of the United States federal government. The SEC holds primary responsibility for enforcing the federal securities laws, proposing securities rules, and regulating the securities industry, the nation's stock and options exchanges, and other activities and organizations, including the electronic securities markets in the United States.

Exam Probability: **Medium**

34. *Answer choices:*

(see index for correct answer)

- a. process perspective
- b. Securities and Exchange Commission
- c. empathy
- d. Sarbanes-Oxley act of 2002

Guidance: level 1

:: Real property law ::

_____ , sometimes colloquially described as 'squatter's rights', is a legal principle under which a person who does not have legal title to a piece of property—usually land—acquires legal ownership based on continuous possession or occupation of the land without the permission of its legal owner.

Exam Probability: **Medium**

35. *Answer choices:*

(see index for correct answer)

- a. Feoffee
- b. Copyhold
- c. Tenancy deposit schemes
- d. Latent defect

Guidance: level 1

:: ::

The _____ Act of 1890 was a United States antitrust law that regulates competition among enterprises, which was passed by Congress under the presidency of Benjamin Harrison.

Exam Probability: **Low**

36. *Answer choices:*

(see index for correct answer)

- a. process perspective
- b. Sarbanes-Oxley act of 2002
- c. surface-level diversity
- d. Sherman Antitrust

Guidance: level 1

:: ::

In general, _____ is a form of dishonesty or criminal activity undertaken by a person or organization entrusted with a position of authority, often to acquire illicit benefit. _____ may include many activities including bribery and embezzlement, though it may also involve practices that are legal in many countries. Political _____ occurs when an office-holder or other governmental employee acts in an official capacity for personal gain. _____ is most commonplace in kleptocracies, oligarchies, narco-states and mafia states.

Exam Probability: **Medium**

37. *Answer choices:*

(see index for correct answer)

- a. interpersonal communication
- b. cultural
- c. Corruption
- d. hierarchical

Guidance: level 1

:: ::

A _____, in common law jurisdictions, is a civil wrong that causes a claimant to suffer loss or harm resulting in legal liability for the person who commits the _____ious act. It can include the intentional infliction of emotional distress, negligence, financial losses, injuries, invasion of privacy, and many other things.

Exam Probability: **Medium**

38. *Answer choices:*

(see index for correct answer)

- a. corporate values
- b. functional perspective
- c. personal values
- d. Tort

Guidance: level 1

:: Business ::

An _____ is a key document used by limited liability companies to outline the business' financial and functional decisions including rules, regulations and provisions. The purpose of the document is to govern the internal operations of the business in a way that suits the specific needs of the business owners. Once the document is signed by the members of the limited liability company, it acts as an official contract binding them to its terms. _____ is mandatory as per laws only in 5 states - California, Delaware, Maine, Missouri, and New York LLCs operating without an _____ are governed by the state's default rules contained in the relevant statute and developed through state court decisions. An _____ is similar in function to corporate by-laws, or analogous to a partnership agreement in multi-member LLCs. In single-member LLCs, an _____ is a declaration of the structure that the member has chosen for the company and sometimes used to prove in court that the LLC structure is separate from that of the individual owner and thus necessary so that the owner has documentation to prove that he or she is indeed separate from the entity itself.

Exam Probability: **Medium**

39. *Answer choices:*

(see index for correct answer)

- a. Signed number
- b. Business strategy mapping
- c. Policy capturing
- d. Values scales

Guidance: level 1

:: Business law ::

A _____ is a group of people who jointly supervise the activities of an organization, which can be either a for-profit business, nonprofit organization, or a government agency. Such a board's powers, duties, and responsibilities are determined by government regulations and the organization's own constitution and bylaws. These authorities may specify the number of members of the board, how they are to be chosen, and how often they are to meet.

Exam Probability: **Medium**

40. *Answer choices:*

(see index for correct answer)

- a. Process agent

- b. Board of directors
- c. Facilitating payment
- d. Power harassment

Guidance: level 1

::: :::

The _____ of 1977 is a United States federal law known primarily for two of its main provisions: one that addresses accounting transparency requirements under the Securities Exchange Act of 1934 and another concerning bribery of foreign officials. The Act was amended in 1988 and in 1998, and has been subject to continued congressional concerns, namely whether its enforcement discourages U.S. companies from investing abroad.

Exam Probability: **Medium**

41. *Answer choices:*

(see index for correct answer)

- a. functional perspective
- b. deep-level diversity
- c. process perspective
- d. empathy

Guidance: level 1

:: Legal doctrines and principles ::

In the United States, the _____ is a legal rule, based on constitutional law, that prevents evidence collected or analyzed in violation of the defendant's constitutional rights from being used in a court of law. This may be considered an example of a prophylactic rule formulated by the judiciary in order to protect a constitutional right. The _____ may also, in some circumstances at least, be considered to follow directly from the constitutional language, such as the Fifth Amendment's command that no person "shall be compelled in any criminal case to be a witness against himself" and that no person "shall be deprived of life, liberty or property without due process of law".

Exam Probability: **Medium**

42. Answer choices:
(see index for correct answer)

- a. negligence
- b. Respondeat superior
- c. Proximate cause
- d. Nonacquiescence

Guidance: level 1

:: ::

_____ is the principled guide to action taken by the administrative executive branches of the state with regard to a class of issues, in a manner consistent with law and institutional customs.

Exam Probability: **High**

43. *Answer choices:*

(see index for correct answer)

- a. Public policy
- b. similarity-attraction theory
- c. information systems assessment
- d. hierarchical perspective

Guidance: level 1

:: ::

_____s and acquisitions are transactions in which the ownership of companies, other business organizations, or their operating units are transferred or consolidated with other entities. As an aspect of strategic management, M&A can allow enterprises to grow or downsize, and change the nature of their business or competitive position.

Exam Probability: **High**

44. *Answer choices:*

(see index for correct answer)

- a. imperative
- b. Merger
- c. Sarbanes-Oxley act of 2002
- d. interpersonal communication

Guidance: level 1

:: Contract law ::

In common law jurisdictions, an _____ is a contract law term for certain assurances that are presumed to be made in the sale of products or real property, due to the circumstances of the sale. These assurances are characterized as warranties irrespective of whether the seller has expressly promised them orally or in writing. They include an _____ of fitness for a particular purpose, an _____ of merchantability for products, _____ of workmanlike quality for services, and an _____ of habitability for a home.

Exam Probability: **Medium**

45. *Answer choices:*
(see index for correct answer)

- a. Contract B
- b. Implied warranty
- c. Duress

- d. Standard form contract

Guidance: level 1

:: ::

_____ is the collection of mechanisms, processes and relations by which corporations are controlled and operated. Governance structures and principles identify the distribution of rights and responsibilities among different participants in the corporation and include the rules and procedures for making decisions in corporate affairs. _____ is necessary because of the possibility of conflicts of interests between stakeholders, primarily between shareholders and upper management or among shareholders.

Exam Probability: **High**

46. *Answer choices:*

(see index for correct answer)

- a. levels of analysis
- b. open system
- c. Corporate governance
- d. cultural

Guidance: level 1

:: ::

_____ is a legal term which, in its broadest sense, is a synonym for anyone in a position of trust and so can refer to any person who holds property, authority, or a position of trust or responsibility for the benefit of another. A _____ can also refer to a person who is allowed to do certain tasks but not able to gain income. Although in the strictest sense of the term a _____ is the holder of property on behalf of a beneficiary, the more expansive sense encompasses persons who serve, for example, on the board of _____ s of an institution that operates for a charity, for the benefit of the general public, or a person in the local government.

Exam Probability: **High**

47. *Answer choices:*

(see index for correct answer)

- a. Trustee
- b. hierarchical perspective
- c. corporate values
- d. similarity-attraction theory

Guidance: level 1

:: Criminal law ::

_____ is the body of law that relates to crime. It proscribes conduct perceived as threatening, harmful, or otherwise endangering to the property, health, safety, and moral welfare of people inclusive of one's self. Most _____ is established by statute, which is to say that the laws are enacted by a legislature. _____ includes the punishment and rehabilitation of people who violate such laws. _____ varies according to jurisdiction, and differs from civil law, where emphasis is more on dispute resolution and victim compensation, rather than on punishment or rehabilitation. Criminal procedure is a formalized official activity that authenticates the fact of commission of a crime and authorizes punitive or rehabilitative treatment of the offender.

Exam Probability: **Medium**

48. *Answer choices:*

(see index for correct answer)

- a. Criminal law
- b. mitigating factor
- c. Mala prohibita
- d. Self-incrimination

Guidance: level 1

A _____ is a sworn body of people convened to render an impartial verdict officially submitted to them by a court, or to set a penalty or judgment. Modern juries tend to be found in courts to ascertain the guilt or lack thereof in a crime. In Anglophone jurisdictions, the verdict may be guilty or not guilty. The old institution of grand juries still exists in some places, particularly the United States, to investigate whether enough evidence of a crime exists to bring someone to trial.

Exam Probability: **Medium**

49. *Answer choices:*

(see index for correct answer)

- a. Character
- b. functional perspective
- c. Jury
- d. Sarbanes-Oxley act of 2002

Guidance: level 1

:: Contract law ::

Offer and acceptance analysis is a traditional approach in contract law. The offer and acceptance formula, developed in the 19th century, identifies a moment of formation when the parties are of one mind. This classical approach to contract formation has been modified by developments in the law of estoppel, misleading conduct, misrepresentation and unjust enrichment.

Exam Probability: **Medium**

50. *Answer choices:*

(see index for correct answer)

- a. Offeror
- b. Baseball business rules
- c. The Death of Contract
- d. Third-party beneficiary

Guidance: level 1

:: Contract law ::

_____ is a doctrine in contract law that describes terms that are so extremely unjust, or overwhelmingly one-sided in favor of the party who has the superior bargaining power, that they are contrary to good conscience. Typically, an unconscionable contract is held to be unenforceable because no reasonable or informed person would otherwise agree to it. The perpetrator of the conduct is not allowed to benefit, because the consideration offered is lacking, or is so obviously inadequate, that to enforce the contract would be unfair to the party seeking to escape the contract.

Exam Probability: **Medium**

51. *Answer choices:*

(see index for correct answer)

- a. Unenforceable contract
- b. Partial integration
- c. Unconscionability
- d. Fair Food Program

Guidance: level 1

:: Trade secrets ::

The _____ of 1996 was a 6 title Act of Congress dealing with a wide range of issues, including not only industrial espionage, but the insanity defense, matters regarding the Boys & Girls Clubs of America, requirements for presentence investigation reports, and the United States Sentencing Commission reports regarding encryption or scrambling technology, and other technical and minor amendments.

Exam Probability: **Medium**

52. *Answer choices:*

(see index for correct answer)

- a. Economic Espionage Act
- b. Exposure
- c. Economic Espionage Act of 1996
- d. Data General Corp. v. Digital Computer Controls, Inc.

Guidance: level 1

:: ::

_____ is a marketing communication that employs an openly sponsored, non-personal message to promote or sell a product, service or idea. Sponsors of _____ are typically businesses wishing to promote their products or services. _____ is differentiated from public relations in that an advertiser pays for and has control over the message. It differs from personal selling in that the message is non-personal, i.e., not directed to a particular individual. _____ is communicated through various mass media, including traditional media such as newspapers, magazines, television, radio, outdoor _____ or direct mail; and new media such as search results, blogs, social media, websites or text messages. The actual presentation of the message in a medium is referred to as an advertisement, or "ad" or advert for short.

Exam Probability: **Low**

53. *Answer choices:*
(see index for correct answer)

- a. process perspective
- b. personal values
- c. levels of analysis
- d. Advertising

Guidance: level 1

:: Legal terms ::

_____, or exemplary damages, are damages assessed in order to punish the defendant for outrageous conduct and/or to reform or deter the defendant and others from engaging in conduct similar to that which formed the basis of the lawsuit. Although the purpose of _____ is not to compensate the plaintiff, the plaintiff will receive all or some of the _____ award.

Exam Probability: **Low**

54. *Answer choices:*

(see index for correct answer)

- a. False pretenses
- b. Original jurisdiction
- c. Punitive damages
- d. Issue

Guidance: level 1

:: Project management ::

_____ is the right to exercise power, which can be formalized by a state and exercised by way of judges, appointed executives of government, or the ecclesiastical or priestly appointed representatives of a God or other deities.

Exam Probability: **High**

55. Answer choices:

(see index for correct answer)

- a. Product flow diagram
- b. Authority
- c. Waterfall model
- d. Organizational project management

Guidance: level 1

:: Legal terms ::

_____ s may be governments, corporations or investment trusts. _____ s are legally responsible for the obligations of the issue and for reporting financial conditions, material developments and any other operational activities as required by the regulations of their jurisdictions.

Exam Probability: **Medium**

56. Answer choices:

(see index for correct answer)

- a. Issuer
- b. Government interest
- c. Partible inheritance
- d. Fact-finding

Guidance: level 1

:: Generally Accepted Accounting Principles ::

In accounting, _____ is the income that a business have from its normal business activities, usually from the sale of goods and services to customers. _____ is also referred to as sales or turnover. Some companies receive _____ from interest, royalties, or other fees. _____ may refer to business income in general, or it may refer to the amount, in a monetary unit, earned during a period of time, as in "Last year, Company X had _____ of $42 million". Profits or net income generally imply total _____ minus total expenses in a given period. In accounting, in the balance statement it is a subsection of the Equity section and _____ increases equity, it is often referred to as the "top line" due to its position on the income statement at the very top. This is to be contrasted with the "bottom line" which denotes net income.

Exam Probability: **Medium**

57. *Answer choices:*
(see index for correct answer)

- a. Gross income
- b. Deferral
- c. Closing entries
- d. Revenue

Guidance: level 1

The _____ is an independent agency of the Federal government of the United States with responsibilities for enforcing U.S. labor law in relation to collective bargaining and unfair labor practices. Under the National Labor Relations Act of 1935 it supervises elections for labor union representation and can investigate and remedy unfair labor practices. Unfair labor practices may involve union-related situations or instances of protected concerted activity. The NLRB is governed by a five-person board and a General Counsel, all of whom are appointed by the President with the consent of the Senate. Board members are appointed to five-year terms and the General Counsel is appointed to a four-year term. The General Counsel acts as a prosecutor and the Board acts as an appellate quasi-judicial body from decisions of administrative law judges.

Exam Probability: **Low**

58. *Answer choices:*

(see index for correct answer)

- a. similarity-attraction theory
- b. National Labor Relations Board
- c. functional perspective
- d. corporate values

Guidance: level 1

A _____ is an aggregate of fundamental principles or established precedents that constitute the legal basis of a polity, organisation or other type of entity, and commonly determine how that entity is to be governed.

Exam Probability: **Low**

59. *Answer choices:*

(see index for correct answer)

- a. process perspective
- b. Constitution
- c. surface-level diversity
- d. personal values

Guidance: level 1

Finance

Finance is a field that is concerned with the allocation (investment) of assets and liabilities over space and time, often under conditions of risk or uncertainty. Finance can also be defined as the science of money management. Participants in the market aim to price assets based on their risk level, fundamental value, and their expected rate of return. Finance can be split into three sub-categories: public finance, corporate finance and personal finance.

:: Financial economics ::

_____ , Inc. is an independent investment research and financial publishing firm based in New York City, New York, United States, founded in 1931 by Arnold Bernhard. _____ is best known for publishing The _____ Investment Survey, a stock analysis newsletter that is among the most highly regarded and widely used independent investment research resources in global investment and trading markets, tracking approximately 1,700 publicly traded stocks in over 99 industries.

Exam Probability: **Low**

1. *Answer choices:*

(see index for correct answer)

- a. Portfolio insurance
- b. Holding value
- c. Value Line
- d. Consumer leverage ratio

Guidance: level 1

:: Capital (economics) ::

In Economics and Accounting, the _____ is the cost of a company's funds , or, from an investor's point of view "the required rate of return on a portfolio company's existing securities". It is used to evaluate new projects of a company. It is the minimum return that investors expect for providing capital to the company, thus setting a benchmark that a new project has to meet.

Exam Probability: **High**

2. *Answer choices:*

(see index for correct answer)

- a. Structural capital
- b. patient capital
- c. Information capital
- d. operating capital

Guidance: level 1

:: Institutional investors ::

A _____ is an investment fund that pools capital from accredited investors or institutional investors and invests in a variety of assets, often with complex portfolio-construction and risk management techniques. It is administered by a professional investment management firm, and often structured as a limited partnership, limited liability company, or similar vehicle. _____ s are generally distinct from mutual funds and regarded as alternative investments, as their use of leverage is not capped by regulators, and distinct from private equity funds, as the majority of _____ s invest in relatively liquid assets. However, funds which operate similarly to _____ s but are regulated similarly to mutual funds are available and known as liquid alternative investments.

Exam Probability: **Medium**

3. *Answer choices:*

(see index for correct answer)

- a. Chartered Financial Analyst
- b. Sampension
- c. Davidson Kempner Capital Management
- d. Capital Introduction

Guidance: level 1

:: Global systemically important banks ::

> The _____ Corporation is an American multinational investment bank and financial services company based in Charlotte, North Carolina with central hubs in New York City, London, Hong Kong, Minneapolis, and Toronto. _____ was formed through NationsBank's acquisition of BankAmerica in 1998. It is the second largest banking institution in the United States, after JP Morgan Chase. As a part of the Big Four, it services approximately 10.73% of all American bank deposits, in direct competition with Citigroup, Wells Fargo, and JPMorgan Chase. Its primary financial services revolve around commercial banking, wealth management, and investment banking.

Exam Probability: **Medium**

4. *Answer choices:*

(see index for correct answer)

- a. BNP Paribas
- b. Banco Bilbao Vizcaya Argentaria
- c. Bank of America

- d. Nordea

Guidance: level 1

:: Costs ::

In microeconomic theory, the _____, or alternative cost, of making a particular choice is the value of the most valuable choice out of those that were not taken. In other words, opportunity that will require sacrifices.

Exam Probability: **High**

5. *Answer choices:*
(see index for correct answer)

- a. Further processing cost
- b. Opportunity cost
- c. Cost of poor quality
- d. Social cost

Guidance: level 1

:: ::

A _____, or holiday, is a leave of absence from a regular occupation, or a specific trip or journey, usually for the purpose of recreation or tourism. People often take a _____ during specific holiday observances, or for specific festivals or celebrations. _____s are often spent with friends or family.

Exam Probability: **Low**

6. *Answer choices:*

(see index for correct answer)

- a. open system
- b. surface-level diversity
- c. Vacation
- d. information systems assessment

Guidance: level 1

:: Finance ::

The _____ of a corporation is the accumulated net income of the corporation that is retained by the corporation at a particular point of time, such as at the end of the reporting period. At the end of that period, the net income at that point is transferred from the Profit and Loss Account to the _____ account. If the balance of the _____ account is negative it may be called accumulated losses, retained losses or accumulated deficit, or similar terminology.

Exam Probability: **Low**

7. *Answer choices:*

(see index for correct answer)

- a. Debt-snowball method
- b. Syndicated loan
- c. Retained earnings
- d. Liabilities Subject to Compromise

Guidance: level 1

:: Shareholders ::

A _____ is a payment made by a corporation to its shareholders, usually as a distribution of profits. When a corporation earns a profit or surplus, the corporation is able to re-invest the profit in the business and pay a proportion of the profit as a _____ to shareholders. Distribution to shareholders may be in cash or, if the corporation has a _____ reinvestment plan, the amount can be paid by the issue of further shares or share repurchase. When _____ s are paid, shareholders typically must pay income taxes, and the corporation does not receive a corporate income tax deduction for the _____ payments.

Exam Probability: **Medium**

8. *Answer choices:*

(see index for correct answer)

- a. Shotgun clause
- b. Shareholder value
- c. Shareholder Protection Act
- d. Derivative suit

Guidance: level 1

:: Commerce ::

A _____ , manufacturing plant or a production plant is an industrial site, usually consisting of buildings and machinery, or more commonly a complex having several buildings, where workers manufacture goods or operate machines processing one product into another.

Exam Probability: **High**

9. *Answer choices:*

(see index for correct answer)

- a. Card association
- b. PIN pad
- c. Closed household economy
- d. Organ trade

Guidance: level 1

:: Marketing ::

_____ or stock is the goods and materials that a business holds for the ultimate goal of resale.

Exam Probability: **Medium**

10. *Answer choices:*

(see index for correct answer)

- a. Emailing
- b. Kano model
- c. Marketing communications planning framework
- d. Multichannel marketing

Guidance: level 1

:: ::

_____ is an eight-block-long street running roughly northwest to southeast from Broadway to South Street, at the East River, in the Financial District of Lower Manhattan in New York City. Over time, the term has become a metonym for the financial markets of the United States as a whole, the American financial services industry, or New York–based financial interests.

Exam Probability: **Medium**

11. *Answer choices:*

(see index for correct answer)

- a. co-culture
- b. hierarchical
- c. Wall Street
- d. empathy

Guidance: level 1

:: Generally Accepted Accounting Principles ::

> Expenditure is an outflow of money to another person or group to pay for an item or service, or for a category of costs. For a tenant, rent is an _____. For students or parents, tuition is an _____. Buying food, clothing, furniture or an automobile is often referred to as an _____. An _____ is a cost that is "paid" or "remitted", usually in exchange for something of value. Something that seems to cost a great deal is "expensive". Something that seems to cost little is "inexpensive". "_____ s of the table" are _____ s of dining, refreshments, a feast, etc.

Exam Probability: **Medium**

12. *Answer choices:*

(see index for correct answer)

- a. Depreciation
- b. Net income

- c. Closing entries
- d. Treasury stock

Guidance: level 1

:: Stock market ::

A _____ or stock divide increases the number of shares in a company. The price is adjusted such that the before and after market capitalization of the company remains the same and dilution does not occur. Options and warrants are included.

Exam Probability: **Medium**

13. *Answer choices:*

(see index for correct answer)

- a. Red chip
- b. Clientele effect
- c. Security
- d. Stock split

Guidance: level 1

:: bad_topic ::

_____ refers to systematic approach to the governance and realization of value from the things that a group or entity is responsible for, over their whole life cycles. It may apply both to tangible assets and to intangible assets. _____ is a systematic process of developing, operating, maintaining, upgrading, and disposing of assets in the most cost-effective manner.

Exam Probability: **Low**

14. *Answer choices:*

(see index for correct answer)

- a. Cognitive appraisal
- b. Sealy Corporation
- c. Asset management
- d. Domain squatting

Guidance: level 1

:: Government bonds ::

A _____, commonly known as a Muni Bond, is a bond issued by a local government or territory, or one of their agencies. It is generally used to finance public projects such as roads, schools, airports and seaports, and infrastructure-related repairs. The term _____ is commonly used in the United States, which has the largest market of such trade-able securities in the world. As of 2011, the _____ market was valued at $3.7 trillion. Potential issuers of _____ s include states, cities, counties, redevelopment agencies, special-purpose districts, school districts, public utility districts, publicly owned airports and seaports, and other governmental entities at or below the state level having more than a de minimis amount of one of the three sovereign powers: the power of taxation, the power of eminent domain or the police power.

Exam Probability: **High**

15. *Answer choices:*

(see index for correct answer)

- a. Municipal bond
- b. War bond
- c. South Carolina v. Baker
- d. Eurobonds

Guidance: level 1

:: ::

_____ is the withdrawal from one's position or occupation or from one's active working life. A person may also semi-retire by reducing work hours.

Exam Probability: **High**

16. *Answer choices:*

(see index for correct answer)

- a. levels of analysis
- b. deep-level diversity
- c. imperative
- d. Retirement

Guidance: level 1

:: Financial ratios ::

A _____ or accounting ratio is a relative magnitude of two selected numerical values taken from an enterprise's financial statements. Often used in accounting, there are many standard ratios used to try to evaluate the overall financial condition of a corporation or other organization. _____ s may be used by managers within a firm, by current and potential shareholders of a firm, and by a firm's creditors. Financial analysts use _____ s to compare the strengths and weaknesses in various companies. If shares in a company are traded in a financial market, the market price of the shares is used in certain _____ s.

Exam Probability: **Medium**

17. *Answer choices:*

(see index for correct answer)

- a. Average collection period
- b. Capitalization rate
- c. Financial ratio
- d. Total expense ratio

Guidance: level 1

:: Scheduling (computing) ::

> Ageing or _____ is the process of becoming older. The term refers especially to human beings, many animals, and fungi, whereas for example bacteria, perennial plants and some simple animals are potentially biologically immortal. In the broader sense, ageing can refer to single cells within an organism which have ceased dividing or to the population of a species.

Exam Probability: **High**

18. *Answer choices:*

(see index for correct answer)

- a. Affinity mask
- b. Aging
- c. Kernel preemption
- d. Run queue

Guidance: level 1

:: Funds ::

_____ value is the value of an entity's assets minus the value of its liabilities, often in relation to open-end or mutual funds, since shares of such funds registered with the U.S. Securities and Exchange Commission are redeemed at their _____ value. It is also a key figure with regard to hedge funds and venture capital funds when calculating the value of the underlying investments in these funds by investors. This may also be the same as the book value or the equity value of a business. _____ value may represent the value of the total equity, or it may be divided by the number of shares outstanding held by investors, thereby representing the _____ value per share.

Exam Probability: **Low**

19. *Answer choices:*

(see index for correct answer)

- a. The Watch Fund
- b. Icapital.biz Berhad
- c. Great Lakes Protection Fund
- d. Glacier National Park Fund

Guidance: level 1

:: Financial risk ::

_____ is the risk that arises for bond owners from fluctuating interest rates. How much _____ a bond has depends on how sensitive its price is to interest rate changes in the market. The sensitivity depends on two things, the bond's time to maturity, and the coupon rate of the bond.

Exam Probability: **High**

20. *Answer choices:*

(see index for correct answer)

- a. Student Investment Advisory Service
- b. Risk-free rate
- c. Investment management
- d. Interest rate risk

Guidance: level 1

:: ::

_____ is a political and social philosophy promoting traditional social institutions in the context of culture and civilization. The central tenets of _____ include tradition, human imperfection, organic society, hierarchy, authority, and property rights. Conservatives seek to preserve a range of institutions such as religion, parliamentary government, and property rights, with the aim of emphasizing social stability and continuity. The more traditional elements—reactionaries—oppose modernism and seek a return to "the way things were".

Exam Probability: **Low**

21. *Answer choices:*

(see index for correct answer)

- a. Character
- b. process perspective
- c. information systems assessment
- d. hierarchical

Guidance: level 1

:: Actuarial science ::

_____ is the possibility of losing something of value. Values can be gained or lost when taking _____ resulting from a given action or inaction, foreseen or unforeseen. _____ can also be defined as the intentional interaction with uncertainty. Uncertainty is a potential, unpredictable, and uncontrollable outcome; _____ is a consequence of action taken in spite of uncertainty.

Exam Probability: **Low**

22. *Answer choices:*

(see index for correct answer)

- a. Risk
- b. Statutory reserve

- c. Esscher principle
- d. Fictional actuaries

Guidance: level 1

:: Separation of investment and commercial banking ::

A _____ is a type of bank that provides services such as accepting deposits, making business loans, and offering basic investment products that is operated as a business for profit.

Exam Probability: **High**

23. *Answer choices:*

(see index for correct answer)

- a. Merchant bank
- b. Depository institution
- c. Bank Holding Company Act
- d. Commercial bank

Guidance: level 1

:: Competition (economics) ::

_____ arises whenever at least two parties strive for a goal which cannot be shared: where one's gain is the other's loss.

Exam Probability: **Low**

24. *Answer choices:*

(see index for correct answer)

- a. Currency competition
- b. National Competitiveness Report of Armenia
- c. Economic forces
- d. Level playing field

Guidance: level 1

:: Inventory ::

Costs are associated with particular goods using one of the several formulas, including specific identification, first-in first-out, or average cost. Costs include all costs of purchase, costs of conversion and other costs that are incurred in bringing the inventories to their present location and condition. Costs of goods made by the businesses include material, labor, and allocated overhead. The costs of those goods which are not yet sold are deferred as costs of inventory until the inventory is sold or written down in value.

Exam Probability: **Low**

25. Answer choices:

(see index for correct answer)

- a. Cost of goods available for sale
- b. Item-level tagging
- c. Cost of goods sold
- d. Stock demands

Guidance: level 1

:: Inventory ::

In business and accounting/accountancy, _____ or continuous inventory describes systems of inventory where information on inventory quantity and availability is updated on a continuous basis as a function of doing business. Generally this is accomplished by connecting the inventory system with order entry and in retail the point of sale system. In this case, book inventory would be exactly the same as, or almost the same, as the real inventory.

Exam Probability: **Low**

26. Answer choices:

(see index for correct answer)

- a. Perpetual inventory
- b. Lower of cost or market
- c. Stock demands
- d. Order fulfillment

Guidance: level 1

:: Banking ::

A _____ is a financial account maintained by a bank for a customer. A _____ can be a deposit account, a credit card account, a current account, or any other type of account offered by a financial institution, and represents the funds that a customer has entrusted to the financial institution and from which the customer can make withdrawals. Alternatively, accounts may be loan accounts in which case the customer owes money to the financial institution.

Exam Probability: **Medium**

27. *Answer choices:*

(see index for correct answer)

- a. Peer-to-peer banking
- b. Joint account
- c. Minimum daily balance
- d. Bank account

Guidance: level 1

:: ::

_____ is a means of protection from financial loss. It is a form of risk management, primarily used to hedge against the risk of a contingent or uncertain loss

Exam Probability: **Medium**

28. *Answer choices:*

(see index for correct answer)

- a. corporate values
- b. similarity-attraction theory
- c. deep-level diversity
- d. Insurance

Guidance: level 1

:: Bonds (finance) ::

An _____ is a legal contract that reflects or covers a debt or purchase obligation. It specifically refers to two types of practices: in historical usage, an _____ d servant status, and in modern usage, it is an instrument used for commercial debt or real estate transaction.

Exam Probability: **Medium**

29. *Answer choices:*

(see index for correct answer)

- a. Indenture
- b. Senior debt
- c. Bond Tender Offer
- d. Dim sum bond

Guidance: level 1

:: Accounting ::

It is the period for which books are balanced and the financial statements are prepared. Generally, the _____ consists of 12 months. However the beginning of the _____ differs according to the jurisdiction. For example, one entity may follow the regular calendar year, i.e. January to December as the accounting year, while another entity may follow April to March as the _____ .

Exam Probability: **Medium**

30. *Answer choices:*

(see index for correct answer)

- a. Accounting research
- b. Accounting period
- c. Legal cashier
- d. Maker-checker

Guidance: level 1

:: Finance ::

A _____ , publicly-traded company, publicly-held company, publicly-listed company, or public limited company is a corporation whose ownership is dispersed among the general public in many shares of stock which are freely traded on a stock exchange or in over-the-counter markets. In some jurisdictions, public companies over a certain size must be listed on an exchange. A _____ can be listed or unlisted .

Exam Probability: **Low**

31. *Answer choices:*

(see index for correct answer)

- a. Public company
- b. Tear sheet
- c. Numbrs
- d. Purchase price adjustment

Guidance: level 1

:: Manufacturing ::

_____ s are goods that have completed the manufacturing process but have not yet been sold or distributed to the end user.

Exam Probability: **Medium**

32. *Answer choices:*

(see index for correct answer)

- a. Acheson process
- b. Component engineering
- c. International Material Data System
- d. Manufacturing Engineering Centre

Guidance: level 1

:: Inventory ::

It requires a detailed physical count, so that the company knows exactly how many of each goods brought on specific dates remained at year end inventory. When this information is found, the amount of goods are multiplied by their purchase cost at their purchase date, to get a number for the ending inventory cost.

Exam Probability: **Low**

33. *Answer choices:*

(see index for correct answer)

- a. Inventory optimization
- b. Specific identification

- c. Consignment stock
- d. Lower of cost or market

Guidance: level 1

:: Generally Accepted Accounting Principles ::

In accrual accounting, the revenue recognition principle states that expenses should be recorded during the period in which they are incurred, regardless of when the transfer of cash occurs. Conversely, cash basis accounting calls for the recognition of an expense when the cash is paid, regardless of when the expense was actually incurred.

Exam Probability: **Low**

34. *Answer choices:*

(see index for correct answer)

- a. Normal balance
- b. Engagement letter
- c. Insurance asset management
- d. Matching principle

Guidance: level 1

:: Money market instruments ::

_____, in the global financial market, is an unsecured promissory note with a fixed maturity of not more than 270 days.

Exam Probability: **Low**

35. *Answer choices:*

(see index for correct answer)

- a. Commercial paper in India
- b. Banker's acceptance

Guidance: level 1

:: United States Generally Accepted Accounting Principles ::

In a companies' financial reporting, _____ "includes all changes in equity during a period except those resulting from investments by owners and distributions to owners". Because that use excludes the effects of changing ownership interest, an economic measure of _____ is necessary for financial analysis from the shareholders' point of view

Exam Probability: **Medium**

36. *Answer choices:*

(see index for correct answer)

- a. Comprehensive income

- b. Available for sale
- c. Accounting for leases in the United States
- d. Cost segregation study

Guidance: level 1

:: ::

An _____ is the production of goods or related services within an economy. The major source of revenue of a group or company is the indicator of its relevant _____. When a large group has multiple sources of revenue generation, it is considered to be working in different industries. Manufacturing _____ became a key sector of production and labour in European and North American countries during the Industrial Revolution, upsetting previous mercantile and feudal economies. This came through many successive rapid advances in technology, such as the production of steel and coal.

Exam Probability: **High**

37. *Answer choices:*

(see index for correct answer)

- a. hierarchical
- b. Sarbanes-Oxley act of 2002
- c. hierarchical perspective
- d. process perspective

Guidance: level 1

:: Business economics ::

A _____ is a term used primarily in cost accounting to describe something to which costs are assigned. Common examples of _____ s are: product lines, geographic territories, customers, departments or anything else for which management would like to quantify cost.

Exam Probability: **Medium**

38. *Answer choices:*

(see index for correct answer)

- a. Risk pool
- b. Function cost analysis
- c. Cost object
- d. Kaizen costing

Guidance: level 1

:: Hazard analysis ::

Broadly speaking, a _____ is the combined effort of 1. identifying and analyzing potential events that may negatively impact individuals, assets, and/or the environment ; and 2. making judgments "on the tolerability of the risk on the basis of a risk analysis" while considering influencing factors . Put in simpler terms, a _____ analyzes what can go wrong, how likely it is to happen, what the potential consequences are, and how tolerable the identified risk is. As part of this process, the resulting determination of risk may be expressed in a quantitative or qualitative fashion. The _____ is an inherent part of an overall risk management strategy, which attempts to, after a _____ , "introduce control measures to eliminate or reduce" any potential risk-related consequences.

Exam Probability: **Medium**

39. *Answer choices:*

(see index for correct answer)

- a. Hazard
- b. Hazardous Materials Identification System
- c. Hazard identification
- d. Swiss cheese model

Guidance: level 1

:: Management ::

The _____ is a strategy performance management tool – a semi-standard structured report, that can be used by managers to keep track of the execution of activities by the staff within their control and to monitor the consequences arising from these actions.

Exam Probability: **Medium**

40. *Answer choices:*

(see index for correct answer)

- a. Focused improvement
- b. Modes of leadership
- c. Balanced scorecard
- d. Project cost management

Guidance: level 1

:: Financial markets ::

A _____ is a financial market in which long-term debt or equity-backed securities are bought and sold. _____ s channel the wealth of savers to those who can put it to long-term productive use, such as companies or governments making long-term investments. Financial regulators like the Bank of England and the U.S. Securities and Exchange Commission oversee _____ s to protect investors against fraud, among other duties.

Exam Probability: **High**

41. *Answer choices:*

(see index for correct answer)

- a. Fundamentally based indexes
- b. Capital market
- c. Advanced Computerized Execution System
- d. Payment schedule

Guidance: level 1

:: Business economics ::

In finance, _____ is the risk of losses caused by interest rate changes. The prices of most financial instruments, such as stocks and bonds move inversely with interest rates, so investors are subject to capital loss when rates rise.

Exam Probability: **Low**

42. *Answer choices:*

(see index for correct answer)

- a. Threshold price-point
- b. Staple financing
- c. Average daily rate
- d. Peer group analysis

Guidance: level 1

:: Real estate valuation ::

_____ or OMV is the price at which an asset would trade in a competitive auction setting. _____ is often used interchangeably with open _____, fair value or fair _____, although these terms have distinct definitions in different standards, and may or may not differ in some circumstances.

Exam Probability: **Medium**

43. *Answer choices:*

(see index for correct answer)

- a. Appraisal Standards Board
- b. cap rate
- c. PropertyShark
- d. Highest and best use

Guidance: level 1

:: Marketing ::

A _____ is something that is necessary for an organism to live a healthy life. _____s are distinguished from wants in that, in the case of a _____, a deficiency causes a clear adverse outcome: a dysfunction or death. In other words, a _____ is something required for a safe, stable and healthy life while a want is a desire, wish or aspiration. When _____s or wants are backed by purchasing power, they have the potential to become economic demands.

Exam Probability: **Low**

44. *Answer choices:*

(see index for correct answer)

- a. Lead management
- b. Digital billboard
- c. Positioning
- d. Need

Guidance: level 1

:: Pharmaceutical industry ::

A _____ is a document in which data collected for a clinical trial is first recorded. This data is usually later entered in the case report form. The International Conference on Harmonisation of Technical Requirements for Registration of Pharmaceuticals for Human Use guidelines define _____ s as "original documents, data, and records." _____ s contain source data, which is defined as "all information in original records and certified copies of original records of clinical findings, observations, or other activities in a clinical trial necessary for the reconstruction and evaluation of the trial."

Exam Probability: **Medium**

45. *Answer choices:*

(see index for correct answer)

- a. FDA Accelerated Approval
- b. Pharmaceutical packaging
- c. International Society for Pharmaceutical Engineering
- d. Microextrusion

Guidance: level 1

:: Accounting in the United States ::

_____ is the title of qualified accountants in numerous countries in the English-speaking world. In the United States, the CPA is a license to provide accounting services to the public. It is awarded by each of the 50 states for practice in that state. Additionally, almost every state has passed mobility laws to allow CPAs from other states to practice in their state. State licensing requirements vary, but the minimum standard requirements include passing the Uniform _____ Examination, 150 semester units of college education, and one year of accounting related experience.

Exam Probability: **Low**

46. *Answer choices:*

(see index for correct answer)

- a. Trueblood Committee
- b. Revolving fund
- c. The Wheat Committee
- d. Certified Public Accountant

Guidance: level 1

:: Asset ::

In accounting, a _____ is any asset which can reasonably be expected to be sold, consumed, or exhausted through the normal operations of a business within the current fiscal year or operating cycle . Typical _____ s include cash, cash equivalents, short-term investments , accounts receivable, stock inventory, supplies, and the portion of prepaid liabilities which will be paid within a year.In simple words, assets which are held for a short period are known as _____ s. Such assets are expected to be realised in cash or consumed during the normal operating cycle of the business.

Exam Probability: **High**

47. *Answer choices:*

(see index for correct answer)

- a. Asset
- b. Current asset

Guidance: level 1

:: ::

_____ refers to a business or organization attempting to acquire goods or services to accomplish its goals. Although there are several organizations that attempt to set standards in the _____ process, processes can vary greatly between organizations. Typically the word "_____" is not used interchangeably with the word "procurement", since procurement typically includes expediting, supplier quality, and transportation and logistics in addition to _____ .

Exam Probability: **Medium**

48. *Answer choices:*

(see index for correct answer)

- a. Purchasing
- b. imperative
- c. personal values
- d. interpersonal communication

Guidance: level 1

:: Stock market ::

_____ or stock market launch is a type of public offering in which shares of a company are sold to institutional investors and usually also retail investors; an IPO is underwritten by one or more investment banks, who also arrange for the shares to be listed on one or more stock exchanges. Through this process, colloquially known as floating, or going public, a privately held company is transformed into a public company. _____ s can be used: to raise new equity capital for the company concerned; to monetize the investments of private shareholders such as company founders or private equity investors; and to enable easy trading of existing holdings or future capital raising by becoming publicly traded enterprises.

Exam Probability: **High**

49. *Answer choices:*

(see index for correct answer)

- a. Free riding
- b. Initial public offering
- c. Stock market
- d. Street name securities

Guidance: level 1

:: Accounting terminology ::

_____ of something is, in finance, the adding together of interest or different investments over a period of time. It holds specific meanings in accounting, where it can refer to accounts on a balance sheet that represent liabilities and non-cash-based assets used in _____ -based accounting. These types of accounts include, among others, accounts payable, accounts receivable, goodwill, deferred tax liability and future interest expense.

Exam Probability: **Medium**

50. *Answer choices:*

(see index for correct answer)

- a. Capital expenditure
- b. Absorption costing
- c. Accrual
- d. Accounts payable

Guidance: level 1

:: ::

Business is the activity of making one's living or making money by producing or buying and selling products. Simply put, it is "any activity or enterprise entered into for profit. It does not mean it is a company, a corporation, partnership, or have any such formal organization, but it can range from a street peddler to General Motors."

Exam Probability: **Medium**

51. *Answer choices:*

(see index for correct answer)

- a. Firm
- b. empathy
- c. Character
- d. similarity-attraction theory

Guidance: level 1

:: Financial markets ::

For an individual, a _____ is the minimum amount of money by which the expected return on a risky asset must exceed the known return on a risk-free asset in order to induce an individual to hold the risky asset rather than the risk-free asset. It is positive if the person is risk averse. Thus it is the minimum willingness to accept compensation for the risk.

Exam Probability: **Low**

52. *Answer choices:*

(see index for correct answer)

- a. Risk premium
- b. Financial instrument
- c. Green trading
- d. Capital market

Guidance: level 1

:: Insolvency ::

_____ is a legal process through which people or other entities who cannot repay debts to creditors may seek relief from some or all of their debts. In most jurisdictions, _____ is imposed by a court order, often initiated by the debtor.

Exam Probability: **Medium**

53. *Answer choices:*

(see index for correct answer)

- a. Debt consolidation
- b. Bankruptcy
- c. Liquidation

- d. George Samuel Ford

Guidance: level 1

:: Options (finance) ::

In finance, a put or _____ is a stock market device which gives the owner the right, but not the obligation, to sell an asset, at a specified price, by a predetermined date to a given party. The purchase of a _____ is interpreted as a negative sentiment about the future value of theunderlying stock. The term "put" comes from the fact that the owner has the right to "put up for sale" the stock or index.

Exam Probability: **High**

54. *Answer choices:*

(see index for correct answer)

- a. Call option
- b. Interest rate guarantee
- c. Put option
- d. Option symbol

Guidance: level 1

:: ::

_____ is the consumption and saving opportunity gained by an entity within a specified timeframe, which is generally expressed in monetary terms. For households and individuals, "_____ is the sum of all the wages, salaries, profits, interest payments, rents, and other forms of earnings received in a given period of time."

Exam Probability: **Medium**

55. *Answer choices:*

(see index for correct answer)

- a. cultural
- b. Income
- c. levels of analysis
- d. information systems assessment

Guidance: level 1

:: Credit cards ::

A _____ is a payment card issued to users to enable the cardholder to pay a merchant for goods and services based on the cardholder's promise to the card issuer to pay them for the amounts plus the other agreed charges. The card issuer creates a revolving account and grants a line of credit to the cardholder, from which the cardholder can borrow money for payment to a merchant or as a cash advance.

Exam Probability: **High**

56. *Answer choices:*

(see index for correct answer)

- a. Credit card
- b. SBI Cards
- c. Visa Black Card
- d. Kisan Credit Card

Guidance: level 1

:: Decision theory ::

A _____ is a deliberate system of principles to guide decisions and achieve rational outcomes. A _____ is a statement of intent, and is implemented as a procedure or protocol. Policies are generally adopted by a governance body within an organization. Policies can assist in both subjective and objective decision making. Policies to assist in subjective decision making usually assist senior management with decisions that must be based on the relative merits of a number of factors, and as a result are often hard to test objectively, e.g. work-life balance _____ . In contrast policies to assist in objective decision making are usually operational in nature and can be objectively tested, e.g. password _____ .

Exam Probability: **Medium**

57. *Answer choices:*

(see index for correct answer)

- a. Ellsberg paradox

- b. Nominal group technique
- c. Ophelimity
- d. Mental accounting

Guidance: level 1

:: ::

_____ is the administration of an organization, whether it is a business, a not-for-profit organization, or government body. _____ includes the activities of setting the strategy of an organization and coordinating the efforts of its employees to accomplish its objectives through the application of available resources, such as financial, natural, technological, and human resources. The term " _____ " may also refer to those people who manage an organization.

Exam Probability: **High**

58. *Answer choices:*

(see index for correct answer)

- a. information systems assessment
- b. Management
- c. personal values
- d. corporate values

Guidance: level 1

:: Accounting terminology ::

_____ are liabilities that reflect expenses that have not yet been paid or logged under accounts payable during an accounting period; in other words, a company's obligation to pay for goods and services that have been provided for which invoices have not yet been received. Examples would include accrued wages payable, accrued sales tax payable, and accrued rent payable.

Exam Probability: **High**

59. *Answer choices:*

(see index for correct answer)

- a. Capital appreciation
- b. Accounts receivable
- c. Accrued liabilities
- d. Internal auditing

Guidance: level 1

Human resource management

Human resource (HR) management is the strategic approach to the effective management of organization workers so that they help the business gain a competitive advantage. It is designed to maximize employee performance in service of an employer's strategic objectives. HR is primarily concerned with the management of people within organizations, focusing on policies and on systems. HR departments are responsible for overseeing employee-benefits design, employee recruitment, training and development, performance appraisal, and rewarding (e.g., managing pay and benefit systems). HR also concerns itself with organizational change and industrial relations, that is, the balancing of organizational practices with requirements arising from collective bargaining and from governmental laws.

:: Working time ::

The shift plan, rota or roster is the central component of a shift schedule in shift work. The schedule includes considerations of shift overlap, shift change times and alignment with the clock, vacation, training, shift differentials, holidays, etc. The shift plan determines the sequence of work and free days within a shift system.

Exam Probability: **High**

1. *Answer choices:*

(see index for correct answer)

- a. Lochner v. New York
- b. Clyde Engineering Co Ltd v Cowburn
- c. Employment law
- d. Blue law

Guidance: level 1

:: ::

_____ is a form of government characterized by strong central power and limited political freedoms. Individual freedoms are subordinate to the state and there is no constitutional accountability and rule of law under an authoritarian regime. Authoritarian regimes can be autocratic with power concentrated in one person or it can be more spread out between multiple officials and government institutions. Juan Linz's influential 1964 description of _____ characterized authoritarian political systems by four qualities.

Exam Probability: **Medium**

2. *Answer choices:*

(see index for correct answer)

- a. open system
- b. hierarchical
- c. surface-level diversity
- d. Authoritarianism

Guidance: level 1

:: Survey methodology ::

A _____ is the procedure of systematically acquiring and recording information about the members of a given population. The term is used mostly in connection with national population and housing _____ es; other common _____ es include agriculture, business, and traffic _____ es. The United Nations defines the essential features of population and housing _____ es as "individual enumeration, universality within a defined territory, simultaneity and defined periodicity", and recommends that population _____ es be taken at least every 10 years. United Nations recommendations also cover _____ topics to be collected, official definitions, classifications and other useful information to co-ordinate international practice.

Exam Probability: **Low**

3. *Answer choices:*

(see index for correct answer)

- a. Group concept mapping
- b. World Association for Public Opinion Research
- c. Census
- d. Data editing

Guidance: level 1

:: Workplace ::

_____ is asystematic determination of a subject's merit, worth and significance, using criteria governed by a set of standards. It can assist an organization, program, design, project or any other intervention or initiative to assess any aim, realisable concept/proposal, or any alternative, to help in decision-making; or to ascertain the degree of achievement or value in regard to the aim and objectives and results of any such action that has been completed. The primary purpose of _____ , in addition to gaining insight into prior or existing initiatives, is to enable reflection and assist in the identification of future change.

Exam Probability: **Medium**

4. *Answer choices:*

(see index for correct answer)

- a. Workplace listening
- b. Workplace deviance
- c. Workplace revenge

- d. Evaluation

Guidance: level 1

:: Network theory ::

A _____ is a social structure made up of a set of social actors, sets of dyadic ties, and other social interactions between actors. The _____ perspective provides a set of methods for analyzing the structure of whole social entities as well as a variety of theories explaining the patterns observed in these structures. The study of these structures uses _____ analysis to identify local and global patterns, locate influential entities, and examine network dynamics.

Exam Probability: **High**

5. *Answer choices:*

(see index for correct answer)

- a. Top 100 historical figures of Wikipedia
- b. Assortativity
- c. Consumer network
- d. Fitness model

Guidance: level 1

:: Human resource management ::

_____ assesses whether a person performs a job well. _____, studied academically as part of industrial and organizational psychology, also forms a part of human resources management. Performance is an important criterion for organizational outcomes and success. John P. Campbell describes _____ as an individual-level variable, or something a single person does. This differentiates it from more encompassing constructs such as organizational performance or national performance, which are higher-level variables.

Exam Probability: **Medium**

6. *Answer choices:*

(see index for correct answer)

- a. Cross-cultural capital
- b. Parallel running
- c. Competency-based job description
- d. Job performance

Guidance: level 1

:: ::

A _____, medical practitioner, medical doctor, or simply doctor, is a professional who practises medicine, which is concerned with promoting, maintaining, or restoring health through the study, diagnosis, prognosis and treatment of disease, injury, and other physical and mental impairments. _____ s may focus their practice on certain disease categories, types of patients, and methods of treatment—known as specialities—or they may assume responsibility for the provision of continuing and comprehensive medical care to individuals, families, and communities—known as general practice. Medical practice properly requires both a detailed knowledge of the academic disciplines, such as anatomy and physiology, underlying diseases and their treatment—the science of medicine—and also a decent competence in its applied practice—the art or craft of medicine.

Exam Probability: **Low**

7. *Answer choices:*

(see index for correct answer)

- a. Physician
- b. information systems assessment
- c. imperative
- d. open system

Guidance: level 1

:: Management ::

_____ is a technique used by some employers to rotate their employees' assigned jobs throughout their employment. Employers practice this technique for a number of reasons. It was designed to promote flexibility of employees and to keep employees interested into staying with the company/organization which employs them. There is also research that shows how _____ s help relieve the stress of employees who work in a job that requires manual labor.

Exam Probability: **Medium**

8. *Answer choices:*

(see index for correct answer)

- a. Financial planning
- b. Innovation leadership
- c. Matrix management
- d. Job rotation

Guidance: level 1

:: ::

In educational development, _____ provides a person, often a student, focus for selecting a career or subject to undertake in the future. Often educational institutions provide career counsellors to assist students with their educational development.

Exam Probability: **Low**

9. *Answer choices:*

(see index for correct answer)

- a. corporate values
- b. cultural
- c. Career development
- d. imperative

Guidance: level 1

:: Human resource management ::

A _____ is a group of people with different functional expertise working toward a common goal. It may include people from finance, marketing, operations, and human resources departments. Typically, it includes employees from all levels of an organization. Members may also come from outside an organization .

Exam Probability: **Medium**

10. *Answer choices:*

(see index for correct answer)

- a. Sham peer review
- b. Trust fall
- c. Induction programme
- d. Restructuring

Guidance: level 1

:: Human resource management ::

_____ means increasing the scope of a job through extending the range of its job duties and responsibilities generally within the same level and periphery. _____ involves combining various activities at the same level in the organization and adding them to the existing job. It is also called the horizontal expansion of job activities. This contradicts the principles of specialisation and the division of labour whereby work is divided into small units, each of which is performed repetitively by an individual worker and the responsibilities are always clear. Some motivational theories suggest that the boredom and alienation caused by the division of labour can actually cause efficiency to fall. Thus, _____ seeks to motivate workers through reversing the process of specialisation. A typical approach might be to replace assembly lines with modular work; instead of an employee repeating the same step on each product, they perform several tasks on a single item. In order for employees to be provided with _____ they will need to be retrained in new fields to understand how each field works.

Exam Probability: **Medium**

11. *Answer choices:*

(see index for correct answer)

- a. Job knowledge
- b. Induction training
- c. Job enlargement
- d. Mechanical aptitude

Guidance: level 1

:: Power (social and political) ::

_____ is a form of reverence gained by a leader who has strong interpersonal relationship skills. _____ , as an aspect of personal power, becomes particularly important as organizational leadership becomes increasingly about collaboration and influence, rather than command and control.

Exam Probability: **High**

12. *Answer choices:*

(see index for correct answer)

- a. need for power
- b. Hard power
- c. Referent power

Guidance: level 1

:: United States employment discrimination case law ::

_____ , 411 U.S. 792 , is a US employment law case by the United States Supreme Court regarding the burdens and nature of proof in proving a Title VII case and the order in which plaintiffs and defendants present proof. It was the seminal case in the McDonnell Douglas burden-shifting framework.

Exam Probability: **High**

13. *Answer choices:*

(see index for correct answer)

- a. McDonnell Douglas Corp. v. Green
- b. Faragher v. City of Boca Raton
- c. Bundy v. Jackson
- d. Dothard v. Rawlinson

Guidance: level 1

:: Employment compensation ::

The formula commonly used by compensation professionals to assess the competitiveness of an employee's pay level involves calculating a " _____ ". _____ is the short form for Comparative ratio.

Exam Probability: **High**

14. *Answer choices:*

(see index for correct answer)

- a. Pension administration in the United States
- b. Cafeteria plan
- c. Compa-ratio
- d. Open compensation plan

Guidance: level 1

:: Problem solving ::

A _____ is a unit or formation established to work on a single defined task or activity. Originally introduced by the United States Navy, the term has now caught on for general usage and is a standard part of NATO terminology. Many non-military organizations now create "_____s" or task groups for temporary activities that might have once been performed by ad hoc committees.

Exam Probability: **Medium**

15. *Answer choices:*
(see index for correct answer)

- a. Hyperfocus
- b. Task force
- c. Trizics
- d. Problem statement

Guidance: level 1

:: ::

A _____ contract is a form of employment that carries fewer hours per week than a full-time job. They work in shifts. The shifts are often rotational. Workers are considered to be _____ if they commonly work fewer than 30 hours per week. According to the International Labour Organization, the number of _____ workers has increased from one-fourth to a half in the past 20 years in most developed countries, excluding the United States. There are many reasons for working _____, including the desire to do so, having one's hours cut back by an employer and being unable to find a full-time job. The International Labour Organisation Convention 175 requires that _____ workers be treated no less favourably than full-time workers.

Exam Probability: **Low**

16. *Answer choices:*

(see index for correct answer)

- a. Character
- b. similarity-attraction theory
- c. corporate values
- d. Part-time

Guidance: level 1

:: ::

The causes of _____ are heavily debated. Classical economics, new classical economics, and the Austrian School of economics argued that market mechanisms are reliable means of resolving _____ . These theories argue against interventions imposed on the labor market from the outside, such as unionization, bureaucratic work rules, minimum wage laws, taxes, and other regulations that they claim discourage the hiring of workers. Keynesian economics emphasizes the cyclical nature of _____ and recommends government interventions in the economy that it claims will reduce _____ during recessions. This theory focuses on recurrent shocks that suddenly reduce aggregate demand for goods and services and thus reduce demand for workers. Keynesian models recommend government interventions designed to increase demand for workers; these can include financial stimuli, publicly funded job creation, and expansionist monetary policies. Its namesake economist, John Maynard Keynes, believed that the root cause of _____ is the desire of investors to receive more money rather than produce more products, which is not possible without public bodies producing new money. A third group of theories emphasize the need for a stable supply of capital and investment to maintain full employment. On this view, government should guarantee full employment through fiscal policy, monetary policy and trade policy as stated, for example, in the US Employment Act of 1946, by counteracting private sector or trade investment volatility, and reducing inequality.

Exam Probability: **Low**

17. *Answer choices:*

(see index for correct answer)

- a. hierarchical
- b. personal values
- c. corporate values
- d. interpersonal communication

Guidance: level 1

:: Occupational safety and health law ::

The _____ of 1970 is a US labor law governing the federal law of occupational health and safety in the private sector and federal government in the United States. It was enacted by Congress in 1970 and was signed by President Richard Nixon on December 29, 1970. Its main goal is to ensure that employers provide employees with an environment free from recognized hazards, such as exposure to toxic chemicals, excessive noise levels, mechanical dangers, heat or cold stress, or unsanitary conditions. The Act created the Occupational Safety and Health Administration and the National Institute for Occupational Safety and Health .

Exam Probability: **Low**

18. *Answer choices:*

(see index for correct answer)

- a. Health and Safety at Work etc. Act 1974
- b. Factory and Workshop Act 1895
- c. Occupational Safety and Health Act
- d. Occupational Safety and Health Act 1994

Guidance: level 1

:: ::

_____ is the moral stance, political philosophy, ideology, or social outlook that emphasizes the moral worth of the individual. Individualists promote the exercise of one's goals and desires and so value independence and self-reliance and advocate that interests of the individual should achieve precedence over the state or a social group, while opposing external interference upon one's own interests by society or institutions such as the government. _____ is often defined in contrast to totalitarianism, collectivism, and more corporate social forms.

Exam Probability: **Low**

19. *Answer choices:*

(see index for correct answer)

- a. co-culture
- b. Individualism
- c. hierarchical perspective
- d. process perspective

Guidance: level 1

:: Foreign workers ::

A _____ or guest worker is a human who works in a country other than the one of which he or she is a citizen. Some _____ s are using a guest worker program in a country with more preferred job prospects than their home country. Guest workers are often either sent or invited to work outside their home country, or have acquired a job before they left their home country, whereas migrant workers often leave their home country without having a specific job at hand.

Exam Probability: **Low**

20. *Answer choices:*

(see index for correct answer)

- a. Host family
- b. Union of Italian Migrant Workers
- c. Foreign worker
- d. Ten Pound Poms

Guidance: level 1

:: Training ::

_____ is the process of ensuring compliance with laws, regulations, rules, standards, or social norms. By enforcing laws and regulations, governments attempt to effectuate successful implementation of policies.

Exam Probability: **Low**

21. *Answer choices:*

(see index for correct answer)

- a. Hot potato
- b. Adobe Captivate
- c. Enforcement
- d. Hypoventilation training

Guidance: level 1

:: Trade unions ::

A _____ , in North America, or union branch , in the United Kingdom and other countries, is a local branch of a usually national trade union. The terms used for sub-branches of _____ s vary from country to country and include "shop committee", "shop floor committee", "board of control", "chapel", and others.

Exam Probability: **Low**

22. *Answer choices:*

(see index for correct answer)

- a. Open-source unionism
- b. Local union
- c. Anti-union violence
- d. Company union

Guidance: level 1

:: Business ethics ::

_____ is a persistent pattern of mistreatment from others in the workplace that causes either physical or emotional harm. It can include such tactics as verbal, nonverbal, psychological, physical abuse and humiliation. This type of workplace aggression is particularly difficult because, unlike the typical school bully, workplace bullies often operate within the established rules and policies of their organization and their society. In the majority of cases, bullying in the workplace is reported as having been by someone who has authority over their victim. However, bullies can also be peers, and occasionally subordinates. Research has also investigated the impact of the larger organizational context on bullying as well as the group-level processes that impact on the incidence and maintenance of bullying behaviour. Bullying can be covert or overt. It may be missed by superiors; it may be known by many throughout the organization. Negative effects are not limited to the targeted individuals, and may lead to a decline in employee morale and a change in organizational culture. It can also take place as overbearing supervision, constant criticism, and blocking promotions.

Exam Probability: **High**

23. *Answer choices:*

(see index for correct answer)

- a. Moral hazard
- b. Workplace bullying
- c. Eating your own dog food
- d. Wheelmen

Guidance: level 1

:: Offshoring ::

Outsourcing is an agreement in which one company hires another company to be responsible for a planned or existing activity that is or could be done internally, and sometimes involves transferring employees and assets from one firm to another.

Exam Probability: **Medium**

24. *Answer choices:*

(see index for correct answer)

- a. Advanced Contact Solutions
- b. Nearshoring
- c. Antex
- d. Sourcing advisory

Guidance: level 1

:: Project management ::

Some scenarios associate "this kind of planning" with learning "life skills". _____ s are necessary, or at least useful, in situations where individuals need to know what time they must be at a specific location to receive a specific service, and where people need to accomplish a set of goals within a set time period.

Exam Probability: **Medium**

25. *Answer choices:*

(see index for correct answer)

- a. Schedule
- b. Project network
- c. Kickoff meeting
- d. Global Alliance for Project Performance Standards

Guidance: level 1

:: Labour relations ::

An _____ is a place of employment at which one is not required to join or financially support a union as a condition of hiring or continued employment. _____ is also known as a merit shop.

Exam Probability: **Medium**

26. *Answer choices:*

(see index for correct answer)

- a. Association of German Chambers of Industry and Commerce
- b. United Students Against Sweatshops
- c. Open shop
- d. Whipsaw strike

Guidance: level 1

:: Management ::

_____ is a set of activities that ensure goals are met in an effective and efficient manner. _____ can focus on the performance of an organization, a department, an employee, or the processes in place to manage particular tasks. _____ standards are generally organized and disseminated by senior leadership at an organization, and by task owners.

Exam Probability: **High**

27. *Answer choices:*

(see index for correct answer)

- a. Business process mapping
- b. Environmental stewardship
- c. Toxic leader
- d. Organizational conflict

Guidance: level 1

:: Labour relations ::

_____ is a form of protest in which people congregate outside a place of work or location where an event is taking place. Often, this is done in an attempt to dissuade others from going in , but it can also be done to draw public attention to a cause. Picketers normally endeavor to be non-violent. It can have a number of aims, but is generally to put pressure on the party targeted to meet particular demands or cease operations. This pressure is achieved by harming the business through loss of customers and negative publicity, or by discouraging or preventing workers or customers from entering the site and thereby preventing the business from operating normally.

Exam Probability: **High**

28. *Answer choices:*

(see index for correct answer)

- a. Picketing
- b. Union representative
- c. Two-tier system
- d. Union shop

Guidance: level 1

:: ::

_____ is the process of gathering and measuring information on targeted variables in an established system, which then enables one to answer relevant questions and evaluate outcomes. _____ is a component of research in all fields of study including physical and social sciences, humanities, and business. While methods vary by discipline, the emphasis on ensuring accurate and honest collection remains the same. The goal for all _____ is to capture quality evidence that allows analysis to lead to the formulation of convincing and credible answers to the questions that have been posed.

Exam Probability: **Low**

29. *Answer choices:*

(see index for correct answer)

- a. surface-level diversity
- b. similarity-attraction theory
- c. Sarbanes-Oxley act of 2002
- d. interpersonal communication

Guidance: level 1

:: ::

Educational technology is "the study and ethical practice of facilitating learning and improving performance by creating, using, and managing appropriate technological processes and resources".

Exam Probability: **High**

30. *Answer choices:*

(see index for correct answer)

- a. interpersonal communication
- b. personal values
- c. E-learning
- d. similarity-attraction theory

Guidance: level 1

:: Validity (statistics) ::

_____ is the extent to which a test accurately measures what it is supposed to measure. In the fields of psychological testing and educational testing, "validity refers to the degree to which evidence and theory support the interpretations of test scores entailed by proposed uses of tests". Although classical models divided the concept into various "validities", the currently dominant view is that validity is a single unitary construct.

Exam Probability: **High**

31. *Answer choices:*

(see index for correct answer)

- a. Criterion validity
- b. Statistical conclusion
- c. Verification and validation
- d. Test validity

Guidance: level 1

:: Occupational safety and health organizations ::

The _____ is the United States federal agency responsible for conducting research and making recommendations for the prevention of work-related injury and illness. NIOSH is part of the Centers for Disease Control and Prevention within the U.S. Department of Health and Human Services.

Exam Probability: **Low**

32. *Answer choices:*

(see index for correct answer)

- a. Health and Safety Executive for Northern Ireland
- b. Dangerous Goods Safety Advisor
- c. National Institute for Occupational Safety and Health
- d. American Conference of Governmental Industrial Hygienists

Guidance: level 1

:: Management ::

The _____ is a strategy performance management tool – a semi-standard structured report, that can be used by managers to keep track of the execution of activities by the staff within their control and to monitor the consequences arising from these actions.

Exam Probability: **High**

33. *Answer choices:*

(see index for correct answer)

- a. Management Week
- b. Balanced scorecard
- c. Action item
- d. Product Development and Systems Engineering Consortium

Guidance: level 1

:: International trade ::

_____ or globalisation is the process of interaction and integration among people, companies, and governments worldwide. As a complex and multifaceted phenomenon, _____ is considered by some as a form of capitalist expansion which entails the integration of local and national economies into a global, unregulated market economy. _____ has grown due to advances in transportation and communication technology. With the increased global interactions comes the growth of international trade, ideas, and culture. _____ is primarily an economic process of interaction and integration that's associated with social and cultural aspects. However, conflicts and diplomacy are also large parts of the history of _____ , and modern _____ .

Exam Probability: **Low**

34. *Answer choices:*

(see index for correct answer)

- a. Import license
- b. Globalization
- c. Competitiveness Policy Council
- d. Swiss Formula

Guidance: level 1

:: Business models ::

A _____ is a diagram that is used to document the primary strategic goals being pursued by an organization or management team. It is an element of the documentation associated with the Balanced Scorecard, and in particular is characteristic of the second generation of Balanced Scorecard designs that first appeared during the mid-1990s. The first diagrams of this type appeared in the early 1990s, and the idea of using this type of diagram to help document Balanced Scorecard was discussed in a paper by Drs. Robert S. Kaplan and David P. Norton in 1996.

Exam Probability: **Low**

35. *Answer choices:*

(see index for correct answer)

- a. Sailing Ship Effect
- b. Strategy map
- c. Low-cost carrier
- d. Small business

Guidance: level 1

:: ::

On December 31, 2016, Xerox separated its business process service operations into a new publicly traded company, Conduent. Xerox focuses on its document technology and document outsourcing business, and continues to trade on the NYSE. On January 31, 2018, Xerox announced that it would sell a controlling stake to Fujifilm, which has maintained a joint venture in the Asia-Pacific region known as Fuji Xerox.

Exam Probability: **Low**

36. *Answer choices:*

(see index for correct answer)

- a. hierarchical
- b. imperative
- c. surface-level diversity
- d. Xerox Corporation

Guidance: level 1

:: Human resource management ::

_____ are the people who make up the workforce of an organization, business sector, or economy. "Human capital" is sometimes used synonymously with " _____ ", although human capital typically refers to a narrower effect. Likewise, other terms sometimes used include manpower, talent, labor, personnel, or simply people.

Exam Probability: **Low**

37. *Answer choices:*

(see index for correct answer)

- a. Service record
- b. Human resources

- c. Restructuring
- d. Domestic inquiry

Guidance: level 1

:: Offshoring ::

A _____ is the temporary suspension or permanent termination of employment of an employee or, more commonly, a group of employees for business reasons, such as personnel management or downsizing an organization. Originally, _____ referred exclusively to a temporary interruption in work, or employment but this has evolved to a permanent elimination of a position in both British and US English, requiring the addition of "temporary" to specify the original meaning of the word. A _____ is not to be confused with wrongful termination. Laid off workers or displaced workers are workers who have lost or left their jobs because their employer has closed or moved, there was insufficient work for them to do, or their position or shift was abolished. Downsizing in a company is defined to involve the reduction of employees in a workforce. Downsizing in companies became a popular practice in the 1980s and early 1990s as it was seen as a way to deliver better shareholder value as it helps to reduce the costs of employers. Indeed, recent research on downsizing in the U.S., UK, and Japan suggests that downsizing is being regarded by management as one of the preferred routes to help declining organizations, cutting unnecessary costs, and improve organizational performance. Usually a _____ occurs as a cost cutting measure.

Exam Probability: **High**

38. *Answer choices:*

(see index for correct answer)

- a. Offshore custom software development
- b. Layoff
- c. Offshore outsourcing
- d. Nearshoring

Guidance: level 1

:: ::

A _____ is a fund into which a sum of money is added during an employee's employment years, and from which payments are drawn to support the person's retirement from work in the form of periodic payments. A _____ may be a "defined benefit plan" where a fixed sum is paid regularly to a person, or a "defined contribution plan" under which a fixed sum is invested and then becomes available at retirement age. _____ s should not be confused with severance pay; the former is usually paid in regular installments for life after retirement, while the latter is typically paid as a fixed amount after involuntary termination of employment prior to retirement.

Exam Probability: **Low**

39. *Answer choices:*

(see index for correct answer)

- a. levels of analysis
- b. Pension
- c. Character
- d. information systems assessment

Guidance: level 1

:: Meetings ::

A _____ is a body of one or more persons that is subordinate to a deliberative assembly. Usually, the assembly sends matters into a _____ as a way to explore them more fully than would be possible if the assembly itself were considering them. _____ s may have different functions and their type of work differ depending on the type of the organization and its needs.

Exam Probability: **Low**

40. *Answer choices:*

(see index for correct answer)

- a. Stammtisch
- b. Open town meeting
- c. Carlton Club meeting
- d. Committee

Guidance: level 1

:: Labor ::

_____ refers to the process of grouping activities into departments. Division of labour creates specialists who need coordination. This coordination is facilitated by grouping specialists together in departments.

Exam Probability: **Low**

41. *Answer choices:*

(see index for correct answer)

- a. Knowledge worker
- b. Ethical Trading Initiative
- c. Dispatched labor
- d. Departmentalization

Guidance: level 1

:: Business ethics cases ::

_____, 477 U.S. 57, is a US labor law case, where the United States Supreme Court, in a 9-0 decision, recognized sexual harassment as a violation of Title VII of the Civil Rights Act of 1964. The case was the first of its kind to reach the Supreme Court and would redefine sexual harassment in the workplace.

Exam Probability: **Low**

42. *Answer choices:*

(see index for correct answer)

- a. Bank of Credit and Commerce International
- b. Meritor Savings Bank v. Vinson
- c. Sandstorm report
- d. United States v. Paramount Pictures, Inc.

Guidance: level 1

:: Recruitment ::

A _____, also referred commonly as a career fair or career expo, is an event in which employers, recruiters, and schools give information to potential employees. Job seekers attend these while trying to make a good impression to potential coworkers by speaking face-to-face with one another, filling out résumés, and asking questions in attempt to get a good feel on the work needed. Likewise, online _____ s are held, giving job seekers another way to get in contact with probable employers using the internet.

Exam Probability: **High**

43. *Answer choices:*

(see index for correct answer)

- a. Curriculum vitae
- b. Europass
- c. Job fair
- d. Probation

Guidance: level 1

A _____ is a technical analysis of a biological specimen, for example urine, hair, blood, breath, sweat, and/or oral fluid/saliva—to determine the presence or absence of specified parent drugs or their metabolites. Major applications of _____ ing include detection of the presence of performance enhancing steroids in sport, employers and parole/probation officers screening for drugs prohibited by law and police officers testing for the presence and concentration of alcohol in the blood commonly referred to as BAC . BAC tests are typically administered via a breathalyzer while urinalysis is used for the vast majority of _____ ing in sports and the workplace. Numerous other methods with varying degrees of accuracy, sensitivity , and detection periods exist.

Exam Probability: **Medium**

44. *Answer choices:*

(see index for correct answer)

- a. functional perspective
- b. Drug test
- c. levels of analysis
- d. deep-level diversity

Guidance: level 1

:: Employment ::

A flat organization has an organizational structure with few or no levels of middle management between staff and executives. An organization's structure refers to the nature of the distribution of the units and positions within it, also to the nature of the relationships among those units and positions. Tall and flat organizations differ based on how many levels of management are present in the organization, and how much control managers are endowed with.

Exam Probability: **High**

45. *Answer choices:*

(see index for correct answer)

- a. Employment
- b. Psychological contract
- c. Fly-in fly-out
- d. Work experience

Guidance: level 1

:: Employment ::

_____ is the probability that an individual will keep his/her job; a job with a high level of _____ is such that a person with the job would have a small chance of losing it.

Exam Probability: **Medium**

46. *Answer choices:*

(see index for correct answer)

- a. Job attitude
- b. Performance improvement
- c. Job security
- d. Jobless claims

Guidance: level 1

:: Business law ::

A _____ is an arrangement where parties, known as partners, agree to cooperate to advance their mutual interests. The partners in a _____ may be individuals, businesses, interest-based organizations, schools, governments or combinations. Organizations may partner to increase the likelihood of each achieving their mission and to amplify their reach. A _____ may result in issuing and holding equity or may be only governed by a contract.

Exam Probability: **Medium**

47. *Answer choices:*

(see index for correct answer)

- a. Partnership
- b. Court auction

- c. Arbitration award
- d. Negotiable instrument

Guidance: level 1

:: Human resource management ::

> _____ is the strategic approach to the effective management of people in an organization so that they help the business to gain a competitive advantage. It is designed to maximize employee performance in service of an employer's strategic objectives. HR is primarily concerned with the management of people within organizations, focusing on policies and on systems. HR departments are responsible for overseeing employee-benefits design, employee recruitment, training and development, performance appraisal, and Reward management . HR also concerns itself with organizational change and industrial relations, that is, the balancing of organizational practices with requirements arising from collective bargaining and from governmental laws.

Exam Probability: **Low**

48. *Answer choices:*
(see index for correct answer)

- a. Chartered Institute of Personnel and Development
- b. Organizational culture
- c. Management by objectives
- d. Human resource management

Guidance: level 1

:: Labour relations ::

_____ is the practice of hiring more workers than are needed to perform a given job, or to adopt work procedures which appear pointless, complex and time-consuming merely to employ additional workers. The term "make-work" is sometimes used as a synonym for _____ .

Exam Probability: **Low**

49. *Answer choices:*
(see index for correct answer)

- a. Two-tier system
- b. Merit shop
- c. Acas
- d. Featherbedding

Guidance: level 1

:: Production and manufacturing ::

_____ is a set of techniques and tools for process improvement. Though as a shortened form it may be found written as 6S, it should not be confused with the methodology known as 6S .

Exam Probability: **Medium**

50. *Answer choices:*

(see index for correct answer)

- a. Plant layout study
- b. Six Sigma
- c. production planning
- d. ISO/TS 16949

Guidance: level 1

:: Belief ::

> _____ is the ability to acquire knowledge without proof, evidence, or conscious reasoning, or without understanding how the knowledge was acquired. Different writers give the word " _____ " a great variety of different meanings, ranging from direct access to unconscious knowledge, unconscious cognition, inner sensing, inner insight to unconscious pattern-recognition and the ability to understand something instinctively, without the need for conscious reasoning.

Exam Probability: **High**

51. *Answer choices:*

(see index for correct answer)

- a. Alief

- b. Sententia probabilis
- c. Ignorance
- d. False pleasure

Guidance: level 1

:: Employment compensation ::

_____ s and benefits in kind include various types of non-wage compensation provided to employees in addition to their normal wages or salaries. Instances where an employee exchanges wages for some other form of benefit is generally referred to as a "salary packaging" or "salary exchange" arrangement. In most countries, most kinds of _____ s are taxable to at least some degree. Examples of these benefits include: housing furnished or not, with or without free utilities; group insurance ; disability income protection; retirement benefits; daycare; tuition reimbursement; sick leave; vacation ; social security; profit sharing; employer student loan contributions; conveyancing; domestic help ; and other specialized benefits.

Exam Probability: **Medium**

52. *Answer choices:*

(see index for correct answer)

- a. Employee benefit
- b. Pay-for-Performance
- c. Equal Pay Act 1970
- d. Seasonal bonuses

Guidance: level 1

:: Ethically disputed business practices ::

An _____ in US labor law refers to certain actions taken by employers or unions that violate the National Labor Relations Act of 1935 29 U.S.C. § 151–169 and other legislation. Such acts are investigated by the National Labor Relations Board .

Exam Probability: **High**

53. *Answer choices:*

(see index for correct answer)

- a. Tobashi scheme
- b. Unfair labor practice
- c. Patent troll
- d. Spamming

Guidance: level 1

:: Business terms ::

A _____ is a short statement of why an organization exists, what its overall goal is, identifying the goal of its operations: what kind of product or service it provides, its primary customers or market, and its geographical region of operation. It may include a short statement of such fundamental matters as the organization's values or philosophies, a business's main competitive advantages, or a desired future state—the "vision".

Exam Probability: **Low**

54. *Answer choices:*

(see index for correct answer)

- a. centralization
- b. Personal selling
- c. Mission statement
- d. organizational capital

Guidance: level 1

:: Social psychology ::

In social psychology, _____ is the phenomenon of a person exerting less effort to achieve a goal when he or she works in a group than when working alone. This is seen as one of the main reasons groups are sometimes less productive than the combined performance of their members working as individuals, but should be distinguished from the accidental coordination problems that groups sometimes experience.

Exam Probability: **High**

55. *Answer choices:*

(see index for correct answer)

- a. Cross-cultural leadership
- b. Social character
- c. Prosocial
- d. Social loafing

Guidance: level 1

:: Human resource management ::

_____ involves improving the effectiveness of organizations and the individuals and teams within them. Training may be viewed as related to immediate changes in organizational effectiveness via organized instruction, while development is related to the progress of longer-term organizational and employee goals. While _____ technically have differing definitions, the two are oftentimes used interchangeably and/or together. _____ has historically been a topic within applied psychology but has within the last two decades become closely associated with human resources management, talent management, human resources development, instructional design, human factors, and knowledge management.

Exam Probability: **High**

56. *Answer choices:*

(see index for correct answer)

- a. Training and development
- b. Open plan
- c. Competency-based recruitment
- d. Organizational culture

Guidance: level 1

:: ::

A _____ is an occupation founded upon specialized educational training, the purpose of which is to supply disinterested objective counsel and service to others, for a direct and definite compensation, wholly apart from expectation of other business gain. The term is a truncation of the term "liberal _____ ", which is, in turn, an Anglicization of the French term " _____ libérale". Originally borrowed by English users in the 19th century, it has been re-borrowed by international users from the late 20th, though the class overtones of the term do not seem to survive retranslation: "liberal _____ s" are, according to the European Union's Directive on Recognition of _____ al Qualifications "those practiced on the basis of relevant _____ al qualifications in a personal, responsible and _____ ally independent capacity by those providing intellectual and conceptual services in the interest of the client and the public".

Exam Probability: **High**

57. *Answer choices:*

(see index for correct answer)

- a. Profession
- b. cultural

- c. process perspective
- d. imperative

Guidance: level 1

:: ::

An _____ is a person temporarily or permanently residing in a country other than their native country. In common usage, the term often refers to professionals, skilled workers, or artists taking positions outside their home country, either independently or sent abroad by their employers, who can be companies, universities, governments, or non-governmental organisations. Effectively migrant workers, they usually earn more than they would at home, and less than local employees. However, the term ` _____ ` is also used for retirees and others who have chosen to live outside their native country. Historically, it has also referred to exiles.

Exam Probability: **Medium**

58. *Answer choices:*

(see index for correct answer)

- a. Expatriate
- b. similarity-attraction theory
- c. surface-level diversity
- d. imperative

Guidance: level 1

:: ::

_____ is an enduring pattern of romantic or sexual attraction to persons of the opposite sex or gender, the same sex or gender, or to both sexes or more than one gender. These attractions are generally subsumed under heterosexuality, homosexuality, and bisexuality, while asexuality is sometimes identified as the fourth category.

Exam Probability: **Medium**

59. *Answer choices:*

(see index for correct answer)

- a. cultural
- b. hierarchical perspective
- c. similarity-attraction theory
- d. corporate values

Guidance: level 1

Information systems

Information systems (IS) are formal, sociotechnical, organizational systems designed to collect, process, store, and distribute information. In a sociotechnical perspective Information Systems are composed by four components: technology, process, people and organizational structure.

:: ::

A _____ is server software, or hardware dedicated to running said software, that can satisfy World Wide Web client requests. A _____ can, in general, contain one or more websites. A _____ processes incoming network requests over HTTP and several other related protocols.

Exam Probability: **High**

1. *Answer choices:*

(see index for correct answer)

- a. process perspective
- b. open system
- c. similarity-attraction theory
- d. cultural

Guidance: level 1

:: Computer access control ::

_____ is the act of confirming the truth of an attribute of a single piece of data claimed true by an entity. In contrast with identification, which refers to the act of stating or otherwise indicating a claim purportedly attesting to a person or thing's identity, _____ is the process of actually confirming that identity. It might involve confirming the identity of a person by validating their identity documents, verifying the authenticity of a website with a digital certificate, determining the age of an artifact by carbon dating, or ensuring that a product is what its packaging and labeling claim to be. In other words, _____ often involves verifying the validity of at least one form of identification.

Exam Probability: **High**

2. *Answer choices:*

(see index for correct answer)

- a. Copy protection
- b. EAuthentication
- c. Authentication
- d. Distributed Access Control System

Guidance: level 1

:: Security compliance ::

A _____ is a communicated intent to inflict harm or loss on another person. A _____ is considered an act of coercion. _____ s are widely observed in animal behavior, particularly in a ritualized form, chiefly in order to avoid the unnecessary physical violence that can lead to physical damage or the death of both conflicting parties.

Exam Probability: **High**

3. *Answer choices:*

(see index for correct answer)

- a. 201 CMR 17.00
- b. Security Content Automation Protocol
- c. North American Electric Reliability Corporation
- d. Threat

Guidance: level 1

:: Payment systems ::

An _____ is an electronic telecommunications device that enables customers of financial institutions to perform financial transactions, such as cash withdrawals, deposits, transfer funds, or obtaining account information, at any time and without the need for direct interaction with bank staff.

Exam Probability: **Low**

4. *Answer choices:*

(see index for correct answer)

- a. Google Wallet
- b. Automated teller machine
- c. Lemon Wallet
- d. Mobile purchasing

Guidance: level 1

:: ::

_____ LLC is an American multinational technology company that specializes in Internet-related services and products, which include online advertising technologies, search engine, cloud computing, software, and hardware. It is considered one of the Big Four technology companies, alongside Amazon, Apple and Facebook.

Exam Probability: **Low**

5. *Answer choices:*

(see index for correct answer)

- a. cultural
- b. hierarchical perspective
- c. empathy
- d. Google

Guidance: level 1

:: Product testing ::

_____ is a characteristic of a product or system, whose interfaces are completely understood, to work with other products or systems, at present or in the future, in either implementation or access, without any restrictions.

Exam Probability: **Low**

6. *Answer choices:*

(see index for correct answer)

- a. Wine tasting
- b. Coffee cupping
- c. Interoperability
- d. Defect tracking

Guidance: level 1

:: Computer memory ::

_____ is a type of non-volatile memory used in computers and other electronic devices. Data stored in ROM can only be modified slowly, with difficulty, or not at all, so it is mainly used to store firmware or application software in plug-in cartridges.

Exam Probability: **High**

7. *Answer choices:*

(see index for correct answer)

- a. Delay line memory
- b. Read-only memory
- c. Interleaved memory
- d. Quad Data Rate SRAM

Guidance: level 1

:: Confidence tricks ::

_____ is the fraudulent attempt to obtain sensitive information such as usernames, passwords and credit card details by disguising oneself as a trustworthy entity in an electronic communication. Typically carried out by email spoofing or instant messaging, it often directs users to enter personal information at a fake website which matches the look and feel of the legitimate site.

Exam Probability: **Low**

8. *Answer choices:*

(see index for correct answer)

- a. Domain name scams
- b. Black money scam
- c. Flim-Flam!
- d. Phishing

Guidance: level 1

:: Business process ::

_____ is a discipline in operations management in which people use various methods to discover, model, analyze, measure, improve, optimize, and automate business processes. BPM focuses on improving corporate performance by managing business processes. Any combination of methods used to manage a company's business processes is BPM. Processes can be structured and repeatable or unstructured and variable. Though not required, enabling technologies are often used with BPM.

Exam Probability: **High**

9. *Answer choices:*

(see index for correct answer)

- a. Business Motivation Model
- b. Business process management
- c. Joget Workflow
- d. Dynamic business process management

Guidance: level 1

:: ::

A _____ is a telecommunications network that extends over a large geographical distance for the primary purpose of computer networking. _____ s are often established with leased telecommunication circuits.

Exam Probability: **Low**

10. *Answer choices:*

(see index for correct answer)

- a. cultural
- b. hierarchical perspective
- c. corporate values
- d. information systems assessment

Guidance: level 1

:: ::

_____ rate is the ratio of users who click on a specific link to the number of total users who view a page, email, or advertisement. It is commonly used to measure the success of an online advertising campaign for a particular website as well as the effectiveness of email campaigns.

Exam Probability: **Low**

11. *Answer choices:*

(see index for correct answer)

- a. surface-level diversity
- b. similarity-attraction theory
- c. open system
- d. functional perspective

Guidance: level 1

:: Identity management ::

_____ is the ability of an individual or group to seclude themselves, or information about themselves, and thereby express themselves selectively. The boundaries and content of what is considered private differ among cultures and individuals, but share common themes. When something is private to a person, it usually means that something is inherently special or sensitive to them. The domain of _____ partially overlaps with security, which can include the concepts of appropriate use, as well as protection of information. _____ may also take the form of bodily integrity.

Exam Probability: **Medium**

12. *Answer choices:*

(see index for correct answer)

- a. Identity verification service
- b. Federated Naming Service
- c. Privacy-enhancing technologies
- d. Privacy

Guidance: level 1

:: Management ::

_____ is the kind of knowledge that is difficult to transfer to another person by means of writing it down or verbalizing it. For example, that London is in the United Kingdom is a piece of explicit knowledge that can be written down, transmitted, and understood by a recipient. However, the ability to speak a language, ride a bicycle, knead dough, play a musical instrument, or design and use complex equipment requires all sorts of knowledge that is not always known explicitly, even by expert practitioners, and which is difficult or impossible to explicitly transfer to other people.

Exam Probability: **Low**

13. *Answer choices:*

(see index for correct answer)

- a. Tacit knowledge
- b. Executive compensation
- c. Private defense agency
- d. Leadership Series

Guidance: level 1

:: IT risk management ::

_____ involves a set of policies, tools and procedures to enable the recovery or continuation of vital technology infrastructure and systems following a natural or human-induced disaster. _____ focuses on the IT or technology systems supporting critical business functions, as opposed to business continuity, which involves keeping all essential aspects of a business functioning despite significant disruptive events. _____ can therefore be considered as a subset of business continuity.

Exam Probability: **High**

14. *Answer choices:*

(see index for correct answer)

- a. Disaster recovery
- b. Information assurance
- c. Incident response team

Guidance: level 1

:: Data management ::

"_____" is a field that treats ways to analyze, systematically extract information from, or otherwise deal with data sets that are too large or complex to be dealt with by traditional data-processing application software. Data with many cases offer greater statistical power, while data with higher complexity may lead to a higher false discovery rate. _____ challenges include capturing data, data storage, data analysis, search, sharing, transfer, visualization, querying, updating, information privacy and data source. _____ was originally associated with three key concepts: volume, variety, and velocity. Other concepts later attributed with _____ are veracity and value.

Exam Probability: **High**

15. *Answer choices:*

(see index for correct answer)

- a. Distributed transaction
- b. EU Open Data Portal
- c. Big data
- d. Data virtualization

Guidance: level 1

:: ::

_____ consists of tailoring a service or a product to accommodate specific individuals, sometimes tied to groups or segments of individuals. A wide variety of organizations use _____ to improve customer satisfaction, digital sales conversion, marketing results, branding, and improved website metrics as well as for advertising. _____ is a key element in social media and recommender systems.

Exam Probability: **Low**

16. *Answer choices:*

(see index for correct answer)

- a. personal values
- b. empathy
- c. cultural
- d. Personalization

Guidance: level 1

A _____ is a structure / access pattern specific to data warehouse environments, used to retrieve client-facing data. The _____ is a subset of the data warehouse and is usually oriented to a specific business line or team. Whereas data warehouses have an enterprise-wide depth, the information in _____ s pertains to a single department. In some deployments, each department or business unit is considered the owner of its _____ including all the hardware, software and data. This enables each department to isolate the use, manipulation and development of their data. In other deployments where conformed dimensions are used, this business unit ownership will not hold true for shared dimensions like customer, product, etc.

Exam Probability: **Low**

17. *Answer choices:*

(see index for correct answer)

- a. corporate values
- b. deep-level diversity
- c. Character
- d. Data mart

Guidance: level 1

:: Enterprise modelling ::

_____ are large-scale application software packages that support business processes, information flows, reporting, and data analytics in complex organizations. While ES are generally packaged enterprise application software systems they can also be bespoke, custom developed systems created to support a specific organization's needs.

Exam Probability: **Low**

18. *Answer choices:*

(see index for correct answer)

- a. Novay
- b. Enterprise engineering
- c. Enterprise systems
- d. Canonical model

Guidance: level 1

:: ::

A _____ is an abstract model that organizes elements of data and standardizes how they relate to one another and to properties of the real world entities. For instance, a _____ may specify that the data element representing a car be composed of a number of other elements which, in turn, represent the color and size of the car and define its owner.

Exam Probability: **Medium**

19. *Answer choices:*

(see index for correct answer)

- a. Data model
- b. open system
- c. imperative
- d. functional perspective

Guidance: level 1

:: Big data ::

_____ is the discovery, interpretation, and communication of meaningful patterns in data; and the process of applying those patterns towards effective decision making. In other words, _____ can be understood as the connective tissue between data and effective decision making, within an organization. Especially valuable in areas rich with recorded information, _____ relies on the simultaneous application of statistics, computer programming and operations research to quantify performance.

Exam Probability: **Medium**

20. *Answer choices:*

(see index for correct answer)

- a. Sogamo
- b. Social IT
- c. RelateIQ

- d. Analytics

Guidance: level 1

:: Information systems ::

_____ , Chief Digital Information Officer or Information Technology Director, is a job title commonly given to the most senior executive in an enterprise who works for the traditional information technology and computer systems that support enterprise goals.

Exam Probability: **Medium**

21. *Answer choices:*

(see index for correct answer)

- a. Chief information officer
- b. Dynamic Business Modeling
- c. Personal knowledge management
- d. Question Manager

Guidance: level 1

:: Information science ::

_____ has been defined as "the branch of ethics that focuses on the relationship between the creation, organization, dissemination, and use of information, and the ethical standards and moral codes governing human conduct in society". It examines the morality that comes from information as a resource, a product, or as a target. It provides a critical framework for considering moral issues concerning informational privacy, moral agency, new environmental issues, problems arising from the life-cycle of information. It is very vital to understand that librarians, archivists, information professionals among others, really understand the importance of knowing how to disseminate proper information as well as being responsible with their actions when addressing information.

Exam Probability: **High**

22. *Answer choices:*

(see index for correct answer)

- a. Informetrics
- b. Scientific communication
- c. Information ethics
- d. Information processing theory

Guidance: level 1

:: Google services ::

_____ is a word processor included as part of a free, web-based software office suite offered by Google within its Google Drive service. This service also includes Google Sheets and Google Slides, a spreadsheet and presentation program respectively. _____ is available as a web application, mobile app for Android, iOS, Windows, BlackBerry, and as a desktop application on Google's ChromeOS. The app is compatible with Microsoft Office file formats. The application allows users to create and edit files online while collaborating with other users in real-time. Edits are tracked by user with a revision history presenting changes. An editor's position is highlighted with an editor-specific color and cursor. A permissions system regulates what users can do. Updates have introduced features using machine learning, including "Explore", offering search results based on the contents of a document, and "Action items", allowing users to assign tasks to other users.

Exam Probability: **High**

23. *Answer choices:*

(see index for correct answer)

- a. Google Books Library Project
- b. Google Compute Engine
- c. Google Consumer Surveys
- d. Google Docs

Guidance: level 1

:: Management ::

_____ is the discipline of strategically planning for, and managing, all interactions with third party organizations that supply goods and/or services to an organization in order to maximize the value of those interactions. In practice, SRM entails creating closer, more collaborative relationships with key suppliers in order to uncover and realize new value and reduce risk of failure.

Exam Probability: **Low**

24. *Answer choices:*

(see index for correct answer)

- a. Reval
- b. Power structure
- c. Organizational hologram
- d. Supplier relationship management

Guidance: level 1

:: Google services ::

Google Ads is an online advertising platform developed by Google, where advertisers pay to display brief advertisements, service offerings, product listings, video content, and generate mobile application installs within the Google ad network to web users.

Exam Probability: **Medium**

25. *Answer choices:*

(see index for correct answer)

- a. Google App Engine
- b. Google eBooks
- c. Google Safe Browsing
- d. Google Consumer Surveys

Guidance: level 1

:: Computer file formats ::

_____ is a communication protocol for peer-to-peer file sharing which is used to distribute data and electronic files over the Internet.

Exam Probability: **Medium**

26. *Answer choices:*

(see index for correct answer)

- a. Computable Document Format
- b. Secure Digital Container
- c. Execute Direct Access Program
- d. Pro-MPEG

Guidance: level 1

:: Data management ::

Given organizations' increasing dependency on information technology to run their operations, Business continuity planning covers the entire organization, and Disaster recovery focuses on IT.

Exam Probability: **Medium**

27. *Answer choices:*

(see index for correct answer)

- a. Disaster recovery plan
- b. Data verification
- c. Savepoint
- d. Reference table

Guidance: level 1

:: Internet advertising ::

_____ is software that aims to gather information about a person or organization, sometimes without their knowledge, that may send such information to another entity without the consumer's consent, that asserts control over a device without the consumer's knowledge, or it may send such information to another entity with the consumer's consent, through cookies.

Exam Probability: **High**

28. *Answer choices:*

(see index for correct answer)

- a. Memolink
- b. Spyware
- c. Filterset.G
- d. Deep linking

Guidance: level 1

:: Tag editors ::

_____ is a media player, media library, Internet radio broadcaster, and mobile device management application developed by Apple Inc. It was announced on January 9, 2001. It is used to play, download, and organize digital multimedia files, including music and video, on personal computers running the macOS and Windows operating systems. Content must be purchased through the _____ Store, whereas _____ is the software letting users manage their purchases.

Exam Probability: **Medium**

29. *Answer choices:*

(see index for correct answer)

- a. ITunes

- b. CD Player
- c. QuuxPlayer
- d. Mp3tag

Guidance: level 1

:: Industrial automation ::

_____ is the technology by which a process or procedure is performed with minimal human assistance. _____ or automatic control is the use of various control systems for operating equipment such as machinery, processes in factories, boilers and heat treating ovens, switching on telephone networks, steering and stabilization of ships, aircraft and other applications and vehicles with minimal or reduced human intervention.

Exam Probability: **Medium**

30. *Answer choices:*

(see index for correct answer)

- a. Advanced Plant Management System
- b. IODD
- c. PLCopen
- d. Collaborative process automation systems

Guidance: level 1

:: Virtual reality ::

An _____ , a concept in Hinduism that means "descent", refers to the material appearance or incarnation of a deity on earth. The relative verb to "alight, to make one's appearance" is sometimes used to refer to any guru or revered human being.

Exam Probability: **Medium**

31. *Answer choices:*

(see index for correct answer)

- a. Avatar
- b. PhysX
- c. Telepointer
- d. Unreal Engine

Guidance: level 1

:: Computer data ::

In computer science, _____ is the ability to access an arbitrary element of a sequence in equal time or any datum from a population of addressable elements roughly as easily and efficiently as any other, no matter how many elements may be in the set. It is typically contrasted to sequential access.

Exam Probability: **Medium**

32. *Answer choices:*

(see index for correct answer)

- a. Compressed pattern matching
- b. Energy Logic
- c. 12-bit
- d. Random access

Guidance: level 1

:: Marketing ::

_____ is a business model in which consumers create value and businesses consume that value. For example, when a consumer writes reviews or when a consumer gives a useful idea for new product development then that consumer is creating value for the business if the business adopts the input. In the C2B model, a reverse auction or demand collection model, enables buyers to name or demand their own price, which is often binding, for a specific good or service. Inside of a consumer to business market the roles involved in the transaction must be established and the consumer must offer something of value to the business.

Exam Probability: **Low**

33. *Answer choices:*

(see index for correct answer)

- a. Business-to-government
- b. Content marketing
- c. Premium pricing
- d. Mass market

Guidance: level 1

:: Business process ::

A _____ or business method is a collection of related, structured activities or tasks by people or equipment which in a specific sequence produce a service or product for a particular customer or customers. _____ es occur at all organizational levels and may or may not be visible to the customers. A _____ may often be visualized as a flowchart of a sequence of activities with interleaving decision points or as a process matrix of a sequence of activities with relevance rules based on data in the process. The benefits of using _____ es include improved customer satisfaction and improved agility for reacting to rapid market change. Process-oriented organizations break down the barriers of structural departments and try to avoid functional silos.

Exam Probability: **Low**

34. *Answer choices:*

(see index for correct answer)

- a. Knowledge process outsourcing
- b. Business Process Definition Metamodel
- c. International business development

- d. Hi-tech export

Guidance: level 1

:: ::

The _____ , commonly known as the Web, is an information system where documents and other web resources are identified by Uniform Resource Locators , which may be interlinked by hypertext, and are accessible over the Internet.
The resources of the WWW may be accessed by users by a software application called a web browser.

Exam Probability: **Medium**

35. *Answer choices:*
(see index for correct answer)

- a. deep-level diversity
- b. World Wide Web
- c. similarity-attraction theory
- d. personal values

Guidance: level 1

:: Computer security standards ::

The _____ for Information Technology Security Evaluation is an international standard for computer security certification. It is currently in version 3.1 revision 5.

Exam Probability: **High**

36. *Answer choices:*

(see index for correct answer)

- a. CTCPEC
- b. Blacker
- c. CVSS
- d. IEC 60870-6

Guidance: level 1

:: Information retrieval ::

_____ is the practice of making content from multiple enterprise-type sources, such as databases and intranets, searchable to a defined audience.

Exam Probability: **Medium**

37. *Answer choices:*

(see index for correct answer)

- a. Concept search
- b. Information Retrieval Specialist Group
- c. Latent semantic indexing
- d. Web search engine

Guidance: level 1

:: Data management ::

_____ means protecting digital data, such as those in a database, from destructive forces and from the unwanted actions of unauthorized users, such as a cyberattack or a data breach.

Exam Probability: **Medium**

38. *Answer choices:*

(see index for correct answer)

- a. Data security
- b. Operational historian
- c. Durability
- d. Edge data integration

Guidance: level 1

:: Information systems ::

_____ is a process used in the life cycle area of the dynamic systems development method to collect business requirements while developing new information systems for a company. "The JAD process also includes approaches for enhancing user participation, expediting development, and improving the quality of specifications." It consists of a workshop where "knowledge workers and IT specialists meet, sometimes for several days, to define and review the business requirements for the system." The attendees include high level management officials who will ensure the product provides the needed reports and information at the end. This acts as "a management process which allows Corporate Information Services departments to work more effectively with users in a shorter time frame".

Exam Probability: **High**

39. *Answer choices:*

(see index for correct answer)

- a. Question Manager
- b. MES Hybrid Document Systems
- c. Joint application design
- d. Information systems

Guidance: level 1

:: Data security ::

In information technology, a _____, or data _____, or the process of backing up, refers to the copying into an archive file of computer data that is already in secondary storage—so that it may be used to restore the original after a data loss event. The verb form is "back up", whereas the noun and adjective form is "_____".

Exam Probability: **Medium**

40. *Answer choices:*

(see index for correct answer)

- a. Guard
- b. Data theft
- c. Backup
- d. First Department

Guidance: level 1

:: ::

A _____ is a knowledge base website on which users collaboratively modify content and structure directly from the web browser. In a typical _____, text is written using a simplified markup language and often edited with the help of a rich-text editor.

Exam Probability: **High**

41. *Answer choices:*

(see index for correct answer)

- a. imperative
- b. Wiki
- c. corporate values
- d. similarity-attraction theory

Guidance: level 1

:: Data security ::

_____ are safeguards or countermeasures to avoid, detect, counteract, or minimize security risks to physical property, information, computer systems, or other assets.

Exam Probability: **High**

42. *Answer choices:*

(see index for correct answer)

- a. Administrative share
- b. Relocatable user backup
- c. Cracking of wireless networks
- d. Security controls

Guidance: level 1

:: Computer memory ::

_____ is an electronic non-volatile computer storage medium that can be electrically erased and reprogrammed.

Exam Probability: **High**

43. *Answer choices:*

(see index for correct answer)

- a. Volatile memory
- b. Sigmaquad
- c. Flash memory
- d. Bank switching

Guidance: level 1

:: Marketing ::

_____, in marketing, manufacturing, call centres and management, is the use of flexible computer-aided manufacturing systems to produce custom output. Such systems combine the low unit costs of mass production processes with the flexibility of individual customization.

Exam Probability: **High**

44. Answer choices:

(see index for correct answer)

- a. Intent scale translation
- b. Mass customization
- c. Buy one, get one free
- d. Geomarketing

Guidance: level 1

:: Distribution, retailing, and wholesaling ::

_____ measures the performance of a system. Certain goals are defined and the _____ gives the percentage to which those goals should be achieved. Fill rate is different from _____ .

Exam Probability: **Low**

45. Answer choices:

(see index for correct answer)

- a. Fast Fiction
- b. National
- c. Hypermarket
- d. Service level

Guidance: level 1

:: Google services ::

_____ is a discontinued image organizer and image viewer for organizing and editing digital photos, plus an integrated photo-sharing website, originally created by a company named Lifescape in 2002. In July 2004, Google acquired _____ from Lifescape and began offering it as freeware. " _____ " is a blend of the name of Spanish painter Pablo Picasso, the phrase mi casa and "pic" for pictures.

Exam Probability: **Medium**

46. *Answer choices:*

(see index for correct answer)

- a. Google Plugin for Eclipse
- b. Picasa
- c. Google Person Finder
- d. Sitemaps

Guidance: level 1

:: Intelligence (information gathering) ::

_____ comprises the strategies and technologies used by enterprises for the data analysis of business information. BI technologies provide historical, current and predictive views of business operations. Common functions of _____ technologies include reporting, online analytical processing, analytics, data mining, process mining, complex event processing, business performance management, benchmarking, text mining, predictive analytics and prescriptive analytics. BI technologies can handle large amounts of structured and sometimes unstructured data to help identify, develop and otherwise create new strategic business opportunities. They aim to allow for the easy interpretation of these big data. Identifying new opportunities and implementing an effective strategy based on insights can provide businesses with a competitive market advantage and long-term stability.

Exam Probability: **Low**

47. *Answer choices:*

(see index for correct answer)

- a. SIGINT Activity Designator
- b. spying
- c. Business intelligence
- d. Human intelligence

Guidance: level 1

:: Consumer behaviour ::

_____ is the ratio of users who click on a specific link to the number of total users who view a page, email, or advertisement. It is commonly used to measure the success of an online advertising campaign for a particular website as well as the effectiveness of email campaigns.

Exam Probability: **Medium**

48. *Answer choices:*

(see index for correct answer)

- a. Internality
- b. Homo consumericus
- c. Click-through rate
- d. Media manipulation

Guidance: level 1

:: E-commerce ::

_____ , and its now-deprecated predecessor, Secure Sockets Layer , are cryptographic protocols designed to provide communications security over a computer network. Several versions of the protocols find widespread use in applications such as web browsing, email, instant messaging, and voice over IP . Websites can use TLS to secure all communications between their servers and web browsers.

Exam Probability: **Medium**

49. *Answer choices:*

(see index for correct answer)

- a. Transport Layer Security
- b. NopCommerce
- c. Piano Media
- d. Shopping directory

Guidance: level 1

:: E-commerce ::

> The phrase _____ was originally coined in 1997 by Kevin Duffey at the launch of the Global _____ Forum, to mean "the delivery of electronic commerce capabilities directly into the consumer's hand, anywhere, via wireless technology." Many choose to think of _____ as meaning "a retail outlet in your customer's pocket."

Exam Probability: **High**

50. *Answer choices:*

(see index for correct answer)

- a. Mobile commerce
- b. Electronic Commerce Regulations 2002
- c. USAePay
- d. Foodie.fm

Guidance: level 1

:: Computer networking ::

_____ is a method of grouping data that is transmitted over a digital network into packets. Packets are made of a header and a payload. Data in the header are used by networking hardware to direct the packet to its destination where the payload is extracted and used by application software. _____ is the primary basis for data communications in computer networks worldwide.

Exam Probability: **Low**

51. *Answer choices:*
(see index for correct answer)

- a. Network agility
- b. Security domain
- c. Northbound interface
- d. STREAMS

Guidance: level 1

:: Data ::

_____ is a branch of mathematics working with data collection, organization, analysis, interpretation and presentation. In applying _____ to, for example, a scientific, industrial, or social problem, it is conventional to begin with a statistical population or a statistical model process to be studied. Populations can be diverse topics such as "all people living in a country" or "every atom composing a crystal". _____ deals with every aspect of data, including the planning of data collection in terms of the design of surveys and experiments. See glossary of probability and _____ .

Exam Probability: **Medium**

52. *Answer choices:*

(see index for correct answer)

- a. Dummy data
- b. Statistics
- c. DataSplice
- d. Sonar

Guidance: level 1

:: Information science ::

The United States National Forum on _____ defines _____ as "... the hyper ability to know when there is a need for information, to be able to identify, locate, evaluate, and effectively use that information for the issue or problem at hand." The American Library Association defines "_____" as a set of abilities requiring individuals to "recognize when information is needed and have the ability to locate, evaluate, and use effectively the needed information. Other definitions incorporate aspects of "skepticism, judgement, free thinking, questioning, and understanding..." or incorporate competencies that an informed citizen of an information society ought to possess to participate intelligently and actively in that society.

Exam Probability: **High**

53. *Answer choices:*

(see index for correct answer)

- a. Memex
- b. Information literacy
- c. Mathematical knowledge management
- d. Information flow

Guidance: level 1

:: Information systems ::

A _____ is an information system that supports business or organizational decision-making activities. DSSs serve the management, operations and planning levels of an organization and help people make decisions about problems that may be rapidly changing and not easily specified in advance—i.e. unstructured and semi-structured decision problems. _____ s can be either fully computerized or human-powered, or a combination of both.

Exam Probability: **Medium**

54. *Answer choices:*

(see index for correct answer)

- a. Digital ecosystem
- b. Decision support system
- c. Geographical Operations System
- d. CountrySTAT

Guidance: level 1

:: Internet marketing ::

_____ is the measurement, collection, analysis and reporting of web data for purposes of understanding and optimizing web usage. However, _____ is not just a process for measuring web traffic but can be used as a tool for business and market research, and to assess and improve the effectiveness of a website. _____ applications can also help companies measure the results of traditional print or broadcast advertising campaigns. It helps one to estimate how traffic to a website changes after the launch of a new advertising campaign. _____ provides information about the number of visitors to a website and the number of page views. It helps gauge traffic and popularity trends which is useful for market research.

Exam Probability: **High**

55. *Answer choices:*

(see index for correct answer)

- a. Interactive advertising
- b. Link bidding
- c. Search retargeting
- d. Web analytics

Guidance: level 1

:: Information technology management ::

____ within quality management systems and information technology systems is a process—either formal or informal—used to ensure that changes to a product or system are introduced in a controlled and coordinated manner. It reduces the possibility that unnecessary changes will be introduced to a system without forethought, introducing faults into the system or undoing changes made by other users of software. The goals of a ____ procedure usually include minimal disruption to services, reduction in back-out activities, and cost-effective utilization of resources involved in implementing change.

Exam Probability: **High**

56. *Answer choices:*

(see index for correct answer)

- a. IT asset management
- b. FORTRAS
- c. Virtual chargeback
- d. Change control

Guidance: level 1

:: Internet governance ::

A _____ is one of the domains at the highest level in the hierarchical Domain Name System of the Internet. The _____ names are installed in the root zone of the name space. For all domains in lower levels, it is the last part of the domain name, that is, the last label of a fully qualified domain name. For example, in the domain name www.example.com, the _____ is com. Responsibility for management of most _____ s is delegated to specific organizations by the Internet Corporation for Assigned Names and Numbers , which operates the Internet Assigned Numbers Authority , and is in charge of maintaining the DNS root zone.

Exam Probability: **High**

57. *Answer choices:*

(see index for correct answer)

- a. Route server
- b. PKNIC
- c. Top-level domain
- d. History of the Internet

Guidance: level 1

:: Marketing ::

_____ is the percentage of a market accounted for by a specific entity. In a survey of nearly 200 senior marketing managers, 67% responded that they found the revenue- "dollar _____ " metric very useful, while 61% found "unit _____ " very useful.

Exam Probability: **High**

58. *Answer choices:*

(see index for correct answer)

- a. Azerbaijan Marketing Society
- b. Exploratory research
- c. Market share
- d. Market sector

Guidance: level 1

:: ::

A _____ is a research instrument consisting of a series of questions for the purpose of gathering information from respondents. The _____ was invented by the Statistical Society of London in 1838.

Exam Probability: **Medium**

59. *Answer choices:*

(see index for correct answer)

- a. functional perspective
- b. hierarchical perspective
- c. co-culture
- d. open system

Guidance: level 1

Marketing

Marketing is the study and management of exchange relationships. Marketing is the business process of creating relationships with and satisfying customers. With its focus on the customer, marketing is one of the premier components of business management.

Marketing is defined by the American Marketing Association as "the activity, set of institutions, and processes for creating, communicating, delivering, and exchanging offerings that have value for customers, clients, partners, and society at large."

:: Marketing techniques ::

_____, also known as embedded marketing, is a marketing technique where references to specific brands or products are incorporated into another work, such as a film or television program, with specific promotional intent.

Exam Probability: **Medium**

1. *Answer choices:*

(see index for correct answer)

- a. Aaker Model
- b. Product placement
- c. Unique selling language
- d. Smarketing

Guidance: level 1

:: Business economics ::

In economics, _____ is demand for a factor of production or intermediate good that occurs as a result of the demand for another intermediate or final good. In essence, the demand for, say, a factor of production by a firm is dependent on the demand by consumers for the product produced by the firm. The term was first introduced by Alfred Marshall in his Principles of Economics in 1890.

Exam Probability: **High**

2. *Answer choices:*

(see index for correct answer)

- a. Incremental operating margin
- b. Units of transportation measurement
- c. Trade sale
- d. Derived demand

Guidance: level 1

:: ::

A _____ is a professional who provides expert advice in a particular area such as security, management, education, accountancy, law, human resources, marketing, finance, engineering, science or any of many other specialized fields.

Exam Probability: **High**

3. *Answer choices:*

(see index for correct answer)

- a. cultural
- b. Consultant
- c. process perspective
- d. hierarchical perspective

Guidance: level 1

:: Types of marketing ::

_____ was first defined as a form of marketing developed from direct response marketing campaigns which emphasizes customer retention and satisfaction, rather than a focus on sales transactions.

Exam Probability: **Low**

4. *Answer choices:*

(see index for correct answer)

- a. Vertical integration
- b. Community marketing
- c. Relationship marketing
- d. Megamarketing

Guidance: level 1

:: Business terms ::

A _____ is a short statement of why an organization exists, what its overall goal is, identifying the goal of its operations: what kind of product or service it provides, its primary customers or market, and its geographical region of operation. It may include a short statement of such fundamental matters as the organization's values or philosophies, a business's main competitive advantages, or a desired future state—the "vision".

Exam Probability: **High**

5. *Answer choices:*

(see index for correct answer)

- a. year-to-date
- b. Mission statement
- c. churn rate
- d. Strategic partner

Guidance: level 1

:: ::

A _____ is an organization, usually a group of people or a company, authorized to act as a single entity and recognized as such in law. Early incorporated entities were established by charter. Most jurisdictions now allow the creation of new _____ s through registration.

Exam Probability: **Low**

6. *Answer choices:*

(see index for correct answer)

- a. personal values
- b. imperative
- c. Character
- d. Corporation

Guidance: level 1

:: Strategic alliances ::

A _____ is an agreement between two or more parties to pursue a set of agreed upon objectives needed while remaining independent organizations. A _____ will usually fall short of a legal partnership entity, agency, or corporate affiliate relationship. Typically, two companies form a _____ when each possesses one or more business assets or have expertise that will help the other by enhancing their businesses. _____ s can develop in outsourcing relationships where the parties desire to achieve long-term win-win benefits and innovation based on mutually desired outcomes.

Exam Probability: **Medium**

7. *Answer choices:*

(see index for correct answer)

- a. Defensive termination
- b. Bridge Alliance

- c. International joint venture
- d. Cross-licensing

Guidance: level 1

:: ::

> Consumer behaviour is the study of individuals, groups, or organizations and all the activities associated with the purchase, use and disposal of goods and services, including the consumer's emotional, mental and behavioural responses that precede or follow these activities. Consumer behaviour emerged in the 1940s and 50s as a distinct sub-discipline in the marketing area.

Exam Probability: **Low**

8. *Answer choices:*

(see index for correct answer)

- a. Character
- b. open system
- c. imperative
- d. Consumer behavior

Guidance: level 1

:: Budgets ::

A _____ is a financial plan for a defined period, often one year. It may also include planned sales volumes and revenues, resource quantities, costs and expenses, assets, liabilities and cash flows. Companies, governments, families and other organizations use it to express strategic plans of activities or events in measurable terms.

Exam Probability: **Low**

9. *Answer choices:*

(see index for correct answer)

- a. Budget
- b. Personal budget
- c. Black budget
- d. Railway Budget

Guidance: level 1

:: Brand management ::

Marketing communications uses different marketing channels and tools in combination: Marketing communication channels focus on any way a business communicates a message to its desired market, or the market in general. A marketing communication tool can be anything from: advertising, personal selling, direct marketing, sponsorship, communication, and promotion to public relations.

Exam Probability: **Medium**

10. *Answer choices:*

(see index for correct answer)

- a. Postmodern marketing
- b. Iconix Brand Group
- c. Brand strength analysis
- d. Integrated marketing

Guidance: level 1

:: Competition (economics) ::

_____ arises whenever at least two parties strive for a goal which cannot be shared: where one's gain is the other's loss.

Exam Probability: **Medium**

11. *Answer choices:*

(see index for correct answer)

- a. Tax competition
- b. Economic forces
- c. Competition
- d. Self-competition

Guidance: level 1

:: Direct selling ::

_____ consists of two main business models: single-level marketing, in which a direct seller makes money by buying products from a parent organization and selling them directly to customers, and multi-level marketing, in which the direct seller may earn money from both direct sales to customers and by sponsoring new direct sellers and potentially earning a commission from their efforts.

Exam Probability: **Low**

12. *Answer choices:*

(see index for correct answer)

- a. Direct Selling News
- b. The Longaberger Company
- c. Direct selling
- d. CVSL

Guidance: level 1

:: Advertising ::

A _____ is a document used by creative professionals and agencies to develop creative deliverables: visual design, copy, advertising, web sites, etc. The document is usually developed by the requestor and approved by the creative team of designers, writers, and project managers. In some cases, the project's _____ may need creative director approval before work will commence.

Exam Probability: **Low**

13. *Answer choices:*

(see index for correct answer)

- a. Retargeter
- b. Issue advocacy ads
- c. Creative brief
- d. Taykey

Guidance: level 1

:: Stock market ::

_____ is freedom from, or resilience against, potential harm caused by others. Beneficiaries of _____ may be of persons and social groups, objects and institutions, ecosystems or any other entity or phenomenon vulnerable to unwanted change by its environment.

Exam Probability: **Medium**

14. *Answer choices:*

(see index for correct answer)

- a. Red herring prospectus
- b. Stop catching
- c. Security
- d. Erie War

Guidance: level 1

:: Legal terms ::

A _____ is a person who is called upon to issue a response to a communication made by another. The term is used in legal contexts, in survey methodology, and in psychological conditioning.

Exam Probability: **Low**

15. *Answer choices:*

(see index for correct answer)

- a. Alluvion
- b. Public Order Act 1986
- c. Commandeering
- d. Natural person

Guidance: level 1

:: ::

A _____ consists of one people who live in the same dwelling and share meals. It may also consist of a single family or another group of people. A dwelling is considered to contain multiple _____ s if meals or living spaces are not shared. The _____ is the basic unit of analysis in many social, microeconomic and government models, and is important to economics and inheritance.

Exam Probability: **Low**

16. *Answer choices:*

(see index for correct answer)

- a. deep-level diversity
- b. functional perspective
- c. interpersonal communication
- d. Household

Guidance: level 1

:: Marketing ::

_____ uses different marketing channels and tools in combination: Marketing communication channels focus on any way a business communicates a message to its desired market, or the market in general. A marketing communication tool can be anything from: advertising, personal selling, direct marketing, sponsorship, communication, and promotion to public relations.

Exam Probability: **Medium**

17. *Answer choices:*
(see index for correct answer)

- a. Customer franchise
- b. Official statistics
- c. Personalized marketing
- d. Marketing communications

Guidance: level 1

:: Brokered programming ::

An _____ is a form of television commercial, which generally includes a toll-free telephone number or website. Most often used as a form of direct response television, long-form _____ s are typically 28:30 or 58:30 minutes in length. _____ s are also known as paid programming. This phenomenon started in the United States, where _____ s were typically shown overnight, outside peak prime time hours for commercial broadcasters. Some television stations chose to air _____ s as an alternative to the former practice of signing off. Some channels air _____ s 24 hours. Some stations also choose to air _____ s during the daytime hours mostly on weekends to fill in for unscheduled network or syndicated programming. By 2009, most _____ spending in the U.S. occurred during the early morning, daytime and evening hours, or in the afternoon. Stations in most countries around the world have instituted similar media structures. The _____ industry is worth over $200 billion.

Exam Probability: **High**

18. *Answer choices:*

(see index for correct answer)

- a. Brokered programming
- b. One Magnificent Morning
- c. Infomercial
- d. Leased access

Guidance: level 1

_____ is an abstract concept of management of complex systems according to a set of rules and trends. In systems theory, these types of rules exist in various fields of biology and society, but the term has slightly different meanings according to context. For example.

Exam Probability: **High**

19. *Answer choices:*
(see index for correct answer)

- a. Regulation
- b. interpersonal communication
- c. imperative
- d. hierarchical perspective

Guidance: level 1

:: Contract law ::

A _____ is a legally-binding agreement which recognises and governs the rights and duties of the parties to the agreement. A _____ is legally enforceable because it meets the requirements and approval of the law. An agreement typically involves the exchange of goods, services, money, or promises of any of those. In the event of breach of _____ , the law awards the injured party access to legal remedies such as damages and cancellation.

Exam Probability: **Low**

20. *Answer choices:*

(see index for correct answer)

- a. Forum selection clause
- b. South African contract law
- c. Partial integration
- d. Principles of International Commercial Contracts

Guidance: level 1

:: Management ::

The term _____ refers to measures designed to increase the degree of autonomy and self-determination in people and in communities in order to enable them to represent their interests in a responsible and self-determined way, acting on their own authority. It is the process of becoming stronger and more confident, especially in controlling one's life and claiming one's rights. _____ as action refers both to the process of self-_____ and to professional support of people, which enables them to overcome their sense of powerlessness and lack of influence, and to recognize and use their resources. To do work with power.

Exam Probability: **Low**

21. *Answer choices:*

(see index for correct answer)

- a. Iterative and incremental development
- b. Managerial Psychology

- c. Empowerment
- d. Business workflow analysis

Guidance: level 1

:: ::

In regulatory jurisdictions that provide for it, _____ is a group of laws and organizations designed to ensure the rights of consumers as well as fair trade, competition and accurate information in the marketplace. The laws are designed to prevent the businesses that engage in fraud or specified unfair practices from gaining an advantage over competitors. They may also provides additional protection for those most vulnerable in society. _____ laws are a form of government regulation that aim to protect the rights of consumers. For example, a government may require businesses to disclose detailed information about products—particularly in areas where safety or public health is an issue, such as food.

Exam Probability: **High**

22. *Answer choices:*

(see index for correct answer)

- a. empathy
- b. Consumer Protection
- c. Character
- d. personal values

Guidance: level 1

:: Decision theory ::

Within economics the concept of _____ is used to model worth or value, but its usage has evolved significantly over time. The term was introduced initially as a measure of pleasure or satisfaction within the theory of utilitarianism by moral philosophers such as Jeremy Bentham and John Stuart Mill. But the term has been adapted and reapplied within neoclassical economics, which dominates modern economic theory, as a _____ function that represents a consumer's preference ordering over a choice set. As such, it is devoid of its original interpretation as a measurement of the pleasure or satisfaction obtained by the consumer from that choice.

Exam Probability: **Low**

23. *Answer choices:*

(see index for correct answer)

- a. Probabilistic prognosis
- b. Multi-attribute global inference of quality
- c. Utility
- d. Weighted sum model

Guidance: level 1

:: Data interchange standards ::

_____ is the concept of businesses electronically communicating information that was traditionally communicated on paper, such as purchase orders and invoices. Technical standards for EDI exist to facilitate parties transacting such instruments without having to make special arrangements.

Exam Probability: **Low**

24. *Answer choices:*

(see index for correct answer)

- a. Electronic data interchange
- b. Domain Application Protocol
- c. Interaction protocol
- d. Data Interchange Standards Association

Guidance: level 1

:: Marketing ::

_____ is the process of using surveys to evaluate consumer acceptance of a new product idea prior to the introduction of a product to the market. It is important not to confuse _____ with advertising testing, brand testing and packaging testing; as is sometimes done. _____ focuses on the basic product idea, without the embellishments and puffery inherent in advertising.

Exam Probability: **Low**

25. *Answer choices:*

(see index for correct answer)

- a. Customer value proposition
- b. Marchitecture
- c. Concept testing
- d. Business stature

Guidance: level 1

:: Logistics ::

_____ is generally the detailed organization and implementation of a complex operation. In a general business sense, _____ is the management of the flow of things between the point of origin and the point of consumption in order to meet requirements of customers or corporations. The resources managed in _____ may include tangible goods such as materials, equipment, and supplies, as well as food and other consumable items. The _____ of physical items usually involves the integration of information flow, materials handling, production, packaging, inventory, transportation, warehousing, and often security.

Exam Probability: **Low**

26. *Answer choices:*

(see index for correct answer)

- a. DASH7
- b. Trailer tracking

- c. Liquid logistics
- d. Logistics

Guidance: level 1

:: Advertising ::

A _____ is a large outdoor advertising structure, typically found in high-traffic areas such as alongside busy roads. _____ s present large advertisements to passing pedestrians and drivers. Typically showing witty slogans and distinctive visuals, _____ s are highly visible in the top designated market areas.

Exam Probability: **Medium**

27. *Answer choices:*

(see index for correct answer)

- a. Jacques Dauphin
- b. Skyscaping
- c. Swipe file
- d. Billboard

Guidance: level 1

:: Data management ::

_____ is a form of intellectual property that grants the creator of an original creative work an exclusive legal right to determine whether and under what conditions this original work may be copied and used by others, usually for a limited term of years. The exclusive rights are not absolute but limited by limitations and exceptions to _____ law, including fair use. A major limitation on _____ on ideas is that _____ protects only the original expression of ideas, and not the underlying ideas themselves.

Exam Probability: **High**

28. *Answer choices:*

(see index for correct answer)

- a. Data management
- b. Copyright
- c. Concurrency control
- d. Data Reference Model

Guidance: level 1

:: ::

_____ is both a research area and a practical skill encompassing the ability of an individual or organization to "lead" or guide other individuals, teams, or entire organizations. Specialist literature debates various viewpoints, contrasting Eastern and Western approaches to _____ , and also United States versus European approaches. U.S. academic environments define _____ as "a process of social influence in which a person can enlist the aid and support of others in the accomplishment of a common task".

Exam Probability: **High**

29. *Answer choices:*

(see index for correct answer)

- a. surface-level diversity
- b. personal values
- c. Leadership
- d. functional perspective

Guidance: level 1

:: Marketing ::

_____s are structured marketing strategies designed by merchants to encourage customers to continue to shop at or use the services of businesses associated with each program. These programs exist covering most types of commerce, each one having varying features and rewards-schemes.

Exam Probability: **High**

30. *Answer choices:*

(see index for correct answer)

- a. Customer franchise
- b. Enterprise relationship management
- c. Net idol

- d. Loyalty program

Guidance: level 1

:: Monopoly (economics) ::

The _____ of 1890 was a United States antitrust law that regulates competition among enterprises, which was passed by Congress under the presidency of Benjamin Harrison.

Exam Probability: **High**

31. *Answer choices:*

(see index for correct answer)

- a. Sherman Antitrust Act
- b. Privatization
- c. Ramsey problem
- d. Monopoly

Guidance: level 1

:: Cultural appropriation ::

_____ is a social and economic order that encourages the acquisition of goods and services in ever-increasing amounts. With the industrial revolution, but particularly in the 20th century, mass production led to an economic crisis: there was overproduction—the supply of goods would grow beyond consumer demand, and so manufacturers turned to planned obsolescence and advertising to manipulate consumer spending. In 1899, a book on _____ published by Thorstein Veblen, called The Theory of the Leisure Class, examined the widespread values and economic institutions emerging along with the widespread "leisure time" in the beginning of the 20th century. In it Veblen "views the activities and spending habits of this leisure class in terms of conspicuous and vicarious consumption and waste. Both are related to the display of status and not to functionality or usefulness."

Exam Probability: **Medium**

32. *Answer choices:*

(see index for correct answer)

- a. Plastic Paddy
- b. California Indian Song
- c. Imaging Blackness
- d. The Rebel Sell

Guidance: level 1

:: ::

_____ or accountancy is the measurement, processing, and communication of financial information about economic entities such as businesses and corporations. The modern field was established by the Italian mathematician Luca Pacioli in 1494. _____, which has been called the "language of business", measures the results of an organization's economic activities and conveys this information to a variety of users, including investors, creditors, management, and regulators. Practitioners of _____ are known as accountants. The terms "_____" and "financial reporting" are often used as synonyms.

Exam Probability: **Medium**

33. *Answer choices:*

(see index for correct answer)

- a. empathy
- b. imperative
- c. Accounting
- d. interpersonal communication

Guidance: level 1

:: Problem solving ::

In other words, _____ is a situation where a group of people meet to generate new ideas and solutions around a specific domain of interest by removing inhibitions. People are able to think more freely and they suggest as many spontaneous new ideas as possible. All the ideas are noted down and those ideas are not criticized and after _____ session the ideas are evaluated. The term was popularized by Alex Faickney Osborn in the 1953 book Applied Imagination.

Exam Probability: **Low**

34. *Answer choices:*

(see index for correct answer)

- a. Encyclopedia of World Problems and Human Potential
- b. Eight Disciplines Problem Solving
- c. Lateral computing
- d. How to Solve It

Guidance: level 1

:: ::

A _____ is a discussion or informational website published on the World Wide Web consisting of discrete, often informal diary-style text entries. Posts are typically displayed in reverse chronological order, so that the most recent post appears first, at the top of the web page. Until 2009, _____ s were usually the work of a single individual, occasionally of a small group, and often covered a single subject or topic. In the 2010s, "multi-author _____ s" emerged, featuring the writing of multiple authors and sometimes professionally edited. MABs from newspapers, other media outlets, universities, think tanks, advocacy groups, and similar institutions account for an increasing quantity of _____ traffic. The rise of Twitter and other "micro _____ ging" systems helps integrate MABs and single-author _____ s into the news media. _____ can also be used as a verb, meaning to maintain or add content to a _____ .

Exam Probability: **High**

35. *Answer choices:*

(see index for correct answer)

- a. process perspective
- b. Blog
- c. information systems assessment
- d. cultural

Guidance: level 1

:: Direct marketing ::

_____ is a form of direct marketing using databases of customers or potential customers to generate personalized communications in order to promote a product or service for marketing purposes. The method of communication can be any addressable medium, as in direct marketing.

Exam Probability: **High**

36. *Answer choices:*

(see index for correct answer)

- a. Database marketing
- b. CornerWorld
- c. American Family Publishers
- d. Telemarketing

Guidance: level 1

:: E-commerce ::

_____ is the activity of buying or selling of products on online services or over the Internet. Electronic commerce draws on technologies such as mobile commerce, electronic funds transfer, supply chain management, Internet marketing, online transaction processing, electronic data interchange, inventory management systems, and automated data collection systems.

Exam Probability: **Low**

37. *Answer choices:*

(see index for correct answer)

- a. ICOCA
- b. Click farm
- c. Allbiz
- d. E-commerce

Guidance: level 1

:: Marketing ::

_____ is a marketing practice of individuals or organizations. It allows them to sell products or services to other companies or organizations that resell them, use them in their products or services or use them to support their works.

Exam Probability: **Low**

38. *Answer choices:*

(see index for correct answer)

- a. Back to school
- b. HyTrust
- c. Customer value proposition
- d. Franchise fee

Guidance: level 1

:: Commerce ::

A _____ is a company or individual that purchases goods or services with the intention of selling them rather than consuming or using them. This is usually done for profit. One example can be found in the industry of telecommunications, where companies buy excess amounts of transmission capacity or call time from other carriers and resell it to smaller carriers.

Exam Probability: **High**

39. *Answer choices:*

(see index for correct answer)

- a. Hauls
- b. Closed household economy
- c. Statutory holdback
- d. Reseller

Guidance: level 1

:: ::

_____ characterises the behaviour of a system or model whose components interact in multiple ways and follow local rules, meaning there is no reasonable higher instruction to define the various possible interactions.

Exam Probability: **Medium**

40. *Answer choices:*

(see index for correct answer)

- a. Sarbanes-Oxley act of 2002
- b. open system
- c. Complexity
- d. empathy

Guidance: level 1

:: ::

_____ is the process of making predictions of the future based on past and present data and most commonly by analysis of trends. A commonplace example might be estimation of some variable of interest at some specified future date. Prediction is a similar, but more general term. Both might refer to formal statistical methods employing time series, cross-sectional or longitudinal data, or alternatively to less formal judgmental methods. Usage can differ between areas of application: for example, in hydrology the terms "forecast" and " _____ " are sometimes reserved for estimates of values at certain specific future times, while the term "prediction" is used for more general estimates, such as the number of times floods will occur over a long period.

Exam Probability: **Medium**

41. *Answer choices:*

(see index for correct answer)

- a. imperative
- b. cultural
- c. hierarchical perspective
- d. Sarbanes-Oxley act of 2002

Guidance: level 1

:: ::

In law, an _____ is the process in which cases are reviewed, where parties request a formal change to an official decision. _____ s function both as a process for error correction as well as a process of clarifying and interpreting law. Although appellate courts have existed for thousands of years, common law countries did not incorporate an affirmative right to _____ into their jurisprudence until the 19th century.

Exam Probability: **High**

42. *Answer choices:*

(see index for correct answer)

- a. corporate values
- b. process perspective

- c. levels of analysis
- d. co-culture

Guidance: level 1

:: Planning ::

_____ is a high level plan to achieve one or more goals under conditions of uncertainty. In the sense of the "art of the general," which included several subsets of skills including tactics, siegecraft, logistics etc., the term came into use in the 6th century C.E. in East Roman terminology, and was translated into Western vernacular languages only in the 18th century. From then until the 20th century, the word "_____" came to denote "a comprehensive way to try to pursue political ends, including the threat or actual use of force, in a dialectic of wills" in a military conflict, in which both adversaries interact.

Exam Probability: **Low**

43. *Answer choices:*

(see index for correct answer)

- a. Counterplan
- b. Commercial area
- c. Strategy
- d. Cross-cultural differences in decision-making

Guidance: level 1

The _____ is a U.S. business-focused, English-language international daily newspaper based in New York City. The Journal, along with its Asian and European editions, is published six days a week by Dow Jones & Company, a division of News Corp. The newspaper is published in the broadsheet format and online. The Journal has been printed continuously since its inception on July 8, 1889, by Charles Dow, Edward Jones, and Charles Bergstresser.

Exam Probability: **Low**

44. *Answer choices:*

(see index for correct answer)

- a. hierarchical
- b. Wall Street Journal
- c. deep-level diversity
- d. hierarchical perspective

Guidance: level 1

Business is the activity of making one's living or making money by producing or buying and selling products. Simply put, it is "any activity or enterprise entered into for profit. It does not mean it is a company, a corporation, partnership, or have any such formal organization, but it can range from a street peddler to General Motors."

Exam Probability: **Low**

45. *Answer choices:*

(see index for correct answer)

- a. Character
- b. interpersonal communication
- c. surface-level diversity
- d. Firm

Guidance: level 1

:: Market research ::

_____ is an organized effort to gather information about target markets or customers. It is a very important component of business strategy. The term is commonly interchanged with marketing research; however, expert practitioners may wish to draw a distinction, in that marketing research is concerned specifically about marketing processes, while _____ is concerned specifically with markets.

Exam Probability: **Low**

46. Answer choices:

(see index for correct answer)

- a. Zyfin
- b. Market research
- c. Cambashi
- d. Software Industry Survey

Guidance: level 1

:: ::

Retail is the process of selling consumer goods or services to customers through multiple channels of distribution to earn a profit. Retailers satisfy demand identified through a supply chain. The term "retailer" is typically applied where a service provider fills the small orders of a large number of individuals, who are end-users, rather than large orders of a small number of wholesale, corporate or government clientele. Shopping generally refers to the act of buying products. Sometimes this is done to obtain final goods, including necessities such as food and clothing; sometimes it takes place as a recreational activity. Recreational shopping often involves window shopping and browsing: it does not always result in a purchase.

Exam Probability: **Medium**

47. Answer choices:

(see index for correct answer)

- a. process perspective

- b. Retailing
- c. Character
- d. corporate values

Guidance: level 1

:: Data ::

Data has two ways of being created or generated. The first is what is called `captured data`, and is found through purposeful investigation or analysis. The second is called `exhaust data`, and is gathered usually by machines or terminals as a secondary function. For example, cash registers, smartphones, and speedometers serve a main function but may collect data as a secondary task. Exhaustive data is usually too large or of little use to process and becomes `transient` or thrown away.

Exam Probability: **Low**

48. *Answer choices:*

(see index for correct answer)

- a. Primary data
- b. GS1 DataBar Coupon
- c. Synthetic data
- d. Data Transmission

Guidance: level 1

:: Progressive Era in the United States ::

The Clayton Antitrust Act of 1914, was a part of United States antitrust law with the goal of adding further substance to the U.S. antitrust law regime; the _____ sought to prevent anticompetitive practices in their incipiency. That regime started with the Sherman Antitrust Act of 1890, the first Federal law outlawing practices considered harmful to consumers. The _____ specified particular prohibited conduct, the three-level enforcement scheme, the exemptions, and the remedial measures.

Exam Probability: **Medium**

49. *Answer choices:*

(see index for correct answer)

- a. Mann Act
- b. pragmatism
- c. Clayton Antitrust Act

Guidance: level 1

:: Financial economics ::

In management, business value is an informal term that includes all forms of value that determine the health and well-being of the firm in the long run. Business value expands concept of value of the firm beyond economic value to include other forms of value such as employee value, _____ , supplier value, channel partner value, alliance partner value, managerial value, and societal value. Many of these forms of value are not directly measured in monetary terms.

Exam Probability: **Medium**

50. *Answer choices:*

(see index for correct answer)

- a. Interest rate parity
- b. Financial export
- c. Customer value
- d. Investment protection

Guidance: level 1

Market segmentation is the activity of dividing a broad consumer or business market, normally consisting of existing and potential customers, into sub-groups of consumers based on some type of shared characteristics. In dividing or segmenting markets, researchers typically look for common characteristics such as shared needs, common interests, similar lifestyles or even similar demographic profiles. The overall aim of segmentation is to identify high yield segments – that is, those segments that are likely to be the most profitable or that have growth potential – so that these can be selected for special attention .

Exam Probability: **Low**

51. *Answer choices:*

(see index for correct answer)

- a. hierarchical
- b. deep-level diversity
- c. functional perspective
- d. Market segments

Guidance: level 1

:: Promotion and marketing communications ::

Advertising mail, also known as _____ , junk mail , mailshot or admail, is the delivery of advertising material to recipients of postal mail. The delivery of advertising mail forms a large and growing service for many postal services, and direct-mail marketing forms a significant portion of the direct marketing industry. Some organizations attempt to help people opt out of receiving advertising mail, in many cases motivated by a concern over its negative environmental impact.

Exam Probability: **Medium**

52. *Answer choices:*

(see index for correct answer)

- a. Direct mail
- b. IB5k
- c. Trade promotion management
- d. CollarCard

Guidance: level 1

:: ::

An _____ is a systematic and independent examination of books, accounts, statutory records, documents and vouchers of an organization to ascertain how far the financial statements as well as non-financial disclosures present a true and fair view of the concern. It also attempts to ensure that the books of accounts are properly maintained by the concern as required by law. _____ ing has become such a ubiquitous phenomenon in the corporate and the public sector that academics started identifying an " _____ Society". The _____ or perceives and recognises the propositions before them for examination, obtains evidence, evaluates the same and formulates an opinion on the basis of his judgement which is communicated through their _____ ing report.

Exam Probability: **Medium**

53. *Answer choices:*

(see index for correct answer)

- a. levels of analysis
- b. similarity-attraction theory
- c. Audit
- d. cultural

Guidance: level 1

:: Evaluation methods ::

_____ is a scientific method of observation to gather non-numerical data. This type of research "refers to the meanings, concepts definitions, characteristics, metaphors, symbols, and description of things" and not to their "counts or measures." This research answers why and how a certain phenomenon may occur rather than how often. _____ approaches are employed across many academic disciplines, focusing particularly on the human elements of the social and natural sciences; in less academic contexts, areas of application include qualitative market research, business, service demonstrations by non-profits, and journalism.

Exam Probability: **High**

54. *Answer choices:*

(see index for correct answer)

- a. Fixtureless in-circuit test
- b. Quantitative research
- c. Alternative assessment
- d. Qualitative research

Guidance: level 1

:: ::

In law, a _____ is a coming together of parties to a dispute, to present information in a tribunal, a formal setting with the authority to adjudicate claims or disputes. One form of tribunal is a court. The tribunal, which may occur before a judge, jury, or other designated trier of fact, aims to achieve a resolution to their dispute.

Exam Probability: **Medium**

55. *Answer choices:*

(see index for correct answer)

- a. Trial
- b. similarity-attraction theory
- c. functional perspective
- d. deep-level diversity

Guidance: level 1

:: Marketing ::

A _____ is a group of customers within a business's serviceable available market at which a business aims its marketing efforts and resources. A _____ is a subset of the total market for a product or service. The _____ typically consists of consumers who exhibit similar characteristics and are considered most likely to buy a business's market offerings or are likely to be the most profitable segments for the business to service.

Exam Probability: **Medium**

56. *Answer choices:*

(see index for correct answer)

- a. Customer insight
- b. Porter hypothesis

- c. Target market
- d. Marketing myopia

Guidance: level 1

:: ::

_____ is the provision of service to customers before, during and after a purchase. The perception of success of such interactions is dependent on employees "who can adjust themselves to the personality of the guest". _____ concerns the priority an organization assigns to _____ relative to components such as product innovation and pricing. In this sense, an organization that values good _____ may spend more money in training employees than the average organization or may proactively interview customers for feedback.

Exam Probability: **Medium**

57. *Answer choices:*

(see index for correct answer)

- a. Customer service
- b. hierarchical
- c. co-culture
- d. hierarchical perspective

Guidance: level 1

:: Generally Accepted Accounting Principles ::

In accounting, _____ is the income that a business have from its normal business activities, usually from the sale of goods and services to customers. _____ is also referred to as sales or turnover. Some companies receive _____ from interest, royalties, or other fees. _____ may refer to business income in general, or it may refer to the amount, in a monetary unit, earned during a period of time, as in "Last year, Company X had _____ of $42 million". Profits or net income generally imply total _____ minus total expenses in a given period. In accounting, in the balance statement it is a subsection of the Equity section and _____ increases equity, it is often referred to as the "top line" due to its position on the income statement at the very top. This is to be contrasted with the "bottom line" which denotes net income .

Exam Probability: **High**

58. *Answer choices:*

(see index for correct answer)

- a. Gross profit
- b. Revenue
- c. Operating statement
- d. Vendor-specific objective evidence

Guidance: level 1

:: Industry ::

_____ describes various measures of the efficiency of production. Often, a _____ measure is expressed as the ratio of an aggregate output to a single input or an aggregate input used in a production process, i.e. output per unit of input. Most common example is the labour _____ measure, e.g., such as GDP per worker. There are many different definitions of _____ and the choice among them depends on the purpose of the _____ measurement and/or data availability. The key source of difference between various _____ measures is also usually related to how the outputs and the inputs are aggregated into scalars to obtain such a ratio-type measure of _____ .

Exam Probability: **High**

59. *Answer choices:*

(see index for correct answer)

- a. Industrial society
- b. Chemical process
- c. Productivity
- d. Takt time

Guidance: level 1

Manufacturing

Manufacturing is the production of merchandise for use or sale using labor and machines, tools, chemical and biological processing, or formulation. The term may refer to a range of human activity, from handicraft to high tech, but is most commonly applied to industrial design, in which raw materials are transformed into finished goods on a large scale. Such finished goods may be sold to other manufacturers for the production of other, more complex products, such as aircraft, household appliances, furniture, sports equipment or automobiles, or sold to wholesalers, who in turn sell them to retailers, who then sell them to end users and consumers.

:: Materials science ::

An _____ is a polymer with viscoelasticity and very weak intermolecular forces, and generally low Young's modulus and high failure strain compared with other materials. The term, a portmanteau of elastic polymer, is often used interchangeably with rubber, although the latter is preferred when referring to vulcanisates. Each of the monomers which link to form the polymer is usually a compound of several elements among carbon, hydrogen, oxygen and silicon. _____ s are amorphous polymers maintained above their glass transition temperature, so that considerable molecular reconformation, without breaking of covalent bonds, is feasible. At ambient temperatures, such rubbers are thus relatively soft and deformable. Their primary uses are for seals, adhesives and molded flexible parts. Application areas for different types of rubber are manifold and cover segments as diverse as tires, soles for shoes, and damping and insulating elements. The importance of these rubbers can be judged from the fact that global revenues are forecast to rise to US$56 billion in 2020.

Exam Probability: **Low**

1. *Answer choices:*

(see index for correct answer)

- a. Elastomer
- b. Zinagizado
- c. Surface stress
- d. Waviness

Guidance: level 1

:: ::

_____ is the quantity of three-dimensional space enclosed by a closed surface, for example, the space that a substance or shape occupies or contains. _____ is often quantified numerically using the SI derived unit, the cubic metre. The _____ of a container is generally understood to be the capacity of the container; i. e., the amount of fluid that the container could hold, rather than the amount of space the container itself displaces. Three dimensional mathematical shapes are also assigned _____ s. _____ s of some simple shapes, such as regular, straight-edged, and circular shapes can be easily calculated using arithmetic formulas. _____ s of complicated shapes can be calculated with integral calculus if a formula exists for the shape's boundary. One-dimensional figures and two-dimensional shapes are assigned zero _____ in the three-dimensional space.

Exam Probability: **High**

2. *Answer choices:*

(see index for correct answer)

- a. cultural
- b. similarity-attraction theory
- c. Volume
- d. surface-level diversity

Guidance: level 1

:: Product management ::

_____ s, also known as Shewhart charts or process-behavior charts, are a statistical process control tool used to determine if a manufacturing or business process is in a state of control.

Exam Probability: **Low**

3. *Answer choices:*

(see index for correct answer)

- a. Control chart
- b. Swing tag
- c. Tipping point
- d. Crossing the Chasm

Guidance: level 1

:: Industrial processes ::

_____ is a technique involving the condensation of vapors and the return of this condensate to the system from which it originated. It is used in industrial and laboratory distillations. It is also used in chemistry to supply energy to reactions over a long period of time.

Exam Probability: **Medium**

4. *Answer choices:*

(see index for correct answer)

- a. Reflux
- b. Basic oxygen steelmaking
- c. Alkylation
- d. Abrasive jet machining

Guidance: level 1

:: ::

The _____ is a project plan of how the production budget will be spent over a given timescale, for every phase of a business project.

Exam Probability: **Low**

5. *Answer choices:*

(see index for correct answer)

- a. cultural
- b. Production schedule
- c. functional perspective
- d. corporate values

Guidance: level 1

:: Industrial organization ::

In economics, specifically general equilibrium theory, a perfect market is defined by several idealizing conditions, collectively called _____. In theoretical models where conditions of _____ hold, it has been theoretically demonstrated that a market will reach an equilibrium in which the quantity supplied for every product or service, including labor, equals the quantity demanded at the current price. This equilibrium would be a Pareto optimum.

Exam Probability: **Low**

6. *Answer choices:*

(see index for correct answer)

- a. Free entry
- b. Organizational studies
- c. American system of manufacturing
- d. Path dependence

Guidance: level 1

:: Management ::

In economics and marketing, _____ is the process of distinguishing a product or service from others, to make it more attractive to a particular target market. This involves differentiating it from competitors' products as well as a firm's own products. The concept was proposed by Edward Chamberlin in his 1933 The Theory of Monopolistic Competition.

Exam Probability: **Low**

7. *Answer choices:*

(see index for correct answer)

- a. Product differentiation
- b. Interim management
- c. Knowledge Based Decision Making
- d. Strategic group

Guidance: level 1

:: Inventory ::

The _____ is the level of inventory which triggers an action to replenish that particular inventory stock. It is a minimum amount of an item which a firm holds in stock, such that, when stock falls to this amount, the item must be reordered. It is normally calculated as the forecast usage during the replenishment lead time plus safety stock. In the EOQ model, it was assumed that there is no time lag between ordering and procuring of materials. Therefore the _____ for replenishing the stocks occurs at that level when the inventory level drops to zero and because instant delivery by suppliers, the stock level bounce back.

Exam Probability: **Low**

8. *Answer choices:*

(see index for correct answer)

- a. Reorder point
- b. Stock-taking
- c. Stock obsolescence
- d. Phantom inventory

Guidance: level 1

:: Teams ::

A _____ usually refers to a group of individuals who work together from different geographic locations and rely on communication technology such as email, FAX, and video or voice conferencing services in order to collaborate. The term can also refer to groups or teams that work together asynchronously or across organizational levels. Powell, Piccoli and Ives define _____ s as "groups of geographically, organizationally and/or time dispersed workers brought together by information and telecommunication technologies to accomplish one or more organizational tasks." According to Ale Ebrahim et. al. , _____ s can also be defined as "small temporary groups of geographically, organizationally and/or time dispersed knowledge workers who coordinate their work predominantly with electronic information and communication technologies in order to accomplish one or more organization tasks."

Exam Probability: **High**

9. Answer choices:

(see index for correct answer)

- a. team composition
- b. Virtual team

Guidance: level 1

:: Project management ::

> Rolling-wave planning is the process of project planning in waves as the project proceeds and later details become clearer; similar to the techniques used in agile software development approaches like Scrum..

Exam Probability: **High**

10. Answer choices:

(see index for correct answer)

- a. Rolling Wave planning
- b. Requirements traceability
- c. Project Initiation Documentation
- d. Lean project management

Guidance: level 1

:: Management ::

_____ is the process of thinking about the activities required to achieve a desired goal. It is the first and foremost activity to achieve desired results. It involves the creation and maintenance of a plan, such as psychological aspects that require conceptual skills. There are even a couple of tests to measure someone's capability of _____ well. As such, _____ is a fundamental property of intelligent behavior. An important further meaning, often just called " _____ " is the legal context of permitted building developments.

Exam Probability: **Low**

11. *Answer choices:*

(see index for correct answer)

- a. Planning
- b. Document automation
- c. Sales outsourcing
- d. Business process interoperability

Guidance: level 1

:: Commercial item transport and distribution ::

In commerce, supply-chain management, the management of the flow of goods and services, involves the movement and storage of raw materials, of work-in-process inventory, and of finished goods from point of origin to point of consumption. Interconnected or interlinked networks, channels and node businesses combine in the provision of products and services required by end customers in a supply chain. Supply-chain management has been defined as the "design, planning, execution, control, and monitoring of supply-chain activities with the objective of creating net value, building a competitive infrastructure, leveraging worldwide logistics, synchronizing supply with demand and measuring performance globally."SCM practice draws heavily from the areas of industrial engineering, systems engineering, operations management, logistics, procurement, information technology, and marketing and strives for an integrated approach. Marketing channels play an important role in supply-chain management. Current research in supply-chain management is concerned with topics related to sustainability and risk management, among others. Some suggest that the "people dimension" of SCM, ethical issues, internal integration, transparency/visibility, and human capital/talent management are topics that have, so far, been underrepresented on the research agenda.

Exam Probability: **Low**

12. *Answer choices:*

(see index for correct answer)

- a. Refrigerator truck
- b. Wine shipping laws in the United States
- c. Retail concentration
- d. Materiel

Guidance: level 1

:: Project management ::

_____ s can take many forms depending on the type of project being implemented and the nature of the organization. The _____ details the project deliverables and describes the major objectives. The objectives should include measurable success criteria for the project.

Exam Probability: **Low**

13. *Answer choices:*

(see index for correct answer)

- a. Scope statement
- b. Operational bill
- c. Punch list
- d. Schedule chicken

Guidance: level 1

:: Computer memory companies ::

_____ Corporation is a Japanese multinational conglomerate headquartered in Tokyo, Japan. Its diversified products and services include information technology and communications equipment and systems, electronic components and materials, power systems, industrial and social infrastructure systems, consumer electronics, household appliances, medical equipment, office equipment, as well as lighting and logistics.

Exam Probability: **High**

14. *Answer choices:*

(see index for correct answer)

- a. Virage Logic
- b. Winbond
- c. Alliance Semiconductor
- d. Crossbar

Guidance: level 1

:: Packaging materials ::

> _____ is a thin material produced by pressing together moist fibres of cellulose pulp derived from wood, rags or grasses, and drying them into flexible sheets. It is a versatile material with many uses, including writing, printing, packaging, cleaning, decorating, and a number of industrial and construction processes. _____ s are essential in legal or non-legal documentation.

Exam Probability: **High**

15. *Answer choices:*

(see index for correct answer)

- a. Waxtite
- b. Metallised film

- c. Paper
- d. Paperboard

Guidance: level 1

:: Management ::

_____ is the discipline of strategically planning for, and managing, all interactions with third party organizations that supply goods and/or services to an organization in order to maximize the value of those interactions. In practice, SRM entails creating closer, more collaborative relationships with key suppliers in order to uncover and realize new value and reduce risk of failure.

Exam Probability: **High**

16. *Answer choices:*

(see index for correct answer)

- a. Management by exception
- b. Logistics management
- c. Quick response manufacturing
- d. Supplier relationship management

Guidance: level 1

:: Production and manufacturing ::

_____ is the production under license of technology developed elsewhere. It is an especially prominent commercial practice in developing nations, which often approach _____ as a starting point for indigenous industrial development.

Exam Probability: **High**

17. *Answer choices:*

(see index for correct answer)

- a. Licensed production
- b. International Automotive Task Force
- c. Economic dispatch
- d. Citect

Guidance: level 1

:: Production and manufacturing ::

An _____ is a manufacturing process in which parts are added as the semi-finished assembly moves from workstation to workstation where the parts are added in sequence until the final assembly is produced. By mechanically moving the parts to the assembly work and moving the semi-finished assembly from work station to work station, a finished product can be assembled faster and with less labor than by having workers carry parts to a stationary piece for assembly.

Exam Probability: **High**

18. *Answer choices:*

(see index for correct answer)

- a. Piece work
- b. DeviceNet
- c. Time to market
- d. Assembly line

Guidance: level 1

:: Project management ::

In political science, an _____ is a means by which a petition signed by a certain minimum number of registered voters can force a government to choose to either enact a law or hold a public vote in parliament in what is called indirect _____, or under direct _____, the proposition is immediately put to a plebiscite or referendum, in what is called a Popular initiated Referendum or citizen-initiated referendum).

Exam Probability: **Low**

19. *Answer choices:*

(see index for correct answer)

- a. Structured data analysis
- b. Social project management
- c. Initiative
- d. Project

Guidance: level 1

:: Process management ::

When used in the context of communication networks, such as Ethernet or packet radio, _____ or network _____ is the rate of successful message delivery over a communication channel. The data these messages belong to may be delivered over a physical or logical link, or it can pass through a certain network node. _____ is usually measured in bits per second, and sometimes in data packets per second or data packets per time slot.

Exam Probability: **High**

20. *Answer choices:*

(see index for correct answer)

- a. Process
- b. business process re-engineering
- c. Throughput
- d. President%27s Quality Award

Guidance: level 1

:: Information technology management ::

_____ within quality management systems and information technology systems is a process—either formal or informal—used to ensure that changes to a product or system are introduced in a controlled and coordinated manner. It reduces the possibility that unnecessary changes will be introduced to a system without forethought, introducing faults into the system or undoing changes made by other users of software. The goals of a _____ procedure usually include minimal disruption to services, reduction in back-out activities, and cost-effective utilization of resources involved in implementing change.

Exam Probability: **Low**

21. *Answer choices:*

(see index for correct answer)

- a. Infrastructure optimization
- b. HP Open Extensibility Platform
- c. Battle command knowledge system
- d. Change control

Guidance: level 1

:: ::

Some scenarios associate "this kind of planning" with learning "life skills".Schedules are necessary, or at least useful, in situations where individuals need to know what time they must be at a specific location to receive a specific service, and where people need to accomplish a set of goals within a set time period.

Exam Probability: **Low**

22. *Answer choices:*

(see index for correct answer)

- a. Sarbanes-Oxley act of 2002
- b. Scheduling
- c. interpersonal communication
- d. hierarchical

Guidance: level 1

:: Project management ::

A _____ is a professional in the field of project management. _____ s have the responsibility of the planning, procurement and execution of a project, in any undertaking that has a defined scope, defined start and a defined finish; regardless of industry. _____ s are first point of contact for any issues or discrepancies arising from within the heads of various departments in an organization before the problem escalates to higher authorities. Project management is the responsibility of a _____ . This individual seldom participates directly in the activities that produce the end result, but rather strives to maintain the progress, mutual interaction and tasks of various parties in such a way that reduces the risk of overall failure, maximizes benefits, and minimizes costs.

Exam Probability: **Low**

23. *Answer choices:*

(see index for correct answer)

- a. Iteration
- b. Global Alliance for Project Performance Standards
- c. Legal matter management
- d. Project manager

Guidance: level 1

:: Management ::

_____ is an iterative four-step management method used in business for the control and continuous improvement of processes and products. It is also known as the Deming circle/cycle/wheel, the Shewhart cycle, the control circle/cycle, or plan–do–study–act . Another version of this _____ cycle is O _____ . The added "O" stands for observation or as some versions say: "Observe the current condition." This emphasis on observation and current condition has currency with the literature on lean manufacturing and the Toyota Production System. The _____ cycle, with Ishikawa's changes, can be traced back to S. Mizuno of the Tokyo Institute of Technology in 1959.

Exam Probability: **High**

24. *Answer choices:*

(see index for correct answer)

- a. Flat organization
- b. PDCA
- c. Total Worker Health

- d. Identity formation

Guidance: level 1

:: Procurement ::

Purchasing is the formal process of buying goods and services. The _____ can vary from one organization to another, but there are some common key elements.

Exam Probability: **Low**

25. *Answer choices:*

(see index for correct answer)

- a. Best value procurement
- b. Bulk purchasing
- c. Purchasing process
- d. Domestic sourcing

Guidance: level 1

:: Commercial item transport and distribution ::

_____ in logistics and supply chain management is an organization's use of third-party businesses to outsource elements of its distribution, warehousing, and fulfillment services.

Exam Probability: **Medium**

26. *Answer choices:*

(see index for correct answer)

- a. Swap body
- b. Oversize load
- c. Gas carrier
- d. Toll Global Forwarding

Guidance: level 1

:: Project management ::

In economics and business decision-making, a sunk cost is a cost that has already been incurred and cannot be recovered.

Exam Probability: **High**

27. *Answer choices:*

(see index for correct answer)

- a. Project management triangle
- b. Life-cycle cost analysis
- c. PM Declaration of Interdependence
- d. NEC Engineering and Construction Contract

Guidance: level 1

:: Management ::

_____ is the practice of initiating, planning, executing, controlling, and closing the work of a team to achieve specific goals and meet specific success criteria at the specified time.

Exam Probability: **Low**

28. *Answer choices:*

(see index for correct answer)

- a. Mushroom management
- b. Community of practice
- c. Management buyout
- d. Project management

Guidance: level 1

:: Management ::

_____, also known as natural process limits, are horizontal lines drawn on a statistical process control chart, usually at a distance of ±3 standard deviations of the plotted statistic from the statistic's mean.

Exam Probability: **Low**

29. *Answer choices:*

(see index for correct answer)

- a. PhD in management
- b. Control limits
- c. Energy monitoring and targeting
- d. Executive development

Guidance: level 1

:: Quality control tools ::

A _____ is a type of diagram that represents an algorithm, workflow or process. _____ can also be defined as a diagramatic representation of an algorithm.

Exam Probability: **Medium**

30. *Answer choices:*

(see index for correct answer)

- a. U-chart
- b. Flowchart
- c. Run chart
- d. Fishbone diagram

Guidance: level 1

:: Time management ::

_____ is the process of planning and exercising conscious control of time spent on specific activities, especially to increase effectiveness, efficiency, and productivity. It involves a juggling act of various demands upon a person relating to work, social life, family, hobbies, personal interests and commitments with the finiteness of time. Using time effectively gives the person "choice" on spending/managing activities at their own time and expediency.

Exam Probability: **Medium**

31. *Answer choices:*

(see index for correct answer)

- a. HabitRPG
- b. Time Trek
- c. Time management
- d. waiting room

Guidance: level 1

:: Project management ::

A _____ is a team whose members usually belong to different groups, functions and are assigned to activities for the same project. A team can be divided into sub-teams according to need. Usually _____ s are only used for a defined period of time. They are disbanded after the project is deemed complete. Due to the nature of the specific formation and disbandment, _____ s are usually in organizations.

Exam Probability: **Low**

32. *Answer choices:*

(see index for correct answer)

- a. The Practice Standard for Scheduling
- b. Cost-benefit
- c. Changes clause
- d. Starmad

Guidance: level 1

:: Information technology management ::

_____ is the discipline of engineering concerned with the principles and practice of product and service quality assurance and control. In the software development, it is the management, development, operation and maintenance of IT systems and enterprise architectures with a high quality standard.

Exam Probability: **High**

33. *Answer choices:*

(see index for correct answer)

- a. Business-to-business
- b. Quality Engineering
- c. High Availability Application Architecture
- d. CatDV

Guidance: level 1

:: Distribution, retailing, and wholesaling ::

The _____ is a distribution channel phenomenon in which forecasts yield supply chain inefficiencies. It refers to increasing swings in inventory in response to shifts in customer demand as one moves further up the supply chain. The concept first appeared in Jay Forrester's Industrial Dynamics and thus it is also known as the Forrester effect. The _____ was named for the way the amplitude of a whip increases down its length. The further from the originating signal, the greater the distortion of the wave pattern. In a similar manner, forecast accuracy decreases as one moves upstream along the supply chain. For example, many consumer goods have fairly consistent consumption at retail but this signal becomes more chaotic and unpredictable as the focus moves away from consumer purchasing behavior.

Exam Probability: **Medium**

34. *Answer choices:*

(see index for correct answer)

- a. Bullwhip effect
- b. Plataforma Europa
- c. False designation of origin
- d. Slab-O-Concrete

Guidance: level 1

:: Project management ::

Contemporary business and science treat as a _____ any undertaking, carried out individually or collaboratively and possibly involving research or design, that is carefully planned to achieve a particular aim.

Exam Probability: **Medium**

35. *Answer choices:*

(see index for correct answer)

- a. project triangle
- b. RationalPlan
- c. Project
- d. Pre-mortem

Guidance: level 1

:: Production and manufacturing ::

_____ is a concept in purchasing and project management for securing the quality and timely delivery of goods and components.

Exam Probability: **Medium**

36. *Answer choices:*

(see index for correct answer)

- a. Expediting
- b. Food processing
- c. production planning
- d. Fieldbus Foundation

Guidance: level 1

:: Management ::

_____ is the identification, evaluation, and prioritization of risks followed by coordinated and economical application of resources to minimize, monitor, and control the probability or impact of unfortunate events or to maximize the realization of opportunities.

Exam Probability: **Low**

37. *Answer choices:*

(see index for correct answer)

- a. Intopia
- b. Top development
- c. Records manager
- d. SimulTrain

Guidance: level 1

:: ::

_____ is the production of products for use or sale using labour and machines, tools, chemical and biological processing, or formulation. The term may refer to a range of human activity, from handicraft to high tech, but is most commonly applied to industrial design, in which raw materials are transformed into finished goods on a large scale. Such finished goods may be sold to other manufacturers for the production of other, more complex products, such as aircraft, household appliances, furniture, sports equipment or automobiles, or sold to wholesalers, who in turn sell them to retailers, who then sell them to end users and consumers.

Exam Probability: **Medium**

38. *Answer choices:*

(see index for correct answer)

- a. deep-level diversity
- b. surface-level diversity
- c. functional perspective
- d. Manufacturing

Guidance: level 1

:: Project management ::

In economics, _____ is the assignment of available resources to various uses. In the context of an entire economy, resources can be allocated by various means, such as markets or central planning.

Exam Probability: **Medium**

39. *Answer choices:*

(see index for correct answer)

- a. Virtual design and construction
- b. Resource allocation
- c. Stakeholder analysis
- d. Problem domain analysis

Guidance: level 1

:: Unit operations ::

_____ is a discipline of thermal engineering that concerns the generation, use, conversion, and exchange of thermal energy between physical systems. _____ is classified into various mechanisms, such as thermal conduction, thermal convection, thermal radiation, and transfer of energy by phase changes. Engineers also consider the transfer of mass of differing chemical species, either cold or hot, to achieve _____ . While these mechanisms have distinct characteristics, they often occur simultaneously in the same system.

Exam Probability: **High**

40. *Answer choices:*

(see index for correct answer)

- a. Heat transfer
- b. Separation process
- c. Settling
- d. Solvent impregnated resin

Guidance: level 1

:: Management ::

In organizational studies, _____ is the efficient and effective development of an organization's resources when they are needed. Such resources may include financial resources, inventory, human skills, production resources, or information technology and natural resources.

Exam Probability: **Low**

41. *Answer choices:*

(see index for correct answer)

- a. Enterprise smart grid
- b. Core competency
- c. Dynamic enterprise modeling
- d. Decentralized decision-making

Guidance: level 1

:: Production and manufacturing ::

_____ is a theory of management that analyzes and synthesizes workflows. Its main objective is improving economic efficiency, especially labor productivity. It was one of the earliest attempts to apply science to the engineering of processes and to management. _____ is sometimes known as Taylorism after its founder, Frederick Winslow Taylor.

Exam Probability: **Low**

42. *Answer choices:*

(see index for correct answer)

- a. Object Process Methodology
- b. Production plan
- c. Scientific management
- d. Advanced Manufacturing Software

Guidance: level 1

:: Process management ::

A _____ is a diagram commonly used in chemical and process engineering to indicate the general flow of plant processes and equipment. The PFD displays the relationship between major equipment of a plant facility and does not show minor details such as piping details and designations. Another commonly used term for a PFD is a flowsheet.

Exam Probability: **High**

43. *Answer choices:*

(see index for correct answer)

- a. Ideal tasks
- b. Process capability index
- c. Proactive contracting
- d. Process consultant

Guidance: level 1

:: Manufacturing ::

A _____ is an object used to extend the ability of an individual to modify features of the surrounding environment. Although many animals use simple _____ s, only human beings, whose use of stone _____ s dates back hundreds of millennia, use _____ s to make other _____ s. The set of _____ s needed to perform different tasks that are part of the same activity is called gear or equipment.

Exam Probability: **High**

44. *Answer choices:*

(see index for correct answer)

- a. Flexlink
- b. Part number

- c. Tool
- d. Rubber technology

Guidance: level 1

:: Costs ::

In economics, _____ is the total economic cost of production and is made up of variable cost, which varies according to the quantity of a good produced and includes inputs such as labour and raw materials, plus fixed cost, which is independent of the quantity of a good produced and includes inputs that cannot be varied in the short term: fixed costs such as buildings and machinery, including sunk costs if any. Since cost is measured per unit of time, it is a flow variable.

Exam Probability: **Low**

45. *Answer choices:*

(see index for correct answer)

- a. Opportunity cost
- b. Total cost
- c. Cost per paper
- d. Explicit cost

Guidance: level 1

:: Metrics ::

_____ is a computer model developed by the University of Idaho, that uses Landsat satellite data to compute and map evapotranspiration . _____ calculates ET as a residual of the surface energy balance, where ET is estimated by keeping account of total net short wave and long wave radiation at the vegetation or soil surface, the amount of heat conducted into soil, and the amount of heat convected into the air above the surface. The difference in these three terms represents the amount of energy absorbed during the conversion of liquid water to vapor, which is ET. _____ expresses near-surface temperature gradients used in heat convection as indexed functions of radio _____ surface temperature, thereby eliminating the need for absolutely accurate surface temperature and the need for air-temperature measurements.

Exam Probability: **Low**

46. *Answer choices:*
(see index for correct answer)

- a. Guide number
- b. Parts-per notation
- c. Software metric
- d. METRIC

Guidance: level 1

:: Marketing ::

_____ or stock control can be broadly defined as "the activity of checking a shop's stock." However, a more focused definition takes into account the more science-based, methodical practice of not only verifying a business' inventory but also focusing on the many related facets of inventory management "within an organisation to meet the demand placed upon that business economically." Other facets of _____ include supply chain management, production control, financial flexibility, and customer satisfaction. At the root of _____, however, is the _____ problem, which involves determining when to order, how much to order, and the logistics of those decisions.

Exam Probability: **High**

47. *Answer choices:*

(see index for correct answer)

- a. Marchitecture
- b. Inventory control
- c. Premium pricing
- d. Patronage concentration

Guidance: level 1

:: Production economics ::

_____ is the joint use of a resource or space. It is also the process of dividing and distributing. In its narrow sense, it refers to joint or alternating use of inherently finite goods, such as a common pasture or a shared residence. Still more loosely, "_____" can actually mean giving something as an outright gift: for example, to "share" one's food really means to give some of it as a gift. _____ is a basic component of human interaction, and is responsible for strengthening social ties and ensuring a person's well-being.

Exam Probability: **Medium**

48. *Answer choices:*

(see index for correct answer)

- a. Sharing
- b. Division of work
- c. Total factor productivity
- d. Average fixed cost

Guidance: level 1

:: Management ::

_____ is a method of quality control which employs statistical methods to monitor and control a process. This helps to ensure that the process operates efficiently, producing more specification-conforming products with less waste . SPC can be applied to any process where the "conforming product" output can be measured. Key tools used in SPC include run charts, control charts, a focus on continuous improvement, and the design of experiments. An example of a process where SPC is applied is manufacturing lines.

Exam Probability: **Medium**

49. *Answer choices:*

(see index for correct answer)

- a. Energy management software
- b. Knowledge ecosystem
- c. Statistical process control
- d. Discovery-driven planning

Guidance: level 1

:: Production and manufacturing ::

In industry, _____ is a system of maintaining and improving the integrity of production and quality systems through the machines, equipment, processes, and employees that add business value to an organization.

Exam Probability: **High**

50. *Answer choices:*

(see index for correct answer)

- a. production planning
- b. Total productive maintenance
- c. Subir Chowdhury
- d. Resource Breakdown

Guidance: level 1

:: Quality management ::

In quality management system, a _____ is a document developed by management to express the directive of the top management with respect to quality. _____ management is a strategic item.

Exam Probability: **Low**

51. *Answer choices:*

(see index for correct answer)

- a. Quality policy
- b. European Quality in Social Services
- c. External quality assessment
- d. Quality circle

Guidance: level 1

:: Elementary mathematics ::

In mathematics, a _____ is an enumerated collection of objects in which repetitions are allowed. Like a set, it contains members. The number of elements is called the length of the _____. Unlike a set, the same elements can appear multiple times at different positions in a _____, and order matters. Formally, a _____ can be defined as a function whose domain is either the set of the natural numbers or the set of the first n natural numbers. The position of an element in a _____ is its rank or index; it is the natural number from which the element is the image. It depends on the context or a specific convention, if the first element has index 0 or 1. When a symbol has been chosen for denoting a _____, the nth element of the _____ is denoted by this symbol with n as subscript; for example, the nth element of the Fibonacci _____ is generally denoted Fn.

Exam Probability: **Medium**

52. *Answer choices:*

(see index for correct answer)

- a. Sequence
- b. Variable
- c. Function
- d. Mathematical problem

Guidance: level 1

:: Accounting source documents ::

A _____ is a commercial document and first official offer issued by a buyer to a seller indicating types, quantities, and agreed prices for products or services. It is used to control the purchasing of products and services from external suppliers. _____ s can be an essential part of enterprise resource planning system orders.

Exam Probability: **Medium**

53. *Answer choices:*

(see index for correct answer)

- a. Superbill
- b. Purchase order
- c. Remittance advice
- d. Invoice

Guidance: level 1

:: Supply chain management ::

A _____ is a type of auction in which the traditional roles of buyer and seller are reversed. Thus, there is one buyer and many potential sellers. In an ordinary auction, buyers compete to obtain goods or services by offering increasingly higher prices. In contrast, in a _____, the sellers compete to obtain business from the buyer and prices will typically decrease as the sellers underbid each other.

Exam Probability: **Medium**

54. *Answer choices:*

(see index for correct answer)

- a. Reverse auction
- b. Dynamic discounting
- c. Customs-Trade Partnership Against Terrorism
- d. Irancode

Guidance: level 1

:: Chemical reactions ::

A _____ is a process that leads to the chemical transformation of one set of chemical substances to another. Classically, _____ s encompass changes that only involve the positions of electrons in the forming and breaking of chemical bonds between atoms, with no change to the nuclei , and can often be described by a chemical equation. Nuclear chemistry is a sub-discipline of chemistry that involves the _____ s of unstable and radioactive elements where both electronic and nuclear changes can occur.

Exam Probability: **Low**

55. *Answer choices:*

(see index for correct answer)

- a. Carbonylation
- b. Elementary reaction
- c. Elimination reaction

- d. Associative substitution

Guidance: level 1

:: Outsourcing ::

A _____ is a document that solicits proposal, often made through a bidding process, by an agency or company interested in procurement of a commodity, service, or valuable asset, to potential suppliers to submit business proposals. It is submitted early in the procurement cycle, either at the preliminary study, or procurement stage.

Exam Probability: **High**

56. *Answer choices:*

(see index for correct answer)

- a. Online outsourcing
- b. Selfsourcing
- c. Affiliated Computer Services
- d. Outsourcing of animation

Guidance: level 1

:: Industries ::

The _____ comprises the companies that produce industrial chemicals. Central to the modern world economy, it converts raw materials into more than 70,000 different products. The plastics industry contains some overlap, as most chemical companies produce plastic as well as other chemicals.

Exam Probability: **Medium**

57. *Answer choices:*

(see index for correct answer)

- a. Chemical industry
- b. Professional audiovisual industry
- c. Software industry
- d. Naval stores industry

Guidance: level 1

:: Information systems ::

_____ is the process of creating, sharing, using and managing the knowledge and information of an organisation. It refers to a multidisciplinary approach to achieving organisational objectives by making the best use of knowledge.

Exam Probability: **Medium**

58. *Answer choices:*

(see index for correct answer)

- a. Internal Market Information System
- b. Value sensitive design
- c. Credit bureau
- d. Knowledge management

Guidance: level 1

:: Retailing ::

_____ is the process of selling consumer goods or services to customers through multiple channels of distribution to earn a profit. _____ ers satisfy demand identified through a supply chain. The term " _____ er" is typically applied where a service provider fills the small orders of a large number of individuals, who are end-users, rather than large orders of a small number of wholesale, corporate or government clientele. Shopping generally refers to the act of buying products. Sometimes this is done to obtain final goods, including necessities such as food and clothing; sometimes it takes place as a recreational activity. Recreational shopping often involves window shopping and browsing: it does not always result in a purchase.

Exam Probability: **Medium**

59. *Answer choices:*
(see index for correct answer)

- a. Confectionery store
- b. Retail

- c. Return fraud
- d. St. Vincent de Paul Thrift Store

Guidance: level 1

Commerce

Commerce relates to "the exchange of goods and services, especially on a large scale." It includes legal, economic, political, social, cultural and technological systems that operate in any country or internationally.

:: International trade ::

An _____ is a good brought into a jurisdiction, especially across a national border, from an external source. The party bringing in the good is called an _____ er. An _____ in the receiving country is an export from the sending country. _____ ation and exportation are the defining financial transactions of international trade.

Exam Probability: **Low**

1. *Answer choices:*

(see index for correct answer)

- a. Import
- b. Mutual recognition agreement
- c. European Union Customs Union
- d. Low-cost country sourcing

Guidance: level 1

:: ::

An _____ is the production of goods or related services within an economy. The major source of revenue of a group or company is the indicator of its relevant _____ . When a large group has multiple sources of revenue generation, it is considered to be working in different industries. Manufacturing _____ became a key sector of production and labour in European and North American countries during the Industrial Revolution, upsetting previous mercantile and feudal economies. This came through many successive rapid advances in technology, such as the production of steel and coal.

Exam Probability: **Low**

2. *Answer choices:*

(see index for correct answer)

- a. hierarchical
- b. personal values
- c. open system
- d. Industry

Guidance: level 1

:: ::

_____ is an abstract concept of management of complex systems according to a set of rules and trends. In systems theory, these types of rules exist in various fields of biology and society, but the term has slightly different meanings according to context. For example.

Exam Probability: **Low**

3. *Answer choices:*

(see index for correct answer)

- a. Regulation
- b. similarity-attraction theory
- c. co-culture
- d. corporate values

Guidance: level 1

:: Management ::

_____ is a process by which entities review the quality of all factors involved in production. ISO 9000 defines _____ as "A part of quality management focused on fulfilling quality requirements".

Exam Probability: **High**

4. *Answer choices:*

(see index for correct answer)

- a. Target operating model
- b. Quality control
- c. Cross ownership
- d. Balanced scorecard

Guidance: level 1

:: Trading posts of the Hanseatic League ::

_____ is a city and unitary authority area in North _____ shire, England, with a population of 208,200 as of 2017. Located at the confluence of the Rivers Ouse and Foss, it is the county town of the historic county of _____ shire and was the home of the House of _____ throughout its existence. The city is known for its famous historical landmarks such as _____ Minster and the city walls, as well as a variety of cultural and sporting activities, which makes it a popular tourist destination in England. The local authority is the City of _____ Council, a single tier governing body responsible for providing all local services and facilities throughout the city. The City of _____ local government district includes rural areas beyond the old city boundaries.

Exam Probability: **High**

5. *Answer choices:*

(see index for correct answer)

- a. Ipswich
- b. York
- c. Novgorod Republic
- d. Polotsk

Guidance: level 1

:: Business law ::

The _____, first published in 1952, is one of a number of Uniform Acts that have been established as law with the goal of harmonizing the laws of sales and other commercial transactions across the United States of America through UCC adoption by all 50 states, the District of Columbia, and the Territories of the United States.

Exam Probability: **Medium**

6. *Answer choices:*
(see index for correct answer)

- a. Statutory authority
- b. Industrial relations
- c. De facto corporation and corporation by estoppel
- d. Limited liability company

Guidance: level 1

:: Payments ::

A _____ or government incentive is a form of financial aid or support extended to an economic sector generally with the aim of promoting economic and social policy. Although commonly extended from government, the term _____ can relate to any type of support – for example from NGOs or as implicit subsidies. Subsidies come in various forms including: direct and indirect.

Exam Probability: **Low**

7. *Answer choices:*

(see index for correct answer)

- a. Payment
- b. Subsidy
- c. KlickEx
- d. Direct Payments

Guidance: level 1

:: Supply chain management ::

_____ is the removal of intermediaries in economics from a supply chain, or cutting out the middlemen in connection with a transaction or a series of transactions. Instead of going through traditional distribution channels, which had some type of intermediary , companies may now deal with customers directly, for example via the Internet. Hence, the use of factory direct and direct from the factory to mean the same thing.

Exam Probability: **Medium**

8. *Answer choices:*

(see index for correct answer)

- a. ERFx
- b. Supply network operations
- c. Supply-chain operations reference
- d. Disintermediation

Guidance: level 1

:: ::

According to the philosopher Piyush Mathur , "Tangibility is the property that a phenomenon exhibits if it has and/or transports mass and/or energy and/or momentum".

Exam Probability: **Medium**

9. *Answer choices:*

(see index for correct answer)

- a. Character
- b. Tangible
- c. surface-level diversity
- d. cultural

Guidance: level 1

:: ::

The _____ is a political and economic union of 28 member states that are located primarily in Europe. It has an area of 4,475,757 km2 and an estimated population of about 513 million. The EU has developed an internal single market through a standardised system of laws that apply in all member states in those matters, and only those matters, where members have agreed to act as one. EU policies aim to ensure the free movement of people, goods, services and capital within the internal market, enact legislation in justice and home affairs and maintain common policies on trade, agriculture, fisheries and regional development. For travel within the Schengen Area, passport controls have been abolished. A monetary union was established in 1999 and came into full force in 2002 and is composed of 19 EU member states which use the euro currency.

Exam Probability: **Medium**

10. *Answer choices:*

(see index for correct answer)

- a. interpersonal communication
- b. corporate values
- c. hierarchical perspective
- d. European Union

Guidance: level 1

:: Organizational structure ::

An _____ defines how activities such as task allocation, coordination, and supervision are directed toward the achievement of organizational aims.

Exam Probability: **High**

11. *Answer choices:*

(see index for correct answer)

- a. Unorganisation
- b. Blessed Unrest
- c. Automated Bureaucracy
- d. The Starfish and the Spider

Guidance: level 1

:: Economic globalization ::

_____ is an agreement in which one company hires another company to be responsible for a planned or existing activity that is or could be done internally, and sometimes involves transferring employees and assets from one firm to another.

Exam Probability: **Low**

12. *Answer choices:*

(see index for correct answer)

- a. Outsourcing
- b. global financial

Guidance: level 1

:: Commodities ::

In economics, a _____ is an economic good or service that has full or substantial fungibility: that is, the market treats instances of the good as equivalent or nearly so with no regard to who produced them. Most commodities are raw materials, basic resources, agricultural, or mining products, such as iron ore, sugar, or grains like rice and wheat. Commodities can also be mass-produced unspecialized products such as chemicals and computer memory.

Exam Probability: **High**

13. *Answer choices:*

(see index for correct answer)

- a. Commodity pathway diversion
- b. Commodity
- c. Sample grade
- d. Commoditization

Guidance: level 1

:: ::

Competition arises whenever at least two parties strive for a goal which cannot be shared: where one's gain is the other's loss.

Exam Probability: **High**

14. *Answer choices:*

(see index for correct answer)

- a. levels of analysis
- b. Competitor
- c. cultural
- d. hierarchical

Guidance: level 1

:: Human resource management ::

_____ are the people who make up the workforce of an organization, business sector, or economy. "Human capital" is sometimes used synonymously with "_____", although human capital typically refers to a narrower effect. Likewise, other terms sometimes used include manpower, talent, labor, personnel, or simply people.

Exam Probability: **Low**

15. *Answer choices:*

(see index for correct answer)

- a. Human resources
- b. Illness rate
- c. Contractor management
- d. Leadership development

Guidance: level 1

:: ::

In the broadest sense, _____ is any practice which contributes to the sale of products to a retail consumer. At a retail in-store level, _____ refers to the variety of products available for sale and the display of those products in such a way that it stimulates interest and entices customers to make a purchase.

Exam Probability: **Medium**

16. *Answer choices:*

(see index for correct answer)

- a. co-culture
- b. hierarchical perspective
- c. functional perspective
- d. Sarbanes-Oxley act of 2002

Guidance: level 1

:: Marketing ::

_____ comes from the Latin neg and otsia referring to businessmen who, unlike the patricians, had no leisure time in their industriousness; it held the meaning of business until the 17th century when it took on the diplomatic connotation as a dialogue between two or more people or parties intended to reach a beneficial outcome over one or more issues where a conflict exists with respect to at least one of these issues. Thus, _____ is a process of combining divergent positions into a joint agreement under a decision rule of unanimity.

Exam Probability: **High**

17. *Answer choices:*

(see index for correct answer)

- a. Point of difference
- b. Postmodern branding
- c. Negotiation
- d. Partnerized inventory management

Guidance: level 1

:: Consortia ::

A _____ is an association of two or more individuals, companies, organizations or governments with the objective of participating in a common activity or pooling their resources for achieving a common goal.

Exam Probability: **High**

18. *Answer choices:*

(see index for correct answer)

- a. Blu-ray Disc Association
- b. Network Test Automation Forum
- c. Consortium
- d. Biometric Consortium

Guidance: level 1

:: ::

_____ refers to a business or organization attempting to acquire goods or services to accomplish its goals. Although there are several organizations that attempt to set standards in the _____ process, processes can vary greatly between organizations. Typically the word " _____ " is not used interchangeably with the word "procurement", since procurement typically includes expediting, supplier quality, and transportation and logistics in addition to _____ .

Exam Probability: **High**

19. *Answer choices:*

(see index for correct answer)

- a. imperative
- b. Character
- c. interpersonal communication
- d. Sarbanes-Oxley act of 2002

Guidance: level 1

:: ::

Regulatory economics is the economics of regulation. It is the application of law by government or independent administrative agencies for various purposes, including remedying market failure, protecting the environment, centrally-planning an economy, enriching well-connected firms, or benefiting politicians.

Exam Probability: **Medium**

20. *Answer choices:*

(see index for correct answer)

- a. process perspective
- b. Economic regulation
- c. surface-level diversity
- d. personal values

Guidance: level 1

:: ::

In Christian denominations that practice infant baptism, confirmation is seen as the sealing of Christianity created in baptism. Those being _____ are known as confirmands. In some denominations, such as the Anglican Communion and Methodist Churches, confirmation bestows full membership in a local congregation upon the recipient. In others, such as the Roman Catholic Church, Confirmation "renders the bond with the Church more perfect", because, while a baptized person is already a member, "reception of the sacrament of Confirmation is necessary for the completion of baptismal grace".

Exam Probability: **High**

21. *Answer choices:*

(see index for correct answer)

- a. information systems assessment
- b. surface-level diversity
- c. functional perspective
- d. Confirmed

Guidance: level 1

:: Meetings ::

A _____ is a body of one or more persons that is subordinate to a deliberative assembly. Usually, the assembly sends matters into a _____ as a way to explore them more fully than would be possible if the assembly itself were considering them. _____ s may have different functions and their type of work differ depending on the type of the organization and its needs.

Exam Probability: **Medium**

22. *Answer choices:*

(see index for correct answer)

- a. Tertulia
- b. Committee
- c. Middle East Electricity
- d. Fishbowl

Guidance: level 1

:: ::

_____ s and acquisitions are transactions in which the ownership of companies, other business organizations, or their operating units are transferred or consolidated with other entities. As an aspect of strategic management, M&A can allow enterprises to grow or downsize, and change the nature of their business or competitive position.

Exam Probability: **Medium**

23. Answer choices:

(see index for correct answer)

- a. Merger
- b. co-culture
- c. functional perspective
- d. cultural

Guidance: level 1

:: ::

Competition law is a law that promotes or seeks to maintain market competition by regulating anti-competitive conduct by companies. Competition law is implemented through public and private enforcement. Competition law is known as "_____ law" in the United States for historical reasons, and as "anti-monopoly law" in China and Russia. In previous years it has been known as trade practices law in the United Kingdom and Australia. In the European Union, it is referred to as both _____ and competition law.

Exam Probability: **Low**

24. Answer choices:

(see index for correct answer)

- a. hierarchical
- b. functional perspective
- c. Character

- d. interpersonal communication

Guidance: level 1

:: Industrial automation ::

_____ is the technology by which a process or procedure is performed with minimal human assistance. _____ or automatic control is the use of various control systems for operating equipment such as machinery, processes in factories, boilers and heat treating ovens, switching on telephone networks, steering and stabilization of ships, aircraft and other applications and vehicles with minimal or reduced human intervention.

Exam Probability: **Medium**

25. *Answer choices:*

(see index for correct answer)

- a. Automation
- b. Process automation system
- c. Automation surprise
- d. IODD

Guidance: level 1

:: Market research ::

_____ is an organized effort to gather information about target markets or customers. It is a very important component of business strategy. The term is commonly interchanged with marketing research; however, expert practitioners may wish to draw a distinction, in that marketing research is concerned specifically about marketing processes, while _____ is concerned specifically with markets.

Exam Probability: **High**

26. *Answer choices:*

(see index for correct answer)

- a. Ad Tracking
- b. Market research
- c. Confidence interval
- d. Respondent error

Guidance: level 1

:: Insolvency ::

_____ is a legal process through which people or other entities who cannot repay debts to creditors may seek relief from some or all of their debts. In most jurisdictions, _____ is imposed by a court order, often initiated by the debtor.

Exam Probability: **High**

27. *Answer choices:*

(see index for correct answer)

- a. Bankruptcy
- b. Insolvency
- c. Financial distress
- d. United Kingdom insolvency law

Guidance: level 1

:: Commerce ::

_____ , also known as duty _____ is defined by the United States Customs and Border Protection as the refund of certain duties, internal and revenue taxes and certain fees collected upon the importation of goods. Such refunds are only allowed upon the exportation or destruction of goods under U.S. Customs and Border Protection supervision. Duty _____ is an export promotions program sanctioned by the World Trade Organization and allows the refund of certain duties taxes and fees paid upon importation which was established in 1789 in order to promote U.S. innovation and manufacturing across the global market.

Exam Probability: **Medium**

28. *Answer choices:*

(see index for correct answer)

- a. Perfect tender rule
- b. Group buying

- c. TradeCard
- d. Requisition

Guidance: level 1

:: Management accounting ::

_____ , or dollar contribution per unit, is the selling price per unit minus the variable cost per unit. "Contribution" represents the portion of sales revenue that is not consumed by variable costs and so contributes to the coverage of fixed costs. This concept is one of the key building blocks of break-even analysis.

Exam Probability: **Low**

29. *Answer choices:*

(see index for correct answer)

- a. Profit center
- b. Standard cost
- c. Pre-determined overhead rate
- d. Accounting management

Guidance: level 1

:: ::

A _____ or GM is an executive who has overall responsibility for managing both the revenue and cost elements of a company's income statement, known as profit & loss responsibility. A _____ usually oversees most or all of the firm's marketing and sales functions as well as the day-to-day operations of the business. Frequently, the _____ is responsible for effective planning, delegating, coordinating, staffing, organizing, and decision making to attain desirable profit making results for an organization.

Exam Probability: **High**

30. *Answer choices:*

(see index for correct answer)

- a. hierarchical
- b. General manager
- c. cultural
- d. hierarchical perspective

Guidance: level 1

:: Confidence tricks ::

_____ is the fraudulent attempt to obtain sensitive information such as usernames, passwords and credit card details by disguising oneself as a trustworthy entity in an electronic communication. Typically carried out by email spoofing or instant messaging, it often directs users to enter personal information at a fake website which matches the look and feel of the legitimate site.

Exam Probability: **High**

31. *Answer choices:*

(see index for correct answer)

- a. Confidence trick
- b. DC Advertising
- c. Art student scam
- d. Phishing

Guidance: level 1

:: ::

In Western musical notation, the staff or stave is a set of five horizontal lines and four spaces that each represent a different musical pitch or in the case of a percussion staff, different percussion instruments. Appropriate music symbols, depending on the intended effect, are placed on the staff according to their corresponding pitch or function. Musical notes are placed by pitch, percussion notes are placed by instrument, and rests and other symbols are placed by convention.

Exam Probability: **Medium**

32. *Answer choices:*

(see index for correct answer)

- a. interpersonal communication

- b. Staff position
- c. personal values
- d. similarity-attraction theory

Guidance: level 1

:: ::

Advertising is a marketing communication that employs an openly sponsored, non-personal message to promote or sell a product, service or idea. Sponsors of advertising are typically businesses wishing to promote their products or services. Advertising is differentiated from public relations in that an advertiser pays for and has control over the message. It differs from personal selling in that the message is non-personal, i.e., not directed to a particular individual.Advertising is communicated through various mass media, including traditional media such as newspapers, magazines, television, radio, outdoor advertising or direct mail; and new media such as search results, blogs, social media, websites or text messages. The actual presentation of the message in a medium is referred to as an _____ , or "ad" or advert for short.

Exam Probability: **Medium**

33. *Answer choices:*

(see index for correct answer)

- a. Character
- b. interpersonal communication
- c. surface-level diversity
- d. Sarbanes-Oxley act of 2002

Guidance: level 1

:: Commerce ::

An _____ is a bank that offers card association branded payment cards directly to consumers. The name is derived from the practice of issuing payment to the acquiring bank on behalf of its customer.

Exam Probability: **Medium**

34. *Answer choices:*

(see index for correct answer)

- a. International Marketmakers Combination
- b. Issuing bank
- c. Organ trade
- d. Sell-side analyst

Guidance: level 1

:: Information technology ::

_____ is the use of computers to store, retrieve, transmit, and manipulate data, or information, often in the context of a business or other enterprise. IT is considered to be a subset of information and communications technology. An _____ system is generally an information system, a communications system or, more specifically speaking, a computer system – including all hardware, software and peripheral equipment – operated by a limited group of users.

Exam Probability: **High**

35. *Answer choices:*

(see index for correct answer)

- a. E-Governance
- b. Information technology
- c. Data center infrastructure management
- d. Information society

Guidance: level 1

:: ::

A _____ is a professional who provides expert advice in a particular area such as security, management, education, accountancy, law, human resources, marketing, finance, engineering, science or any of many other specialized fields.

Exam Probability: **High**

36. *Answer choices:*

(see index for correct answer)

- a. surface-level diversity
- b. Consultant
- c. corporate values
- d. similarity-attraction theory

Guidance: level 1

:: ::

_____ is "property consisting of land and the buildings on it, along with its natural resources such as crops, minerals or water; immovable property of this nature; an interest vested in this an item of real property, buildings or housing in general. Also: the business of _____; the profession of buying, selling, or renting land, buildings, or housing." It is a legal term used in jurisdictions whose legal system is derived from English common law, such as India, England, Wales, Northern Ireland, United States, Canada, Pakistan, Australia, and New Zealand.

Exam Probability: **High**

37. *Answer choices:*

(see index for correct answer)

- a. hierarchical
- b. deep-level diversity

- c. Real estate
- d. corporate values

Guidance: level 1

:: Retailing ::

A _____ or trolley, also known by a variety of other names, is a cart supplied by a shop, especially supermarkets, for use by customers inside the shop for transport of merchandise to the checkout counter during shopping. In many cases customers can then also use the cart to transport their purchased goods to their vehicles, but some carts are designed to prevent them from leaving the shop.

Exam Probability: **Low**

38. *Answer choices:*

(see index for correct answer)

- a. Shopping cart
- b. Scrapstore
- c. Catalog merchant
- d. Same-store sales

Guidance: level 1

:: Management ::

_____ is the process of thinking about the activities required to achieve a desired goal. It is the first and foremost activity to achieve desired results. It involves the creation and maintenance of a plan, such as psychological aspects that require conceptual skills. There are even a couple of tests to measure someone's capability of _____ well. As such, _____ is a fundamental property of intelligent behavior. An important further meaning, often just called "_____" is the legal context of permitted building developments.

Exam Probability: **Medium**

39. *Answer choices:*

(see index for correct answer)

- a. Performance indicator
- b. Planning
- c. Project cost management
- d. Scenario planning

Guidance: level 1

:: Basic financial concepts ::

_____ is a sustained increase in the general price level of goods and services in an economy over a period of time. When the general price level rises, each unit of currency buys fewer goods and services; consequently, _____ reflects a reduction in the purchasing power per unit of money a loss of real value in the medium of exchange and unit of account within the economy. The measure of _____ is the _____ rate, the annualized percentage change in a general price index, usually the consumer price index, over time. The opposite of _____ is deflation.

Exam Probability: **Low**

40. *Answer choices:*

(see index for correct answer)

- a. Short interest
- b. Inflation
- c. Tax shield
- d. Maturity

Guidance: level 1

:: Consumer theory ::

A _____ is a technical term in psychology, economics and philosophy usually used in relation to choosing between alternatives. For example, someone prefers A over B if they would rather choose A than B.

Exam Probability: **Medium**

41. *Answer choices:*

(see index for correct answer)

- a. Demand
- b. Income elasticity of demand
- c. Engel curve
- d. Compensated demand

Guidance: level 1

:: Marketing ::

_____ is a concept introduced in a book of the same name in 1999 by marketing expert Seth Godin. _____ is a non-traditional marketing technique that advertises goods and services when advance consent is given.

Exam Probability: **High**

42. *Answer choices:*

(see index for correct answer)

- a. Gatefold
- b. Permission marketing
- c. Demand generation
- d. Dialogue marketing

Guidance: level 1

:: ::

A _____ is an organization, usually a group of people or a company, authorized to act as a single entity and recognized as such in law. Early incorporated entities were established by charter. Most jurisdictions now allow the creation of new _____ s through registration.

Exam Probability: **High**

43. *Answer choices:*

(see index for correct answer)

- a. empathy
- b. information systems assessment
- c. process perspective
- d. Corporation

Guidance: level 1

:: Real estate ::

_____ s serve several societal needs – primarily as shelter from weather, security, living space, privacy, to store belongings, and to comfortably live and work. A _____ as a shelter represents a physical division of the human habitat and the outside.

Exam Probability: **Medium**

44. *Answer choices:*

(see index for correct answer)

- a. Building
- b. Originating application
- c. E-Pro
- d. Earnest payment

Guidance: level 1

:: Economics terminology ::

_____ is the total receipts a seller can obtain from selling goods or services to buyers. It can be written as P × Q, which is the price of the goods multiplied by the quantity of the sold goods.

Exam Probability: **High**

45. *Answer choices:*

(see index for correct answer)

- a. Normal profit
- b. Currency trading
- c. fungible
- d. marginal revenue

Guidance: level 1

:: ::

The _____ is a U.S. business-focused, English-language international daily newspaper based in New York City. The Journal, along with its Asian and European editions, is published six days a week by Dow Jones & Company, a division of News Corp. The newspaper is published in the broadsheet format and online. The Journal has been printed continuously since its inception on July 8, 1889, by Charles Dow, Edward Jones, and Charles Bergstresser.

Exam Probability: **Medium**

46. *Answer choices:*

(see index for correct answer)

- a. corporate values
- b. Wall Street Journal
- c. imperative
- d. empathy

Guidance: level 1

:: ::

An _____ is a systematic and independent examination of books, accounts, statutory records, documents and vouchers of an organization to ascertain how far the financial statements as well as non-financial disclosures present a true and fair view of the concern. It also attempts to ensure that the books of accounts are properly maintained by the concern as required by law. _____ing has become such a ubiquitous phenomenon in the corporate and the public sector that academics started identifying an " _____ Society". The _____ or perceives and recognises the propositions before them for examination, obtains evidence, evaluates the same and formulates an opinion on the basis of his judgement which is communicated through their _____ing report.

Exam Probability: **Medium**

47. *Answer choices:*

(see index for correct answer)

- a. co-culture
- b. imperative
- c. similarity-attraction theory
- d. open system

Guidance: level 1

:: Costs ::

In economics, _____ is the total economic cost of production and is made up of variable cost, which varies according to the quantity of a good produced and includes inputs such as labour and raw materials, plus fixed cost, which is independent of the quantity of a good produced and includes inputs that cannot be varied in the short term: fixed costs such as buildings and machinery, including sunk costs if any. Since cost is measured per unit of time, it is a flow variable.

Exam Probability: **Low**

48. *Answer choices:*

(see index for correct answer)

- a. Sliding scale
- b. Average variable cost
- c. Social cost
- d. Total cost

Guidance: level 1

_____ or standardisation is the process of implementing and developing technical standards based on the consensus of different parties that include firms, users, interest groups, standards organizations and governments. _____ can help maximize compatibility, interoperability, safety, repeatability, or quality. It can also facilitate commoditization of formerly custom processes. In social sciences, including economics, the idea of _____ is close to the solution for a coordination problem, a situation in which all parties can realize mutual gains, but only by making mutually consistent decisions. This view includes the case of "spontaneous _____ processes", to produce de facto standards.

Exam Probability: **High**

49. *Answer choices:*

(see index for correct answer)

- a. levels of analysis
- b. Sarbanes-Oxley act of 2002
- c. Standardization
- d. hierarchical

Guidance: level 1

:: Management accounting ::

In economics, _____ s, indirect costs or overheads are business expenses that are not dependent on the level of goods or services produced by the business. They tend to be time-related, such as interest or rents being paid per month, and are often referred to as overhead costs. This is in contrast to variable costs, which are volume-related and unknown at the beginning of the accounting year. For a simple example, such as a bakery, the monthly rent for the baking facilities, and the monthly payments for the security system and basic phone line are _____ s, as they do not change according to how much bread the bakery produces and sells. On the other hand, the wage costs of the bakery are variable, as the bakery will have to hire more workers if the production of bread increases. Economists reckon _____ as a entry barrier for new entrepreneurs.

Exam Probability: **Low**

50. *Answer choices:*

(see index for correct answer)

- a. Profit center
- b. Fixed cost
- c. Invested capital
- d. Job costing

Guidance: level 1

:: ::

_____, or auditory perception, is the ability to perceive sounds by detecting vibrations, changes in the pressure of the surrounding medium through time, through an organ such as the ear. The academic field concerned with _____ is auditory science.

Exam Probability: **High**

51. *Answer choices:*

(see index for correct answer)

- a. information systems assessment
- b. levels of analysis
- c. hierarchical perspective
- d. Hearing

Guidance: level 1

:: ::

_____ is a qualitative measure used to relate the quality of motor vehicle traffic service. LOS is used to analyze roadways and intersections by categorizing traffic flow and assigning quality levels of traffic based on performance measure like vehicle speed, density, congestion, etc.

Exam Probability: **Low**

52. *Answer choices:*

(see index for correct answer)

- a. interpersonal communication
- b. empathy
- c. Level of service
- d. corporate values

Guidance: level 1

:: Project management ::

Contemporary business and science treat as a _____ any undertaking, carried out individually or collaboratively and possibly involving research or design, that is carefully planned to achieve a particular aim.

Exam Probability: **Medium**

53. *Answer choices:*

(see index for correct answer)

- a. Project management office
- b. Project
- c. Transfer of Burden
- d. Expected commercial value

Guidance: level 1

:: Management accounting ::

_____s are costs that change as the quantity of the good or service that a business produces changes. _____s are the sum of marginal costs over all units produced. They can also be considered normal costs. Fixed costs and _____s make up the two components of total cost. Direct costs are costs that can easily be associated with a particular cost object. However, not all _____s are direct costs. For example, variable manufacturing overhead costs are _____s that are indirect costs, not direct costs. _____s are sometimes called unit-level costs as they vary with the number of units produced.

Exam Probability: **Low**

54. *Answer choices:*

(see index for correct answer)

- a. Variance
- b. Management accounting
- c. Spend management
- d. Variable cost

Guidance: level 1

:: Auctioneering ::

Unlike sealed-bid auctions, an _____ is "open" or fully transparent, as the identity of all bidders is disclosed to each other during the auction. More generally, an auction mechanism is considered "English" if it involves an iterative process of adjusting the price in a direction that is unfavorable to the bidders. In contrast, a Dutch auction would adjust the price in a direction that favored the bidders.

Exam Probability: **High**

55. *Answer choices:*

(see index for correct answer)

- a. Wine auction
- b. Unique bid auction
- c. English auction
- d. Pie supper

Guidance: level 1

:: ::

A _____ is a graphic mark, emblem, or symbol used to aid and promote public identification and recognition. It may be of an abstract or figurative design or include the text of the name it represents as in a wordmark.

Exam Probability: **Low**

56. Answer choices:

(see index for correct answer)

- a. Logo
- b. similarity-attraction theory
- c. personal values
- d. levels of analysis

Guidance: level 1

:: Information technology management ::

_____ s or pop-ups are forms of online advertising on the World Wide Web. A pop-up is a graphical user interface display area, usually a small window, that suddenly appears in the foreground of the visual interface. The pop-up window containing an advertisement is usually generated by JavaScript that uses cross-site scripting, sometimes with a secondary payload that uses Adobe Flash. They can also be generated by other vulnerabilities/security holes in browser security.

Exam Probability: **Low**

57. Answer choices:

(see index for correct answer)

- a. Pop-up ad
- b. HP Open Extensibility Platform
- c. Incident management

- d. Autonomic networking

Guidance: level 1

:: ::

_____ Corporation is an American multinational technology company with headquarters in Redmond, Washington. It develops, manufactures, licenses, supports and sells computer software, consumer electronics, personal computers, and related services. Its best known software products are the _____ Windows line of operating systems, the _____ Office suite, and the Internet Explorer and Edge Web browsers. Its flagship hardware products are the Xbox video game consoles and the _____ Surface lineup of touchscreen personal computers. As of 2016, it is the world's largest software maker by revenue, and one of the world's most valuable companies. The word "_____" is a portmanteau of "microcomputer" and "software". _____ is ranked No. 30 in the 2018 Fortune 500 rankings of the largest United States corporations by total revenue.

Exam Probability: **High**

58. *Answer choices:*

(see index for correct answer)

- a. deep-level diversity
- b. Microsoft
- c. hierarchical
- d. empathy

Guidance: level 1

:: Accounting source documents ::

A _____ is a commercial document and first official offer issued by a buyer to a seller indicating types, quantities, and agreed prices for products or services. It is used to control the purchasing of products and services from external suppliers. _____ s can be an essential part of enterprise resource planning system orders.

Exam Probability: **Low**

59. *Answer choices:*

(see index for correct answer)

- a. Remittance advice
- b. Banknote
- c. Parcel audit
- d. Credit memo

Guidance: level 1

Business ethics

Business ethics (also known as corporate ethics) is a form of applied ethics or professional ethics, that examines ethical principles and moral or ethical problems that can arise in a business environment. It applies to all aspects of business conduct and is relevant to the conduct of individuals and entire organizations. These ethics originate from individuals, organizational statements or from the legal system. These norms, values, ethical, and unethical practices are what is used to guide business. They help those businesses maintain a better connection with their stakeholders.

:: Price fixing convictions ::

_____ AG is a German multinational conglomerate company headquartered in Berlin and Munich and the largest industrial manufacturing company in Europe with branch offices abroad.

Exam Probability: **High**

1. *Answer choices:*

(see index for correct answer)

- a. JJB Sports
- b. Siemens
- c. Christmas tree production in Denmark
- d. AGC Glass Europe

Guidance: level 1

:: ::

The Ethics & Compliance Initiative was formed in 2015 and consists of three nonprofit organizations: the Ethics Research Center, the Ethics & Compliance Association, and the Ethics & Compliance Certification Institute. Based in Arlington, Virginia, United States, ECI is devoted to the advancement of high ethical standards and practices in public and private institutions, and provides research about ethical standards, workplace integrity, and compliance practices and processes.

Exam Probability: **Medium**

2. *Answer choices:*

(see index for correct answer)

- a. process perspective
- b. Ethics Resource Center
- c. cultural
- d. functional perspective

Guidance: level 1

:: Ethical banking ::

A _____ or community development finance institution - abbreviated in both cases to CDFI - is a financial institution that provides credit and financial services to underserved markets and populations, primarily in the USA but also in the UK. A CDFI may be a community development bank, a community development credit union, a community development loan fund, a community development venture capital fund, a microenterprise development loan fund, or a community development corporation.

Exam Probability: **Medium**

3. *Answer choices:*

(see index for correct answer)

- a. Shared Interest
- b. Charity Bank
- c. Triodos Bank

- d. Wilhelm Ernst Barkhoff

Guidance: level 1

:: Law ::

_____ is a body of law which defines the role, powers, and structure of different entities within a state, namely, the executive, the parliament or legislature, and the judiciary; as well as the basic rights of citizens and, in federal countries such as the United States and Canada, the relationship between the central government and state, provincial, or territorial governments.

Exam Probability: **High**

4. *Answer choices:*
(see index for correct answer)

- a. Constitutional law
- b. Legal case

Guidance: level 1

:: ::

Competition law is a law that promotes or seeks to maintain market competition by regulating anti-competitive conduct by companies. Competition law is implemented through public and private enforcement. Competition law is known as "_____ law" in the United States for historical reasons, and as "anti-monopoly law" in China and Russia. In previous years it has been known as trade practices law in the United Kingdom and Australia. In the European Union, it is referred to as both _____ and competition law.

Exam Probability: **Low**

5. *Answer choices:*

(see index for correct answer)

- a. Antitrust
- b. imperative
- c. cultural
- d. surface-level diversity

Guidance: level 1

:: ::

_____ is a region of India consisting of the Indian states of Bihar, Jharkhand, West Bengal, Odisha and also the union territory Andaman and Nicobar Islands. West Bengal's capital Kolkata is the largest city of this region. The Kolkata Metropolitan Area is the country's third largest.

Exam Probability: **High**

6. *Answer choices:*

(see index for correct answer)

- a. East India
- b. hierarchical
- c. cultural
- d. empathy

Guidance: level 1

:: Globalization-related theories ::

_____ is an economic system based on the private ownership of the means of production and their operation for profit. Characteristics central to _____ include private property, capital accumulation, wage labor, voluntary exchange, a price system, and competitive markets. In a capitalist market economy, decision-making and investment are determined by every owner of wealth, property or production ability in financial and capital markets, whereas prices and the distribution of goods and services are mainly determined by competition in goods and services markets.

Exam Probability: **Medium**

7. *Answer choices:*

(see index for correct answer)

- a. postmodernism
- b. Economic Development

- c. Capitalism

Guidance: level 1

:: ::

Oriental Nicety, formerly _____ , Exxon Mediterranean, SeaRiver Mediterranean, S/R Mediterranean, Mediterranean, and Dong Fang Ocean, was an oil tanker that gained notoriety after running aground in Prince William Sound spilling hundreds of thousands of barrels of crude oil in Alaska. On March 24, 1989, while owned by the former Exxon Shipping Company, and captained by Joseph Hazelwood and First Mate James Kunkel bound for Long Beach, California, the vessel ran aground on the Bligh Reef resulting in the second largest oil spill in United States history. The size of the spill is estimated to have been 40,900 to 120,000 m3 , or 257,000 to 750,000 barrels. In 1989, the _____ oil spill was listed as the 54th largest spill in history.

Exam Probability: **Medium**

8. *Answer choices:*

(see index for correct answer)

- a. Sarbanes-Oxley act of 2002
- b. Character
- c. functional perspective
- d. similarity-attraction theory

Guidance: level 1

:: Waste ::

_____ is any unwanted material in all forms that can cause harm. Many of today's household products such as televisions, computers and phones contain toxic chemicals that can pollute the air and contaminate soil and water. Disposing of such waste is a major public health issue.

Exam Probability: **High**

9. *Answer choices:*

(see index for correct answer)

- a. Controlled waste
- b. Sharps waste
- c. Uncontrolled waste
- d. Clinker

Guidance: level 1

:: ::

_____ is a bundle of characteristics, including ways of thinking, feeling, and acting, which humans are said to have naturally. The term is often regarded as capturing what it is to be human, or the essence of humanity. The term is controversial because it is disputed whether or not such an essence exists. Arguments about _____ have been a mainstay of philosophy for centuries and the concept continues to provoke lively philosophical debate. The concept also continues to play a role in science, with neuroscientists, psychologists and social scientists sometimes claiming that their results have yielded insight into _____ . _____ is traditionally contrasted with characteristics that vary among humans, such as characteristics associated with specific cultures. Debates about _____ are related to, although not the same as, debates about the comparative importance of genes and environment in development.

Exam Probability: **High**

10. *Answer choices:*

(see index for correct answer)

- a. open system
- b. Sarbanes-Oxley act of 2002
- c. Human nature
- d. process perspective

Guidance: level 1

:: Dutch inventions ::

> The Fairtrade certification initiative was created to form a new method for economic trade. This method takes an ethical standpoint, and considers the producers first.

Exam Probability: **Low**

11. *Answer choices:*

(see index for correct answer)

- a. Dijkstra's algorithm
- b. Fair Trade Certified

Guidance: level 1

:: ::

> An _____ is the release of a liquid petroleum hydrocarbon into the environment, especially the marine ecosystem, due to human activity, and is a form of pollution. The term is usually given to marine _____ s, where oil is released into the ocean or coastal waters, but spills may also occur on land. _____ s may be due to releases of crude oil from tankers, offshore platforms, drilling rigs and wells, as well as spills of refined petroleum products and their by-products, heavier fuels used by large ships such as bunker fuel, or the spill of any oily refuse or waste oil.

Exam Probability: **High**

12. *Answer choices:*

(see index for correct answer)

- a. Oil spill
- b. interpersonal communication
- c. levels of analysis
- d. imperative

Guidance: level 1

:: Fraud ::

In law, _____ is intentional deception to secure unfair or unlawful gain, or to deprive a victim of a legal right. _____ can violate civil law, a criminal law, or it may cause no loss of money, property or legal right but still be an element of another civil or criminal wrong. The purpose of _____ may be monetary gain or other benefits, for example by obtaining a passport, travel document, or driver's license, or mortgage _____, where the perpetrator may attempt to qualify for a mortgage by way of false statements.

Exam Probability: **High**

13. *Answer choices:*
(see index for correct answer)

- a. Wangiri
- b. Emil Rupp
- c. Employment fraud

- d. Fraud

Guidance: level 1

:: ::

_____ or accountancy is the measurement, processing, and communication of financial information about economic entities such as businesses and corporations. The modern field was established by the Italian mathematician Luca Pacioli in 1494. _____, which has been called the "language of business", measures the results of an organization's economic activities and conveys this information to a variety of users, including investors, creditors, management, and regulators. Practitioners of _____ are known as accountants. The terms "_____" and "financial reporting" are often used as synonyms.

Exam Probability: **Low**

14. *Answer choices:*
(see index for correct answer)

- a. Accounting
- b. Sarbanes-Oxley act of 2002
- c. similarity-attraction theory
- d. hierarchical

Guidance: level 1

The _____ of 1906 was the first of a series of significant consumer protection laws which was enacted by Congress in the 20th century and led to the creation of the Food and Drug Administration. Its main purpose was to ban foreign and interstate traffic in adulterated or mislabeled food and drug products, and it directed the U.S. Bureau of Chemistry to inspect products and refer offenders to prosecutors. It required that active ingredients be placed on the label of a drug's packaging and that drugs could not fall below purity levels established by the United States Pharmacopeia or the National Formulary. The Jungle by Upton Sinclair with its graphic and revolting descriptions of unsanitary conditions and unscrupulous practices rampant in the meatpacking industry, was an inspirational piece that kept the public's attention on the important issue of unhygienic meat processing plants that later led to food inspection legislation. Sinclair quipped, "I aimed at the public's heart and by accident I hit it in the stomach," as outraged readers demanded and got the pure food law.

Exam Probability: **Medium**

15. *Answer choices:*

(see index for correct answer)

- a. functional perspective
- b. information systems assessment
- c. empathy
- d. imperative

Guidance: level 1

:: Criminal law ::

_____ is the body of law that relates to crime. It proscribes conduct perceived as threatening, harmful, or otherwise endangering to the property, health, safety, and moral welfare of people inclusive of one's self. Most _____ is established by statute, which is to say that the laws are enacted by a legislature. _____ includes the punishment and rehabilitation of people who violate such laws. _____ varies according to jurisdiction, and differs from civil law, where emphasis is more on dispute resolution and victim compensation, rather than on punishment or rehabilitation. Criminal procedure is a formalized official activity that authenticates the fact of commission of a crime and authorizes punitive or rehabilitative treatment of the offender.

Exam Probability: **Low**

16. *Answer choices:*

(see index for correct answer)

- a. Mala in se
- b. Criminal law
- c. mitigating factor
- d. complicit

Guidance: level 1

:: Writs ::

In common law, a writ of _____ is a writ whereby a private individual who assists a prosecution can receive all or part of any penalty imposed. Its name is an abbreviation of the Latin phrase _____ pro domino rege quam pro se ipso in hac parte sequitur, meaning "[he] who sues in this matter for the king as well as for himself."

Exam Probability: **High**

17. *Answer choices:*

(see index for correct answer)

- a. Writ of execution
- b. Writ of assistance

Guidance: level 1

:: ::

The _____, the Calvinist work ethic or the Puritan work ethic is a work ethic concept in theology, sociology, economics and history that emphasizes that hard work, discipline and frugality are a result of a person's subscription to the values espoused by the Protestant faith, particularly Calvinism. The phrase was initially coined in 1904–1905 by Max Weber in his book The Protestant Ethic and the Spirit of Capitalism.

Exam Probability: **Low**

18. *Answer choices:*

(see index for correct answer)

- a. Character
- b. imperative
- c. open system
- d. levels of analysis

Guidance: level 1

:: ::

In regulatory jurisdictions that provide for it, _____ is a group of laws and organizations designed to ensure the rights of consumers as well as fair trade, competition and accurate information in the marketplace. The laws are designed to prevent the businesses that engage in fraud or specified unfair practices from gaining an advantage over competitors. They may also provides additional protection for those most vulnerable in society. _____ laws are a form of government regulation that aim to protect the rights of consumers. For example, a government may require businesses to disclose detailed information about products—particularly in areas where safety or public health is an issue, such as food.

Exam Probability: **High**

19. *Answer choices:*
(see index for correct answer)

- a. empathy
- b. process perspective

- c. Consumer Protection
- d. personal values

Guidance: level 1

:: Monopoly (economics) ::

A _____ is a form of intellectual property that gives its owner the legal right to exclude others from making, using, selling, and importing an invention for a limited period of years, in exchange for publishing an enabling public disclosure of the invention. In most countries _____ rights fall under civil law and the _____ holder needs to sue someone infringing the _____ in order to enforce his or her rights. In some industries _____ s are an essential form of competitive advantage; in others they are irrelevant.

Exam Probability: **High**

20. *Answer choices:*

(see index for correct answer)

- a. Dominance
- b. Privatization
- c. Patent
- d. Statute of Monopolies

Guidance: level 1

:: False advertising law ::

The Lanham Act is the primary federal trademark statute of law in the United States. The Act prohibits a number of activities, including trademark infringement, trademark dilution, and false advertising.

Exam Probability: **Medium**

21. *Answer choices:*

(see index for correct answer)

- a. Lanham Act
- b. POM Wonderful LLC v. Coca-Cola Co.

Guidance: level 1

:: ::

A _____ is the ability to carry out a task with determined results often within a given amount of time, energy, or both. _____ s can often be divided into domain-general and domain-specific _____ s. For example, in the domain of work, some general _____ s would include time management, teamwork and leadership, self-motivation and others, whereas domain-specific _____ s would be used only for a certain job. _____ usually requires certain environmental stimuli and situations to assess the level of _____ being shown and used.

Exam Probability: **Low**

22. *Answer choices:*

(see index for correct answer)

- a. open system
- b. Skill
- c. corporate values
- d. personal values

Guidance: level 1

:: Parental leave ::

_____ , or family leave, is an employee benefit available in almost all countries. The term " _____ " may include maternity, paternity, and adoption leave; or may be used distinctively from "maternity leave" and "paternity leave" to describe separate family leave available to either parent to care for small children. In some countries and jurisdictions, "family leave" also includes leave provided to care for ill family members. Often, the minimum benefits and eligibility requirements are stipulated by law.

Exam Probability: **High**

23. *Answer choices:*

(see index for correct answer)

- a. Additional Paternity Leave Regulations 2010
- b. Parental leave
- c. Parental leave economics

- d. Geduldig v. Aiello

Guidance: level 1

:: Types of marketing ::

_____ is an advertisement strategy in which a company uses surprise and/or unconventional interactions in order to promote a product or service. It is a type of publicity. The term was popularized by Jay Conrad Levinson's 1984 book _____ .

Exam Probability: **Low**

24. *Answer choices:*
(see index for correct answer)

- a. Secret brand
- b. Community marketing
- c. Guerrilla Marketing
- d. Ambush marketing

Guidance: level 1

:: Reputation management ::

_____ or image of a social entity is an opinion about that entity, typically as a result of social evaluation on a set of criteria.

Exam Probability: **Medium**

25. *Answer choices:*

(see index for correct answer)

- a. personal brand
- b. Moderation system
- c. Yasni
- d. Reputation

Guidance: level 1

:: ::

The _____ was a severe worldwide economic depression that took place mostly during the 1930s, beginning in the United States. The timing of the _____ varied across nations; in most countries it started in 1929 and lasted until the late-1930s. It was the longest, deepest, and most widespread depression of the 20th century. In the 21st century, the _____ is commonly used as an example of how intensely the world's economy can decline.

Exam Probability: **Medium**

26. *Answer choices:*

(see index for correct answer)

- a. personal values
- b. open system
- c. cultural
- d. Great Depression

Guidance: level 1

:: Business ethics ::

_____ is a type of harassment technique that relates to a sexual nature and the unwelcome or inappropriate promise of rewards in exchange for sexual favors. _____ includes a range of actions from mild transgressions to sexual abuse or assault. Harassment can occur in many different social settings such as the workplace, the home, school, churches, etc. Harassers or victims may be of any gender.

Exam Probability: **High**

27. *Answer choices:*

(see index for correct answer)

- a. United Nations Global Compact
- b. MBA Oath
- c. Corporate crime
- d. Sexual harassment

Guidance: level 1

:: Business ethics ::

_____ is an area of applied ethics which deals with the moral principles behind the operation and regulation of marketing. Some areas of _____ overlap with media ethics.

Exam Probability: **Low**

28. *Answer choices:*

(see index for correct answer)

- a. Salad Oil Scandal
- b. Impact investing
- c. Wheelmen
- d. The Crooked E: The Unshredded Truth About Enron

Guidance: level 1

:: Industry ::

_____ is the manner in which a given entity has decided to address issues of energy development including energy production, distribution and consumption. The attributes of _____ may include legislation, international treaties, incentives to investment, guidelines for energy conservation, taxation and other public policy techniques. Energy is a core component of modern economies. A functioning economy requires not only labor and capital but also energy, for manufacturing processes, transportation, communication, agriculture, and more.

Exam Probability: **Low**

29. *Answer choices:*

(see index for correct answer)

- a. Thomson Reuters Business Classification
- b. Energy policy
- c. Industrial safety system
- d. Cartoning machine

Guidance: level 1

:: Labor rights ::

The _____ is the concept that people have a human _____, or engage in productive employment, and may not be prevented from doing so. The _____ is enshrined in the Universal Declaration of Human Rights and recognized in international human rights law through its inclusion in the International Covenant on Economic, Social and Cultural Rights, where the _____ emphasizes economic, social and cultural development.

Exam Probability: **Low**

30. *Answer choices:*

(see index for correct answer)

- a. Kate Mullany House
- b. Labor rights
- c. Right to work
- d. The Hyatt 100

Guidance: level 1

:: Hazard analysis ::

Broadly speaking, a _____ is the combined effort of 1. identifying and analyzing potential events that may negatively impact individuals, assets, and/or the environment ; and 2. making judgments "on the tolerability of the risk on the basis of a risk analysis" while considering influencing factors . Put in simpler terms, a _____ analyzes what can go wrong, how likely it is to happen, what the potential consequences are, and how tolerable the identified risk is. As part of this process, the resulting determination of risk may be expressed in a quantitative or qualitative fashion. The _____ is an inherent part of an overall risk management strategy, which attempts to, after a _____ , "introduce control measures to eliminate or reduce" any potential risk-related consequences.

Exam Probability: **Medium**

31. *Answer choices:*

(see index for correct answer)

- a. Hazardous Materials Identification System
- b. Swiss cheese model
- c. Hazard identification

Guidance: level 1

:: ::

The _____ is an agency of the United States Department of Labor. Congress established the agency under the Occupational Safety and Health Act, which President Richard M. Nixon signed into law on December 29, 1970. OSHA's mission is to "assure safe and healthy working conditions for working men and women by setting and enforcing standards and by providing training, outreach, education and assistance". The agency is also charged with enforcing a variety of whistleblower statutes and regulations. OSHA is currently headed by Acting Assistant Secretary of Labor Loren Sweatt. OSHA's workplace safety inspections have been shown to reduce injury rates and injury costs without adverse effects to employment, sales, credit ratings, or firm survival.

Exam Probability: **Medium**

32. *Answer choices:*
(see index for correct answer)

- a. levels of analysis
- b. personal values
- c. Occupational Safety and Health Administration

- d. corporate values

Guidance: level 1

:: Social responsibility ::

The United Nations Global Compact is a non-binding United Nations pact to encourage businesses worldwide to adopt sustainable and socially responsible policies, and to report on their implementation. The _____ is a principle-based framework for businesses, stating ten principles in the areas of human rights, labor, the environment and anti-corruption. Under the Global Compact, companies are brought together with UN agencies, labor groups and civil society. Cities can join the Global Compact through the Cities Programme.

Exam Probability: **Medium**

33. *Answer choices:*
(see index for correct answer)

- a. Strategic corporate social responsibility
- b. Footprints network
- c. Stakeholder engagement
- d. Enterprise 2020

Guidance: level 1

:: Office work ::

_____ is the process and behavior in human interactions involving power and authority. It is also a tool to assess the operational capacity and to balance diverse views of interested parties. It is also known as office politics and organizational politics.It is the use of power and social networking within an organization to achieve changes that benefit the organization or individuals within it. Influence by individuals may serve personal interests without regard to their effect on the organization itself. Some of the personal advantages may include access to tangible assets, or intangible benefits such as status or pseudo-authority that influences the behavior of others. On the other hand, organizational politics can increase efficiency, form interpersonal relationships, expedite change, and profit the organization and its members simultaneously.Both individuals and groups may engage in office politics which can be highly destructive, as people focus on personal gains at the expense of the organization. "Self-serving political actions can negatively influence our social groupings, cooperation, information sharing, and many other organizational functions." Thus, it is vital to pay attention to organizational politics and create the right political landscape. "Politics is the lubricant that oils your organization's internal gears."
Office politics has also been described as "simply how power gets worked out on a practical, day-to-day basis."

Exam Probability: **Low**

34. *Answer choices:*

(see index for correct answer)

- a. Office of the future
- b. Mobile office
- c. Peter Principle
- d. Workplace politics

Guidance: level 1

:: Electronic waste ::

_____ or e-waste describes discarded electrical or electronic devices. Used electronics which are destined for refurbishment, reuse, resale, salvage, recycling through material recovery, or disposal are also considered e-waste. Informal processing of e-waste in developing countries can lead to adverse human health effects and environmental pollution.

Exam Probability: **Medium**

35. *Answer choices:*

(see index for correct answer)

- a. E-Stewards
- b. Solving the E-waste Problem
- c. Electronic waste
- d. ReGlobe

Guidance: level 1

:: Social enterprise ::

Corporate social responsibility is a type of international private business self-regulation. While once it was possible to describe CSR as an internal organisational policy or a corporate ethic strategy, that time has passed as various international laws have been developed and various organisations have used their authority to push it beyond individual or even industry-wide initiatives. While it has been considered a form of corporate self-regulation for some time, over the last decade or so it has moved considerably from voluntary decisions at the level of individual organisations, to mandatory schemes at regional, national and even transnational levels.

Exam Probability: **Low**

36. *Answer choices:*

(see index for correct answer)

- a. Social enterprise
- b. Social venture

Guidance: level 1

:: Progressive Era in the United States ::

The Clayton Antitrust Act of 1914, was a part of United States antitrust law with the goal of adding further substance to the U.S. antitrust law regime; the _____ sought to prevent anticompetitive practices in their incipiency. That regime started with the Sherman Antitrust Act of 1890, the first Federal law outlawing practices considered harmful to consumers. The _____ specified particular prohibited conduct, the three-level enforcement scheme, the exemptions, and the remedial measures.

Exam Probability: **High**

37. *Answer choices:*

(see index for correct answer)

- a. pragmatism
- b. Mann Act
- c. Clayton Antitrust Act

Guidance: level 1

:: Supply chain management terms ::

In business and finance, _____ is a system of organizations, people, activities, information, and resources involved in moving a product or service from supplier to customer. _____ activities involve the transformation of natural resources, raw materials, and components into a finished product that is delivered to the end customer. In sophisticated _____ systems, used products may re-enter the _____ at any point where residual value is recyclable. _____ s link value chains.

Exam Probability: **High**

38. *Answer choices:*

(see index for correct answer)

- a. Supply Chain
- b. Capital spare

- c. Widget
- d. Most valuable customers

Guidance: level 1

:: Corporate scandals ::

_____ was a bank based in the Caribbean, which operated from 1986 to 2009 when it went into receivership. It was an affiliate of the Stanford Financial Group and failed when the its parent was seized by United States authorities in early 2009 as part of the investigation into Allen Stanford.

Exam Probability: **Low**

39. *Answer choices:*

(see index for correct answer)

- a. Service Corporation of America
- b. Peter R. Harris
- c. Patent encumbrance of large automotive NiMH batteries
- d. Terra Securities scandal

Guidance: level 1

:: ::

The _____ is an institution of the European Union, responsible for proposing legislation, implementing decisions, upholding the EU treaties and managing the day-to-day business of the EU. Commissioners swear an oath at the European Court of Justice in Luxembourg City, pledging to respect the treaties and to be completely independent in carrying out their duties during their mandate. Unlike in the Council of the European Union, where members are directly and indirectly elected, and the European Parliament, where members are directly elected, the Commissioners are proposed by the Council of the European Union, on the basis of suggestions made by the national governments, and then appointed by the European Council after the approval of the European Parliament.

Exam Probability: **High**

40. *Answer choices:*

(see index for correct answer)

- a. European Commission
- b. imperative
- c. Sarbanes-Oxley act of 2002
- d. similarity-attraction theory

Guidance: level 1

:: ::

_____, O.S.A. was a German professor of theology, composer, priest, monk, and a seminal figure in the Protestant Reformation.

Exam Probability: **Low**

41. *Answer choices:*

(see index for correct answer)

- a. corporate values
- b. Martin Luther
- c. open system
- d. functional perspective

Guidance: level 1

:: Environmental economics ::

_____ is an institutional arrangement designed to help producers in developing countries achieve better trading conditions. Members of the _____ movement advocate the payment of higher prices to exporters, as well as improved social and environmental standards. The movement focuses in particular on commodities, or products which are typically exported from developing countries to developed countries, but also consumed in domestic markets most notably handicrafts, coffee, cocoa, wine, sugar, fresh fruit, chocolate, flowers and gold. The movement seeks to promote greater equity in international trading partnerships through dialogue, transparency, and respect. It promotes sustainable development by offering better trading conditions to, and securing the rights of, marginalized producers and workers in developing countries. _____ is grounded in three core beliefs: first, producers have the power to express unity with consumers. Secondly, the world trade practices that currently exist promote the unequal distribution of wealth between nations. Lastly, buying products from producers in developing countries at a fair price is a more efficient way of promoting sustainable development than traditional charity and aid.

Exam Probability: **High**

42. *Answer choices:*

(see index for correct answer)

- a. Bequest value
- b. Carbon accounting
- c. Green growth
- d. Fair trade

Guidance: level 1

:: Anti-Revisionism ::

_____, officially the German Democratic Republic, was a country that existed from 1949 to 1990, when the eastern portion of Germany was part of the Eastern Bloc during the Cold War. It described itself as a socialist "workers' and peasants' state", and the territory was administered and occupied by Soviet forces at the end of World War II — the Soviet Occupation Zone of the Potsdam Agreement, bounded on the east by the Oder–Neisse line. The Soviet zone surrounded West Berlin but did not include it; as a result, West Berlin remained outside the jurisdiction of the GDR.

Exam Probability: **Medium**

43. *Answer choices:*

(see index for correct answer)

- a. New Communist Movement
- b. Chilean Communist Party
- c. Anti-Party Group
- d. East Germany

Guidance: level 1

:: ::

_____ refers to a business initiative to increase the access between a company and their current and potential customers through the use of the Internet. The Internet allows the company to market themselves and attract new customers to their website where they can provide product information and better customer service. Customers can place orders electronically, therefore reducing expensive long distant phone calls and postage costs of placing orders, while saving time on behalf of the customer and company.

Exam Probability: **High**

44. *Answer choices:*

(see index for correct answer)

- a. functional perspective
- b. open system
- c. Global reach
- d. co-culture

Guidance: level 1

:: Nepotism ::

_____ is the granting of favour to relatives in various fields, including business, politics, entertainment, sports, religion and other activities. The term originated with the assignment of nephews to important positions by Catholic popes and bishops. Trading parliamentary employment for favors is a modern-day example of _____ . Criticism of _____ , however, can be found in ancient Indian texts such as the Kural literature.

Exam Probability: **High**

45. *Answer choices:*

(see index for correct answer)

- a. Nepotism
- b. Wasta
- c. Cronyism
- d. Cardinal-nephew

Guidance: level 1

:: Minimum wage ::

A _____ is the lowest remuneration that employers can legally pay their workers—the price floor below which workers may not sell their labor. Most countries had introduced _____ legislation by the end of the 20th century.

Exam Probability: **High**

46. *Answer choices:*

(see index for correct answer)

- a. National Anti-Sweating League
- b. Minimum wage
- c. Working poor
- d. Minimum wage in Taiwan

Guidance: level 1

:: ::

Cannabis, also known as _____ among other names, is a psychoactive drug from the Cannabis plant used for medical or recreational purposes. The main psychoactive part of cannabis is tetrahydrocannabinol, one of 483 known compounds in the plant, including at least 65 other cannabinoids. Cannabis can be used by smoking, vaporizing, within food, or as an extract.

Exam Probability: **Low**

47. *Answer choices:*

(see index for correct answer)

- a. co-culture
- b. information systems assessment
- c. Marijuana
- d. hierarchical perspective

Guidance: level 1

:: Socialism ::

_____ is a label used to define the first currents of modern socialist thought as exemplified by the work of Henri de Saint-Simon, Charles Fourier, Étienne Cabet and Robert Owen.

Exam Probability: **Low**

48. *Answer choices:*

(see index for correct answer)

- a. Goulash Communism
- b. Socialist economics
- c. World Socialist Movement
- d. Utopian socialism

Guidance: level 1

:: Commercial crimes ::

_____ is an agreement between participants on the same side in a market to buy or sell a product, service, or commodity only at a fixed price, or maintain the market conditions such that the price is maintained at a given level by controlling supply and demand.

Exam Probability: **High**

49. *Answer choices:*

(see index for correct answer)

- a. Shill
- b. Price fixing
- c. Credit card hijacking
- d. Counterfeit consumer goods

Guidance: level 1

:: ::

The Federal National Mortgage Association, commonly known as _____, is a United States government-sponsored enterprise and, since 1968, a publicly traded company. Founded in 1938 during the Great Depression as part of the New Deal, the corporation's purpose is to expand the secondary mortgage market by securitizing mortgage loans in the form of mortgage-backed securities, allowing lenders to reinvest their assets into more lending and in effect increasing the number of lenders in the mortgage market by reducing the reliance on locally based savings and loan associations. Its brother organization is the Federal Home Loan Mortgage Corporation, better known as Freddie Mac. As of 2018, _____ is ranked #21 on the Fortune 500 rankings of the largest United States corporations by total revenue.

Exam Probability: **Low**

50. *Answer choices:*

(see index for correct answer)

- a. Character
- b. interpersonal communication
- c. Fannie Mae
- d. functional perspective

Guidance: level 1

_____ is the study and management of exchange relationships. _____ is the business process of creating relationships with and satisfying customers. With its focus on the customer, _____ is one of the premier components of business management.

Exam Probability: **Low**

51. *Answer choices:*

(see index for correct answer)

- a. Marketing
- b. personal values
- c. surface-level diversity
- d. Character

Guidance: level 1

:: Cognitive biases ::

In personality psychology, _____ is the degree to which people believe that they have control over the outcome of events in their lives, as opposed to external forces beyond their control. Understanding of the concept was developed by Julian B. Rotter in 1954, and has since become an aspect of personality studies. A person's "locus" is conceptualized as internal or external.

Exam Probability: **Medium**

52. Answer choices:

(see index for correct answer)

- a. Out-group homogeneity
- b. Overconfidence effect
- c. Telescoping effect
- d. Locus of control

Guidance: level 1

:: Utilitarianism ::

> _____ is a school of thought that argues that the pursuit of pleasure and intrinsic goods are the primary or most important goals of human life. A hedonist strives to maximize net pleasure. However upon finally gaining said pleasure, happiness may remain stationary.

Exam Probability: **High**

53. Answer choices:

(see index for correct answer)

- a. Hedonism
- b. Equal consideration of interests
- c. Act utilitarianism
- d. Informed judge

Guidance: level 1

:: Confidence tricks ::

A _____ is a business model that recruits members via a promise of payments or services for enrolling others into the scheme, rather than supplying investments or sale of products. As recruiting multiplies, recruiting becomes quickly impossible, and most members are unable to profit; as such, _____ s are unsustainable and often illegal.

Exam Probability: **Medium**

54. *Answer choices:*

(see index for correct answer)

- a. BioPerformance
- b. Black money scam
- c. Pyramid scheme
- d. Shyster

Guidance: level 1

:: ::

A _____ is a form of business network, for example, a local organization of businesses whose goal is to further the interests of businesses. Business owners in towns and cities form these local societies to advocate on behalf of the business community. Local businesses are members, and they elect a board of directors or executive council to set policy for the chamber. The board or council then hires a President, CEO or Executive Director, plus staffing appropriate to size, to run the organization.

Exam Probability: **Medium**

55. *Answer choices:*

(see index for correct answer)

- a. Chamber of Commerce
- b. co-culture
- c. open system
- d. personal values

Guidance: level 1

:: Labour relations ::

_____ is a field of study that can have different meanings depending on the context in which it is used. In an international context, it is a subfield of labor history that studies the human relations with regard to work – in its broadest sense – and how this connects to questions of social inequality. It explicitly encompasses unregulated, historical, and non-Western forms of labor. Here, _____ define "for or with whom one works and under what rules. These rules determine the type of work, type and amount of remuneration, working hours, degrees of physical and psychological strain, as well as the degree of freedom and autonomy associated with the work."

Exam Probability: **Medium**

56. *Answer choices:*

(see index for correct answer)

- a. Whipsaw strike
- b. Association of German Chambers of Industry and Commerce
- c. Labor relations
- d. Two-tier system

Guidance: level 1

:: Euthenics ::

_____ is an ethical framework and suggests that an entity, be it an organization or individual, has an obligation to act for the benefit of society at large. _____ is a duty every individual has to perform so as to maintain a balance between the economy and the ecosystems. A trade-off may exist between economic development, in the material sense, and the welfare of the society and environment, though this has been challenged by many reports over the past decade. _____ means sustaining the equilibrium between the two. It pertains not only to business organizations but also to everyone whose any action impacts the environment. This responsibility can be passive, by avoiding engaging in socially harmful acts, or active, by performing activities that directly advance social goals. _____ must be intergenerational since the actions of one generation have consequences on those following.

Exam Probability: **High**

57. *Answer choices:*

(see index for correct answer)

- a. Family and consumer science
- b. Minnie Cumnock Blodgett
- c. Euthenics
- d. Social responsibility

Guidance: level 1

:: Cultural appropriation ::

_____ is a social and economic order that encourages the acquisition of goods and services in ever-increasing amounts. With the industrial revolution, but particularly in the 20th century, mass production led to an economic crisis: there was overproduction—the supply of goods would grow beyond consumer demand, and so manufacturers turned to planned obsolescence and advertising to manipulate consumer spending. In 1899, a book on _____ published by Thorstein Veblen, called The Theory of the Leisure Class, examined the widespread values and economic institutions emerging along with the widespread "leisure time" in the beginning of the 20th century. In it Veblen "views the activities and spending habits of this leisure class in terms of conspicuous and vicarious consumption and waste. Both are related to the display of status and not to functionality or usefulness."

Exam Probability: **Low**

58. *Answer choices:*

(see index for correct answer)

- a. Aunt Jemima
- b. Cleveland Indians
- c. Representation of African Americans in media
- d. Blackface

Guidance: level 1

:: Minimum wage ::

The _____ are working people whose incomes fall below a given poverty line due to lack of work hours and/or low wages. Largely because they are earning such low wages, the _____ face numerous obstacles that make it difficult for many of them to find and keep a job, save up money, and maintain a sense of self-worth.

Exam Probability: **Low**

59. *Answer choices:*

(see index for correct answer)

- a. Minimum wage in the United States
- b. National Anti-Sweating League
- c. Minimum Wage Fairness Act
- d. Guaranteed minimum income

Guidance: level 1

Accounting

Accounting or accountancy is the measurement, processing, and communication of financial information about economic entities such as businesses and corporations. The modern field was established by the Italian mathematician Luca Pacioli in 1494. Accounting, which has been called the "language of business", measures the results of an organization's economic activities and conveys this information to a variety of users, including investors, creditors, management, and regulators.

:: Pricing ::

_____ is the difference between a lower selling price and a higher purchase price, resulting in a financial loss for the seller.

Exam Probability: **Medium**

1. *Answer choices:*

(see index for correct answer)

- a. Capital loss
- b. Natural gas prices
- c. Factor price equalization
- d. Local exchange trading system

Guidance: level 1

:: Generally Accepted Accounting Principles ::

The first published description of the process is found in Luca Pacioli's 1494 work Summa de arithmetica, in the section titled Particularis de Computis et Scripturis. Although he did not use the term, he essentially prescribed a technique similar to a post-closing _____ .

Exam Probability: **Medium**

2. *Answer choices:*

(see index for correct answer)

- a. Paid in capital
- b. Trial balance
- c. Net profit
- d. Chinese accounting standards

Guidance: level 1

:: Finance ::

In accounting, _____ is the portion of a subsidiary corporation's stock that is not owned by the parent corporation. The magnitude of the _____ in the subsidiary company is generally less than 50% of outstanding shares, or the corporation would generally cease to be a subsidiary of the parent.

Exam Probability: **Medium**

3. *Answer choices:*

(see index for correct answer)

- a. Dedicated Portfolio Theory
- b. Pooled income fund
- c. Minority interest
- d. Failure to deliver

Guidance: level 1

:: Accounting source documents ::

A _____ or account statement is a summary of financial transactions which have occurred over a given period on a bank account held by a person or business with a financial institution.

Exam Probability: **Low**

4. *Answer choices:*
(see index for correct answer)

- a. Credit memorandum
- b. Bank statement
- c. Remittance advice
- d. Superbill

Guidance: level 1

:: Generally Accepted Accounting Principles ::

In accounting, _____ is the income that a business have from its normal business activities, usually from the sale of goods and services to customers. _____ is also referred to as sales or turnover. Some companies receive _____ from interest, royalties, or other fees. _____ may refer to business income in general, or it may refer to the amount, in a monetary unit, earned during a period of time, as in "Last year, Company X had _____ of $42 million". Profits or net income generally imply total _____ minus total expenses in a given period. In accounting, in the balance statement it is a subsection of the Equity section and _____ increases equity, it is often referred to as the "top line" due to its position on the income statement at the very top. This is to be contrasted with the "bottom line" which denotes net income.

Exam Probability: **Low**

5. *Answer choices:*
(see index for correct answer)

- a. Contributed capital
- b. Generally accepted accounting principles
- c. Revenue
- d. Net income

Guidance: level 1

:: Financial accounting ::

A _____ is an ownership interest in a corporation with enough voting stock shares to prevail in any stockholders' motion. A majority of voting shares is always a _____. When a party holds less than the majority of the voting shares, other present circumstances can be considered to determine whether that party is still considered to hold a controlling ownership interest.

Exam Probability: **High**

6. *Answer choices:*

(see index for correct answer)

- a. Working capital
- b. Valuation
- c. SEC filing
- d. Hidden asset

Guidance: level 1

:: Management accounting ::

_____ is a method of identifying and evaluating activities that a business performs, using activity-based costing to carry out a value chain analysis or a re-engineering initiative to improve strategic and operational decisions in an organization.

Exam Probability: **Low**

7. *Answer choices:*

(see index for correct answer)

- a. Certified Management Accountants of Canada
- b. Target costing
- c. Activity-based management
- d. Chartered Cost Accountant

Guidance: level 1

:: Tax law ::

_____ or revenue law is an area of legal study which deals with the constitutional, common-law, statutory, tax treaty, and regulatory rules that constitute the law applicable to taxation.

Exam Probability: **Medium**

8. *Answer choices:*

(see index for correct answer)

- a. First-tier Tribunal
- b. Tax Court of Canada
- c. Taxable wages
- d. Tax law

Guidance: level 1

:: Accounting organizations ::

The _____ promotes accounting education, research and practice. Founded in 1916 as the American Association of University Instructors in Accounting, its present name was adopted in 1936. The Association is a voluntary group of persons interested in accounting education and research.

Exam Probability: **Low**

9. *Answer choices:*

(see index for correct answer)

- a. American Accounting Association
- b. Taxand
- c. Southern African Institute for Business Accountants
- d. National Board of Accountants and Auditors

Guidance: level 1

:: Real property law ::

A _____ or millage rate is an ad valorem tax on the value of a property, usually levied on real estate. The tax is levied by the governing authority of the jurisdiction in which the property is located. This can be a national government, a federated state, a county or geographical region or a municipality. Multiple jurisdictions may tax the same property. This tax can be contrasted to a rent tax which is based on rental income or imputed rent, and a land value tax, which is a levy on the value of land, excluding the value of buildings and other improvements.

Exam Probability: **Medium**

10. *Answer choices:*

(see index for correct answer)

- a. Purveyance
- b. Right of entry
- c. Concurrent estate
- d. Cape

Guidance: level 1

:: ::

_____ is a costing method that identifies activities in an organization and assigns the cost of each activity to all products and services according to the actual consumption by each. This model assigns more indirect costs into direct costs compared to conventional costing.

Exam Probability: **High**

11. *Answer choices:*

(see index for correct answer)

- a. process perspective
- b. hierarchical perspective
- c. co-culture
- d. Activity-based costing

Guidance: level 1

:: ::

Accounts _____ is a legally enforceable claim for payment held by a business for goods supplied and/or services rendered that customers/clients have ordered but not paid for. These are generally in the form of invoices raised by a business and delivered to the customer for payment within an agreed time frame. Accounts _____ is shown in a balance sheet as an asset. It is one of a series of accounting transactions dealing with the billing of a customer for goods and services that the customer has ordered. These may be distinguished from notes _____ , which are debts created through formal legal instruments called promissory notes.

Exam Probability: **Medium**

12. *Answer choices:*

(see index for correct answer)

- a. Receivable
- b. functional perspective
- c. Sarbanes-Oxley act of 2002
- d. surface-level diversity

Guidance: level 1

:: ::

An _____ is a systematic and independent examination of books, accounts, statutory records, documents and vouchers of an organization to ascertain how far the financial statements as well as non-financial disclosures present a true and fair view of the concern. It also attempts to ensure that the books of accounts are properly maintained by the concern as required by law. _____ing has become such a ubiquitous phenomenon in the corporate and the public sector that academics started identifying an " _____ Society". The _____ or perceives and recognises the propositions before them for examination, obtains evidence, evaluates the same and formulates an opinion on the basis of his judgement which is communicated through their _____ing report.

Exam Probability: **High**

13. *Answer choices:*

(see index for correct answer)

- a. co-culture
- b. levels of analysis
- c. hierarchical

- d. surface-level diversity

Guidance: level 1

:: Accounting in the United States ::

_____ were documents issued by the Committee on Accounting Procedure between 1938 and 1959 on various accounting problems. They were discontinued with the dissolution of the Committee in 1959 under a recommendation from the Special Committee on Research Program. In all, 17 bulletins were issued; however, the lack of binding authority over AICPA's membership reduced the influence of, and compliance with the content of the bulletins. The _____ have all been superseded by the Accounting Standards Codification .

Exam Probability: **Low**

14. *Answer choices:*

(see index for correct answer)

- a. Cotton Plantation Record and Account Book
- b. Governmental Accounting Standards Board
- c. Federal Accounting Standards Advisory Board
- d. Accounting Research Bulletins

Guidance: level 1

:: Inventory ::

_____ is the amount of inventory a company has in stock at the end of its fiscal year. It is closely related with _____ cost, which is the amount of money spent to get these goods in stock. It should be calculated at the lower of cost or market.

Exam Probability: **High**

15. *Answer choices:*

(see index for correct answer)

- a. Order picking
- b. Inventory control problem
- c. Ending inventory
- d. Stock obsolescence

Guidance: level 1

:: Management accounting ::

In _____ or managerial accounting, managers use the provisions of accounting information in order to better inform themselves before they decide matters within their organizations, which aids their management and performance of control functions.

Exam Probability: **Low**

16. *Answer choices:*

(see index for correct answer)

- a. Hedge accounting
- b. Grenzplankostenrechnung
- c. Institute of Cost and Management Accountants of Bangladesh
- d. Dual overhead rate

Guidance: level 1

:: Economics terminology ::

A corporation's share capital or _____ is the portion of a corporation's equity that has been obtained by the issue of shares in the corporation to a shareholder, usually for cash. "Share capital" may also denote the number and types of shares that compose a corporation's share structure.

Exam Probability: **High**

17. *Answer choices:*

(see index for correct answer)

- a. Price variance
- b. Capital stock
- c. payee
- d. marginal revenue

Guidance: level 1

:: International Financial Reporting Standards ::

_____ , usually called IFRS, are standards issued by the IFRS Foundation and the International Accounting Standards Board to provide a common global language for business affairs so that company accounts are understandable and comparable across international boundaries. They are a consequence of growing international shareholding and trade and are particularly important for companies that have dealings in several countries. They are progressively replacing the many different national accounting standards. They are the rules to be followed by accountants to maintain books of accounts which are comparable, understandable, reliable and relevant as per the users internal or external. IFRS, with the exception of IAS 29 Financial Reporting in Hyperinflationary Economies and IFRIC 7 Applying the Restatement Approach under IAS 29, are authorized in terms of the historical cost paradigm. IAS 29 and IFRIC 7 are authorized in terms of the units of constant purchasing power paradigm.IAS 2 is related to inventories in this standard we talk about the stock its production process etcIFRS began as an attempt to harmonize accounting across the European Union but the value of harmonization quickly made the concept attractive around the world. However, it has been debated whether or not de facto harmonization has occurred. Standards that were issued by IASC are still within use today and go by the name International Accounting Standards , while standards issued by IASB are called IFRS. IAS were issued between 1973 and 2001 by the Board of the International Accounting Standards Committee . On 1 April 2001, the new International Accounting Standards Board took over from the IASC the responsibility for setting International Accounting Standards. During its first meeting the new Board adopted existing IAS and Standing Interpretations Committee standards . The IASB has continued to develop standards calling the new standards " _____ ".

Exam Probability: **Medium**

18. *Answer choices:*

(see index for correct answer)

- a. IAS 2
- b. International Financial Reporting Standards
- c. IFRS 2
- d. IAS 37

Guidance: level 1

:: United States Generally Accepted Accounting Principles ::

> In a companies' financial reporting, _____ "includes all changes in equity during a period except those resulting from investments by owners and distributions to owners". Because that use excludes the effects of changing ownership interest, an economic measure of _____ is necessary for financial analysis from the shareholders' point of view

Exam Probability: **Low**

19. *Answer choices:*

(see index for correct answer)

- a. GASB 45
- b. Comprehensive income
- c. Cost segregation study
- d. FIN 46

Guidance: level 1

:: Financial accounting ::

_____ in accounting is the process of treating investments in associate companies. Equity accounting is usually applied where an investor entity holds 20–50% of the voting stock of the associate company. The investor records such investments as an asset on its balance sheet. The investor's proportional share of the associate company's net income increases the investment, and proportional payments of dividends decrease it. In the investor's income statement, the proportional share of the investor's net income or net loss is reported as a single-line item.

Exam Probability: **High**

20. *Answer choices:*

(see index for correct answer)

- a. Deferred Acquisition Costs
- b. Intangibles
- c. Convenience translation
- d. Equity method

Guidance: level 1

:: Capital gains taxes ::

A _____ refers to profit that results from a sale of a capital asset, such as stock, bond or real estate, where the sale price exceeds the purchase price. The gain is the difference between a higher selling price and a lower purchase price. Conversely, a capital loss arises if the proceeds from the sale of a capital asset are less than the purchase price.

Exam Probability: **Low**

21. *Answer choices:*

(see index for correct answer)

- a. Capital gain
- b. Capital cost tax factor
- c. Capital Cost Allowance

Guidance: level 1

:: ::

_____ is the collection of mechanisms, processes and relations by which corporations are controlled and operated. Governance structures and principles identify the distribution of rights and responsibilities among different participants in the corporation and include the rules and procedures for making decisions in corporate affairs. _____ is necessary because of the possibility of conflicts of interests between stakeholders, primarily between shareholders and upper management or among shareholders.

Exam Probability: **Medium**

22. Answer choices:

(see index for correct answer)

- a. Character
- b. corporate values
- c. Sarbanes-Oxley act of 2002
- d. functional perspective

Guidance: level 1

:: Generally Accepted Accounting Principles ::

Financial statements prepared and presented by a company typically follow an external standard that specifically guides their preparation. These standards vary across the globe and are typically overseen by some combination of the private accounting profession in that specific nation and the various government regulators. Variations across countries may be considerable, making cross-country evaluation of financial data challenging.

Exam Probability: **Low**

23. Answer choices:

(see index for correct answer)

- a. Contributed capital
- b. Pro forma
- c. Expense
- d. Operating profit

Guidance: level 1

:: Project management ::

In economics, _____ is the assignment of available resources to various uses. In the context of an entire economy, resources can be allocated by various means, such as markets or central planning.

Exam Probability: **Medium**

24. *Answer choices:*

(see index for correct answer)

- a. Feature-driven development
- b. Time horizon
- c. P3M3
- d. project triangle

Guidance: level 1

:: Data security ::

_____ is the concept of having more than one person required to complete a task. In business the separation by sharing of more than one individual in one single task is an internal control intended to prevent fraud and error. The concept is alternatively called segregation of duties or, in the political realm, separation of powers. In democracies, the separation of legislation from administration serves a similar purpose. The concept is addressed in technical systems and in information technology equivalently and generally addressed as redundancy.

Exam Probability: **Low**

25. *Answer choices:*

(see index for correct answer)

- a. Backup validation
- b. Titan Rain
- c. Separation of duties
- d. First Department

Guidance: level 1

:: Accounting in the United States ::

Founded in 1887, the _____ is the national professional organization of Certified Public Accountants in the United States, with more than 418,000 members in 143 countries in business and industry, public practice, government, education, student affiliates and international associates. It sets ethical standards for the profession and U.S. auditing standards for audits of private companies, non-profit organizations, federal, state and local governments. It also develops and grades the Uniform CPA Examination. The AICPA maintains offices in New York City; Washington, DC; Durham, NC; and Ewing, NJ. The AICPA celebrated the 125th anniversary of its founding in 2012.

Exam Probability: **Low**

26. *Answer choices:*

(see index for correct answer)

- a. Plug
- b. Financial Accounting Foundation
- c. Trueblood Committee
- d. American Institute of Certified Public Accountants

Guidance: level 1

:: ::

_____ science is the application of science to criminal and civil laws, mainly—on the criminal side—during criminal investigation, as governed by the legal standards of admissible evidence and criminal procedure.

Exam Probability: **Low**

27. *Answer choices:*

(see index for correct answer)

- a. functional perspective
- b. deep-level diversity
- c. Forensic
- d. hierarchical perspective

Guidance: level 1

:: Financial accounting ::

_____ refers to any one of several methods by which a company, for `financial accounting` or tax purposes, depreciates a fixed asset in such a way that the amount of depreciation taken each year is higher during the earlier years of an asset's life. For financial accounting purposes, _____ is expected to be much more productive during its early years, so that depreciation expense will more accurately represent how much of an asset's usefulness is being used up each year. For tax purposes, _____ provides a way of deferring corporate income taxes by reducing taxable income in current years, in exchange for increased taxable income in future years. This is a valuable tax incentive that encourages businesses to purchase new assets.

Exam Probability: **High**

28. *Answer choices:*

(see index for correct answer)

- a. Mark-to-market accounting
- b. Accelerated depreciation
- c. Convenience translation
- d. Asset swap

Guidance: level 1

:: Tax reform ::

_____ is the process of changing the way taxes are collected or managed by the government and is usually undertaken to improve tax administration or to provide economic or social benefits. _____ can include reducing the level of taxation of all people by the government, making the tax system more progressive or less progressive, or simplifying the tax system and making the system more understandable or more accountable.

Exam Probability: **Medium**

29. *Answer choices:*
(see index for correct answer)

- a. Enterprise Value Tax
- b. Tax reform
- c. Rational economic exchange
- d. Goods and Services Tax

Guidance: level 1

:: Competition (economics) ::

In taxation and accounting, _____ refers to the rules and methods for pricing transactions within and between enterprises under common ownership or control. Because of the potential for cross-border controlled transactions to distort taxable income, tax authorities in many countries can adjust intragroup transfer prices that differ from what would have been charged by unrelated enterprises dealing at arm's length. The OECD and World Bank recommend intragroup pricing rules based on the arm's-length principle, and 19 of the 20 members of the G20 have adopted similar measures through bilateral treaties and domestic legislation, regulations, or administrative practice. Countries with _____ legislation generally follow the OECD _____ Guidelines for Multinational Enterprises and Tax Administrations in most respects, although their rules can differ on some important details.

Exam Probability: **High**

30. *Answer choices:*
(see index for correct answer)

- a. Regulatory competition
- b. Transfer pricing
- c. Self-competition
- d. Category killer

Guidance: level 1

:: Financial economics ::

A _____ is defined to include property of any kind held by an assessee, whether connected with their business or profession or not connected with their business or profession. It includes all kinds of property, movable or immovable, tangible or intangible, fixed or circulating. Thus, land and building, plant and machinery, motorcar, furniture, jewellery, route permits, goodwill, tenancy rights, patents, trademarks, shares, debentures, securities, units, mutual funds, zero-coupon bonds etc. are _____ s.

Exam Probability: **Medium**

31. *Answer choices:*

(see index for correct answer)

- a. Single-index model
- b. Cyclical asymmetry
- c. Added value
- d. Capital asset

Guidance: level 1

:: ::

The _____ is a private, non-profit organization standard-setting body whose primary purpose is to establish and improve Generally Accepted Accounting Principles within the United States in the public's interest. The Securities and Exchange Commission designated the FASB as the organization responsible for setting accounting standards for public companies in the US. The FASB replaced the American Institute of Certified Public Accountants' Accounting Principles Board on July 1, 1973.

Exam Probability: **Low**

32. *Answer choices:*

(see index for correct answer)

- a. information systems assessment
- b. Financial Accounting Standards Board
- c. levels of analysis
- d. functional perspective

Guidance: level 1

:: Financial ratios ::

_____ is a measure of how revenue growth translates into growth in operating income. It is a measure of leverage, and of how risky, or volatile, a company's operating income is.

Exam Probability: **Low**

33. *Answer choices:*

(see index for correct answer)

- a. Times interest earned
- b. Put/call ratio
- c. Operating leverage
- d. Net capital outflow

Guidance: level 1

:: Real estate valuation ::

_____ or OMV is the price at which an asset would trade in a competitive auction setting. _____ is often used interchangeably with open _____, fair value or fair _____, although these terms have distinct definitions in different standards, and may or may not differ in some circumstances.

Exam Probability: **Low**

34. *Answer choices:*

(see index for correct answer)

- a. E.surv
- b. Hedonic regression
- c. Uniform Standards of Professional Appraisal Practice
- d. Market value

Guidance: level 1

:: Commerce ::

A _____ , is a document acknowledging that a person has received money or property in payment following a sale or other transfer of goods or provision of a service. All _____ s must have the date of purchase on them. If the recipient of the payment is legally required to collect sales tax or VAT from the customer, the amount would be added to the _____ and the collection would be deemed to have been on behalf of the relevant tax authority. In many countries, a retailer is required to include the sales tax or VAT in the displayed price of goods sold, from which the tax amount would be calculated at point of sale and remitted to the tax authorities in due course. Similarly, amounts may be deducted from amounts payable, as in the case of wage withholding taxes. On the other hand, tips or other gratuities given by a customer, for example in a restaurant, would not form part of the payment amount or appear on the _____ .

Exam Probability: **Low**

35. *Answer choices:*

(see index for correct answer)

- a. Trading post
- b. Safe harbor
- c. Custom house
- d. Receipt

Guidance: level 1

:: Legal terms ::

An _____ is an action which is inaccurate or incorrect. In some usages, an _____ is synonymous with a mistake. In statistics, "_____" refers to the difference between the value which has been computed and the correct value. An _____ could result in failure or in a deviation from the intended performance or behaviour.

Exam Probability: **High**

36. *Answer choices:*

(see index for correct answer)

- a. Parental consent
- b. Error
- c. Offer of proof
- d. Legal transplant

Guidance: level 1

:: Accounting software ::

_____ is a freely available and global framework for exchanging business information. _____ allows the expression of semantic meaning commonly required in business reporting. The language is XML-based and uses the XML syntax and related XML technologies such as XML Schema, XLink, XPath, and Namespaces. One use of _____ is to define and exchange financial information, such as a financial statement. The _____ Specification is developed and published by _____ International, Inc. .

Exam Probability: **High**

37. *Answer choices:*

(see index for correct answer)

- a. Fortora Fresh Finance
- b. Procurify
- c. Digital Insight
- d. Billback

Guidance: level 1

:: Accounting terminology ::

In management accounting or _____ , managers use the provisions of accounting information in order to better inform themselves before they decide matters within their organizations, which aids their management and performance of control functions.

Exam Probability: **Low**

38. *Answer choices:*

(see index for correct answer)

- a. Accrued liabilities
- b. Managerial accounting
- c. Fund accounting

- d. Statement of financial position

Guidance: level 1

:: Financial ratios ::

The _____ or dividend-price ratio of a share is the dividend per share, divided by the price per share. It is also a company's total annual dividend payments divided by its market capitalization, assuming the number of shares is constant. It is often expressed as a percentage.

Exam Probability: **High**

39. *Answer choices:*

(see index for correct answer)

- a. Quick ratio
- b. Texas ratio
- c. Net profit margin
- d. Dividend yield

Guidance: level 1

:: Management accounting ::

_____ is an accountancy practice, the aim of which is to provide an offset to the mark-to-market movement of the derivative in the profit and loss account. There are two types of hedge recognized. For a fair value hedge the offset is achieved either by marking-to-market an asset or a liability which offsets the P&L movement of the derivative. For a cash flow hedge some of the derivative volatility into a separate component of the entity's equity called the cash flow hedge reserve. Where a hedge relationship is effective, most of the mark-to-market derivative volatility will be offset in the profit and loss account. _____ entails much compliance - involving documenting the hedge relationship and both prospectively and retrospectively proving that the hedge relationship is effective.

Exam Probability: **Low**

40. *Answer choices:*

(see index for correct answer)

- a. Fixed assets management
- b. Throughput accounting
- c. Hedge accounting
- d. Direct material total variance

Guidance: level 1

:: Accounting in the United States ::

_____ refers to a Memorandum of Understanding signed in September 2002 between the Financial Accounting Standards Board, the US standard setter, and the International Accounting Standards Board. The agreement is so called as it was reached in Norwalk.

Exam Probability: **Low**

41. *Answer choices:*

(see index for correct answer)

- a. Other comprehensive income
- b. Norwalk Agreement
- c. Accounting Principles Board
- d. American Institute of Certified Public Accountants

Guidance: level 1

:: Business law ::

A _____, also known as the sole trader, individual entrepreneurship or proprietorship, is a type of enterprise that is owned and run by one person and in which there is no legal distinction between the owner and the business entity. A sole trader does not necessarily work 'alone'—it is possible for the sole trader to employ other people.

Exam Probability: **Medium**

42. Answer choices:

(see index for correct answer)

- a. Trading while insolvent
- b. Unfair competition
- c. Sole proprietorship
- d. Arbitration clause

Guidance: level 1

:: Accounting ::

It is the period for which books are balanced and the financial statements are prepared. Generally, the _____ consists of 12 months. However the beginning of the _____ differs according to the jurisdiction. For example, one entity may follow the regular calendar year, i.e. January to December as the accounting year, while another entity may follow April to March as the _____ .

Exam Probability: **Medium**

43. Answer choices:

(see index for correct answer)

- a. Trading statement
- b. Cash sweep
- c. INPACT International
- d. Earnings surprise

Guidance: level 1

:: Generally Accepted Accounting Principles ::

Expenditure is an outflow of money to another person or group to pay for an item or service, or for a category of costs. For a tenant, rent is an _____. For students or parents, tuition is an _____. Buying food, clothing, furniture or an automobile is often referred to as an _____. An _____ is a cost that is "paid" or "remitted", usually in exchange for something of value. Something that seems to cost a great deal is "expensive". Something that seems to cost little is "inexpensive". "_____ s of the table" are _____ s of dining, refreshments, a feast, etc.

Exam Probability: **Medium**

44. *Answer choices:*

(see index for correct answer)

- a. Expense
- b. Construction in progress
- c. Gross profit
- d. Vendor-specific objective evidence

Guidance: level 1

:: Insolvency ::

_____ is the process in accounting by which a company is brought to an end in the United Kingdom, Republic of Ireland and United States. The assets and property of the company are redistributed. _____ is also sometimes referred to as winding-up or dissolution, although dissolution technically refers to the last stage of _____ . The process of _____ also arises when customs, an authority or agency in a country responsible for collecting and safeguarding customs duties, determines the final computation or ascertainment of the duties or drawback accruing on an entry.

Exam Probability: **High**

45. *Answer choices:*

(see index for correct answer)

- a. Liquidation
- b. United Kingdom insolvency law
- c. Conservatorship
- d. Official Committee of Equity Security Holders

Guidance: level 1

:: Management accounting ::

_____ is the process of reviewing and analyzing a company's financial statements to make better economic decisions to earn income in future. These statements include the income statement, balance sheet, statement of cash flows, notes to accounts and a statement of changes in equity . _____ is a method or process involving specific techniques for evaluating risks, performance, financial health, and future prospects of an organization.

Exam Probability: **Medium**

46. *Answer choices:*

(see index for correct answer)

- a. Grenzplankostenrechnung
- b. Fixed assets management
- c. Spend management
- d. Target costing

Guidance: level 1

:: Financial ratios ::

The _____ is a financial ratio indicating the relative proportion of equity used to finance a company's assets. The two components are often taken from the firm's balance sheet or statement of financial position, but the ratio may also be calculated using market values for both, if the company's equities are publicly traded.

Exam Probability: **Low**

47. *Answer choices:*

(see index for correct answer)

- a. stock turnover
- b. efficiency ratio

- c. Equity ratio
- d. CROCI

Guidance: level 1

:: Generally Accepted Accounting Principles ::

_____ is a measure of a fixed or current asset's worth when held in inventory, in the field of accounting. NRV is part of the Generally Accepted Accounting Principles and International Financial Reporting Standards that apply to valuing inventory, so as to not overstate or understate the value of inventory goods. _____ is generally equal to the selling price of the inventory goods less the selling costs. Therefore, it is expected sales price less selling costs. NRV prevents overstating or understating of an assets value. NRV is the price cap when using the Lower of Cost or Market Rule.

Exam Probability: **High**

48. *Answer choices:*

(see index for correct answer)

- a. Net realizable value
- b. Closing entries
- c. Normal balance
- d. Standard Business Reporting

Guidance: level 1

:: ::

A _____, in the word's original meaning, is a sheet of paper on which one performs work. They come in many forms, most commonly associated with children's school work assignments, tax forms, and accounting or other business environments. Software is increasingly taking over the paper-based _____.

Exam Probability: **High**

49. *Answer choices:*

(see index for correct answer)

- a. Worksheet
- b. imperative
- c. functional perspective
- d. Sarbanes-Oxley act of 2002

Guidance: level 1

:: Asset ::

In financial accounting, an _____ is any resource owned by the business. Anything tangible or intangible that can be owned or controlled to produce value and that is held by a company to produce positive economic value is an _____. Simply stated, _____ s represent value of ownership that can be converted into cash. The balance sheet of a firm records the monetary value of the _____ s owned by that firm. It covers money and other valuables belonging to an individual or to a business.

Exam Probability: **Medium**

50. *Answer choices:*

(see index for correct answer)

- a. Current asset
- b. Fixed asset

Guidance: level 1

:: Management accounting ::

_____ accounting is a traditional cost accounting method introduced in the 1920s, as an alternative for the traditional cost accounting method based on historical costs.

Exam Probability: **High**

51. *Answer choices:*

(see index for correct answer)

- a. Throughput accounting
- b. Indirect costs
- c. Accounting management
- d. Activity-based management

Guidance: level 1

:: Inventory ::

In business and accounting/accountancy, _____ or continuous inventory describes systems of inventory where information on inventory quantity and availability is updated on a continuous basis as a function of doing business. Generally this is accomplished by connecting the inventory system with order entry and in retail the point of sale system. In this case, book inventory would be exactly the same as, or almost the same, as the real inventory.

Exam Probability: **Medium**

52. *Answer choices:*

(see index for correct answer)

- a. Inventory control problem
- b. Perpetual inventory
- c. Stock demands
- d. Phantom inventory

Guidance: level 1

:: Expense ::

An _____ is the right to reimbursement of money spent by employees for work-related purposes. Some common _____ s are: administrative expense, amortization expense, bad debt expense, cost of goods sold, depreciation expense, freight-out, income tax expense, insurance expense, interest expense, loss on disposal of plant assets, maintenance and repairs expense, rent expense, salaries and wages expense, selling expense, supplies expense and utilities expense.

Exam Probability: **Medium**

53. *Answer choices:*

(see index for correct answer)

- a. Expense account
- b. Corporate travel
- c. Operating expense
- d. Freight expense

Guidance: level 1

:: ::

A _____ is an individual or institution that legally owns one or more shares of stock in a public or private corporation. _____ s may be referred to as members of a corporation. Legally, a person is not a _____ in a corporation until their name and other details are entered in the corporation's register of _____ s or members.

Exam Probability: **Low**

54. *Answer choices:*

(see index for correct answer)

- a. levels of analysis
- b. co-culture
- c. Shareholder
- d. corporate values

Guidance: level 1

:: Banking ::

A _____ is a financial institution that accepts deposits from the public and creates credit. Lending activities can be performed either directly or indirectly through capital markets. Due to their importance in the financial stability of a country, _____ s are highly regulated in most countries. Most nations have institutionalized a system known as fractional reserve _____ ing under which _____ s hold liquid assets equal to only a portion of their current liabilities. In addition to other regulations intended to ensure liquidity, _____ s are generally subject to minimum capital requirements based on an international set of capital standards, known as the Basel Accords.

Exam Probability: **Medium**

55. *Answer choices:*

(see index for correct answer)

- a. Common equity
- b. Monetary base
- c. Peer-to-peer banking
- d. Bank

Guidance: level 1

:: ::

The _____ or just chief executive, is the most senior corporate, executive, or administrative officer in charge of managing an organization especially an independent legal entity such as a company or nonprofit institution. CEOs lead a range of organizations, including public and private corporations, non-profit organizations and even some government organizations. The CEO of a corporation or company typically reports to the board of directors and is charged with maximizing the value of the entity, which may include maximizing the share price, market share, revenues or another element. In the non-profit and government sector, CEOs typically aim at achieving outcomes related to the organization's mission, such as reducing poverty, increasing literacy, etc.

Exam Probability: **Medium**

56. *Answer choices:*

(see index for correct answer)

- a. hierarchical perspective
- b. personal values
- c. deep-level diversity

- d. co-culture

Guidance: level 1

:: E-commerce ::

_____ is an e-commerce payment system used in the Netherlands, based on online banking. Introduced in 2005, this payment method allows customers to buy on the Internet using direct online transfers from their bank account.

Exam Probability: **Low**

57. *Answer choices:*

(see index for correct answer)

- a. Feefighters
- b. Computer security
- c. Dragonpay
- d. AsiaPay

Guidance: level 1

:: ::

An _____, for United States federal income tax, is a closely held corporation that makes a valid election to be taxed under Subchapter S of Chapter 1 of the Internal Revenue Code. In general, _____ s do not pay any income taxes. Instead, the corporation's income or losses are divided among and passed through to its shareholders. The shareholders must then report the income or loss on their own individual income tax returns.

Exam Probability: **High**

58. *Answer choices:*

(see index for correct answer)

- a. process perspective
- b. S corporation
- c. open system
- d. Character

Guidance: level 1

:: ::

_____ are electronic transfer of money from one bank account to another, either within a single financial institution or across multiple institutions, via computer-based systems, without the direct intervention of bank staff.

Exam Probability: **Medium**

59. *Answer choices:*

(see index for correct answer)

- a. corporate values
- b. hierarchical perspective
- c. surface-level diversity
- d. Character

Guidance: level 1

INDEX: Correct Answers

Foundations of Business

1. b: Contract

2. : Health

3. : Privacy

4. : Energies

5. c: Trademark

6. : Accounting

7. c: Partnership

8. b: Money

9. c: Incentive

10. a: Planning

11. a: Inventory

12. b: Income statement

13. b: Benchmarking

14. c: Demand

15. b: Loan

16. : Problem

17. d: Commerce

18. a: Career

19. a: ASEAN

20. c: Expense

21. c: Variable cost

22. c: Analysis

23. : Price

24. c: Raw material

25. d: Schedule

26. : Corporate governance

27. c: Solution

28. : Management

29. c: Strategic planning

30. : Policy

31. a: Political risk

32. : Utility

33. d: Opportunity cost

34. c: Fixed cost

35. a: Strategic alliance

36. : Size

37. d: Fraud

38. : Quality control

39. b: Currency

40. : Marketing

41. b: Availability

42. d: Net income

43. : Payment

44. c: Cash

45. d: Best practice

46. a: Number

47. d: Target market

48. d: Small business

49. b: Quality management

50. b: Federal Trade Commission

51. a: Patent

52. : Tariff

53. b: Land

54. d: Balanced scorecard

55. b: Market value

56. c: Question

57. d: Restructuring

58. b: Technology

59. b: Ownership

Management

1. c: Entrepreneurship

2. a: Job enrichment

3. d: Negotiation

4. : Autonomy

5. d: Board of directors

6. d: Initiative

7. : Discipline

8. : Strategy

9. d: Employment

10. c: Certification

11. c: Customer

12. a: Bureaucracy

13. b: Statistical process control

14. a: Management system

15. c: Enron

16. b: Supply chain management

17. a: Competitive advantage

18. c: Feedback

19. a: Business plan

20. d: Threat

21. c: Emotional intelligence

22. a: Supply chain

23. b: Telecommuting

24. d: Offshoring

25. c: Wage

26. : Mediation

27. a: Self-assessment

28. c: Shareholder

29. b: Patent

30. a: Compromise

31. : Quality assurance

32. a: Transformational leadership

33. c: Control chart

34. : Committee

35. b: Purchasing

36. c: Cooperation

37. c: Mission statement

38. c: Recession

39. a: Job analysis

40. a: Productivity

41. a: Law

42. d: Quality management

43. c: Management

44. b: Performance appraisal

45. : Mass customization

46. d: Job design

47. : Product life cycle

48. d: Proactive

49. b: Human resources

50. a: Collaboration

51. b: Career

52. c: Bargaining

53. b: Intranet

54. b: Organizational structure

55. : Management by objectives

56. a: Outsourcing

57. d: Coaching

58. b: Planning

59. : Export

Business law

1. c: Disclaimer

2. c: Economy

3. : Tangible

4. d: Creditor

5. a: Insolvency

6. c: Clayton Act

7. d: Resource

8. c: Administrative law

9. a: Shareholder

10. b: Liquidated damages

11. c: Fee simple

12. : Certiorari

13. b: Commercial Paper

14. b: S corporation

15. c: Proximate cause

16. : Undue influence

17. c: Prohibition

18. b: Procedural law

19. : Inventory

20. : Apparent authority

21. d: Security

22. d: Preference

23. b: Disparagement

24. d: Plaintiff

25. a: Perfection

26. : Bill of lading

27. a: Respondeat superior

28. a: Condition precedent

29. a: Deed

30. : Wage

31. a: Brand

32. c: Employment discrimination

33. b: Federal question

34. b: Securities and Exchange Commission

35. : Adverse possession

36. d: Sherman Antitrust

37. c: Corruption

38. d: Tort

39. : Operating agreement

40. b: Board of directors

41. : Foreign Corrupt Practices Act

42. : Exclusionary rule

43. a: Public policy

44. b: Merger

45. b: Implied warranty

46. c: Corporate governance

47. a: Trustee

48. a: Criminal law

49. c: Jury

50. a: Offeror

51. c: Unconscionability

52. a: Economic Espionage Act

53. d: Advertising

54. c: Punitive damages

55. b: Authority

56. a: Issuer

57. d: Revenue

58. b: National Labor Relations Board

59. b: Constitution

Finance

1. c: Value Line

2. : Cost of capital

3. : Hedge fund

4. c: Bank of America

5. b: Opportunity cost

6. c: Vacation

7. c: Retained earnings

8. : Dividend

9. : Factory

10. : Inventory

11. c: Wall Street

12. : Expense

13. d: Stock split

14. c: Asset management

15. a: Municipal bond

16. d: Retirement

17. c: Financial ratio

18. b: Aging

19. : Net asset

20. d: Interest rate risk

21. : Conservatism

22. a: Risk

23. d: Commercial bank

24. : Competition

25. c: Cost of goods sold

26. a: Perpetual inventory

27. d: Bank account

28. d: Insurance

29. a: Indenture

30. b: Accounting period

31. a: Public company

32. : Finished good

33. b: Specific identification

34. d: Matching principle

35. c: Commercial paper

36. a: Comprehensive income

37. : Industry

38. c: Cost object

39. : Risk assessment

40. c: Balanced scorecard

41. b: Capital market

42. : Rate risk

43. : Market value

44. d: Need

45. : Source document

46. d: Certified Public Accountant

47. b: Current asset

48. a: Purchasing

49. b: Initial public offering

50. c: Accrual

51. a: Firm

52. a: Risk premium

53. b: Bankruptcy

54. c: Put option

55. b: Income

56. a: Credit card

57. : Policy

58. b: Management

59. c: Accrued liabilities

Human resource management

1. : Graveyard shift

2. d: Authoritarianism

3. c: Census

4. d: Evaluation

5. : Social network

6. d: Job performance

7. a: Physician

8. d: Job rotation

9. c: Career development

10. : Cross-functional team

11. c: Job enlargement

12. c: Referent power

13. a: McDonnell Douglas Corp. v. Green

14. c: Compa-ratio

15. b: Task force

16. d: Part-time

17. : Unemployment

18. c: Occupational Safety and Health Act

19. b: Individualism

20. c: Foreign worker

21. c: Enforcement

22. b: Local union

23. b: Workplace bullying

24. b: Nearshoring

25. a: Schedule

26. c: Open shop

27. : Performance management

28. a: Picketing

29. : Data collection

30. c: E-learning

31. d: Test validity

32. c: National Institute for Occupational Safety and Health

33. b: Balanced scorecard

34. b: Globalization

35. b: Strategy map

36. d: Xerox Corporation

37. b: Human resources

38. b: Layoff

39. b: Pension

40. d: Committee

41. d: Departmentalization

42. b: Meritor Savings Bank v. Vinson

43. c: Job fair

44. b: Drug test

45. : Delayering

46. c: Job security

47. a: Partnership

48. d: Human resource management

49. d: Featherbedding

50. b: Six Sigma

51. : Intuition

52. a: Employee benefit

53. b: Unfair labor practice

54. c: Mission statement

55. d: Social loafing

56. a: Training and development

57. a: Profession

58. a: Expatriate

59. : Sexual orientation

Information systems

1. : Web server

2. c: Authentication

3. d: Threat

4. b: Automated teller machine

5. d: Google

6. c: Interoperability

7. b: Read-only memory

8. d: Phishing

9. b: Business process management

10. : Wide Area Network

11. : Click-through

12. d: Privacy

13. a: Tacit knowledge

14. a: Disaster recovery

15. c: Big data

16. d: Personalization

17. d: Data mart

18. c: Enterprise systems

19. a: Data model

20. d: Analytics

21. a: Chief information officer

22. c: Information ethics

23. d: Google Docs

24. d: Supplier relationship management

25. : AdWords

26. : BitTorrent

27. a: Disaster recovery plan

28. b: Spyware

29. a: ITunes

30. : Automation

31. a: Avatar

32. d: Random access

33. : Consumer-to-business

34. : Business process

35. b: World Wide Web

36. : Common Criteria

37. : Enterprise search

38. a: Data security

39. c: Joint application design

40. c: Backup

41. b: Wiki

42. d: Security controls

43. c: Flash memory

44. b: Mass customization

45. d: Service level

46. b: Picasa

47. c: Business intelligence

48. c: Click-through rate

49. a: Transport Layer Security

50. a: Mobile commerce

51. : Packet switching

52. b: Statistics

53. b: Information literacy

54. b: Decision support system

55. d: Web analytics

56. d: Change control

57. c: Top-level domain

58. c: Market share

59. : Questionnaire

Marketing

1. b: Product placement

2. d: Derived demand

3. b: Consultant

4. c: Relationship marketing

5. b: Mission statement

6. d: Corporation

7. : Strategic alliance

8. d: Consumer behavior

9. a: Budget

10. d: Integrated marketing

11. c: Competition

12. c: Direct selling

13. c: Creative brief

14. c: Security

15. : Respondent

16. d: Household

17. d: Marketing communications

18. c: Infomercial

19. a: Regulation

20. : Contract

21. c: Empowerment

22. b: Consumer Protection

23. c: Utility

24. a: Electronic data interchange

25. c: Concept testing

26. d: Logistics

27. d: Billboard

28. b: Copyright

29. c: Leadership

30. d: Loyalty program

31. a: Sherman Antitrust Act

32. : Consumerism

33. c: Accounting

34. : Brainstorming

35. b: Blog

36. a: Database marketing

37. d: E-commerce

38. : Business marketing

39. d: Reseller

40. c: Complexity

41. : Forecasting

42. : Appeal

43. c: Strategy

44. b: Wall Street Journal

45. d: Firm

46. b: Market research

47. b: Retailing

48. a: Primary data

49. d: Clayton Act

50. c: Customer value

51. d: Market segments

52. a: Direct mail

53. c: Audit

54. d: Qualitative research

55. a: Trial

56. c: Target market

57. a: Customer service

58. b: Revenue

59. c: Productivity

Manufacturing

1. a: Elastomer

2. c: Volume

3. a: Control chart

4. a: Reflux

5. b: Production schedule

6. : Perfect competition

7. a: Product differentiation

8. a: Reorder point

9. b: Virtual team

10. a: Rolling Wave planning

11. a: Planning

12. : Supply chain management

13. a: Scope statement

14. : Toshiba

15. c: Paper

16. d: Supplier relationship management

17. a: Licensed production

18. d: Assembly line

19. c: Initiative

20. c: Throughput

21. d: Change control

22. b: Scheduling

23. d: Project manager

24. b: PDCA

25. c: Purchasing process

26. : Third-party logistics

27. : Sunk costs

28. d: Project management

29. b: Control limits

30. b: Flowchart

31. c: Time management

32. : Project team

33. b: Quality Engineering

34. a: Bullwhip effect

35. c: Project

36. a: Expediting

37. : Risk management

38. d: Manufacturing

39. b: Resource allocation

40. a: Heat transfer

41. : Resource management

42. c: Scientific management

43. : Process flow diagram

44. c: Tool

45. b: Total cost

46. d: METRIC

47. b: Inventory control

48. a: Sharing

49. c: Statistical process control

50. b: Total productive maintenance

51. a: Quality policy

52. a: Sequence

53. b: Purchase order

54. a: Reverse auction

55. : Chemical reaction

56. : Request for proposal

57. a: Chemical industry

58. d: Knowledge management

59. b: Retail

Commerce

1. a: Import

2. d: Industry

3. a: Regulation

4. b: Quality control

5. b: York

6. : Uniform Commercial Code

7. b: Subsidy

8. d: Disintermediation

9. b: Tangible

10. d: European Union

11. : Organizational structure

12. a: Outsourcing

13. b: Commodity

14. b: Competitor

15. a: Human resources

16. : Merchandising

17. c: Negotiation

18. c: Consortium

19. : Purchasing

20. b: Economic regulation

21. d: Confirmed

22. b: Committee

23. a: Merger

24. : Antitrust

25. a: Automation

26. b: Market research

27. a: Bankruptcy

28. : Drawback

29. : Contribution margin

30. b: General manager

31. d: Phishing

32. b: Staff position

33. : Advertisement

34. b: Issuing bank

35. b: Information technology

36. b: Consultant

37. c: Real estate

38. a: Shopping cart

39. b: Planning

40. b: Inflation

41. : Preference

42. b: Permission marketing

43. d: Corporation

44. a: Building

45. : Total revenue

46. b: Wall Street Journal

47. : Audit

48. d: Total cost

49. c: Standardization

50. b: Fixed cost

51. d: Hearing

52. c: Level of service

53. b: Project

54. d: Variable cost

55. c: English auction

56. a: Logo

57. a: Pop-up ad

58. b: Microsoft

59. : Purchase order

Business ethics

1. b: Siemens

2. b: Ethics Resource Center

3. : Community development financial institution

4. a: Constitutional law

5. a: Antitrust

6. a: East India

7. c: Capitalism

8. : Exxon Valdez

9. : Toxic waste

10. c: Human nature

11. b: Fair Trade Certified

12. a: Oil spill

13. d: Fraud

14. a: Accounting

15. : Pure Food and Drug Act

16. b: Criminal law

17. c: Qui tam

18. : Protestant work ethic

19. c: Consumer Protection

20. c: Patent

21. a: Lanham Act

22. b: Skill

23. b: Parental leave

24. c: Guerrilla Marketing

25. d: Reputation

26. d: Great Depression

27. d: Sexual harassment

28. : Marketing ethics

29. b: Energy policy

30. c: Right to work

31. d: Risk assessment

32. c: Occupational Safety and Health Administration

33. : UN Global Compact

34. d: Workplace politics

35. c: Electronic waste

36. c: Corporate citizenship

37. d: Clayton Act

38. a: Supply Chain

39. : Stanford International Bank

40. a: European Commission

41. b: Martin Luther

42. d: Fair trade

43. d: East Germany

44. c: Global reach

45. a: Nepotism

46. b: Minimum wage

47. c: Marijuana

48. d: Utopian socialism

49. b: Price fixing

50. c: Fannie Mae

51. a: Marketing

52. d: Locus of control

53. a: Hedonism

54. c: Pyramid scheme

55. a: Chamber of Commerce

56. c: Labor relations

57. d: Social responsibility

58. : Consumerism

59. : Working poor

Accounting

1. a: Capital loss

2. b: Trial balance

3. c: Minority interest

4. b: Bank statement

5. c: Revenue

6. : Controlling interest

7. c: Activity-based management

8. d: Tax law

9. a: American Accounting Association

10. : Property tax

11. d: Activity-based costing

12. a: Receivable

13. : Audit

14. d: Accounting Research Bulletins

15. c: Ending inventory

16. : Management accounting

17. b: Capital stock

18. b: International Financial Reporting Standards

19. b: Comprehensive income

20. d: Equity method

21. a: Capital gain

22. : Corporate governance

23. : Generally Accepted Accounting Principles

24. : Resource allocation

25. c: Separation of duties

26. d: American Institute of Certified Public Accountants

27. c: Forensic

28. b: Accelerated depreciation

29. b: Tax reform

30. b: Transfer pricing

31. d: Capital asset

32. b: Financial Accounting Standards Board

33. c: Operating leverage

34. d: Market value

35. d: Receipt

36. b: Error

37. : XBRL

38. b: Managerial accounting

39. d: Dividend yield

40. c: Hedge accounting

41. b: Norwalk Agreement

42. c: Sole proprietorship

43. : Accounting period

44. a: Expense

45. a: Liquidation

46. : Financial statement analysis

47. c: Equity ratio

48. a: Net realizable value

49. a: Worksheet

50. c: Asset

51. : Standard cost

52. b: Perpetual inventory

53. a: Expense account

54. c: Shareholder

55. d: Bank

56. : Chief executive officer

57. : IDEAL

58. b: S corporation

59. : Electronic funds transfer

CPSIA information can be obtained
at www.ICGtesting.com
Printed in the USA
LVHW031221301019
635717LV00006B/695/P